DO NO HARM

DO NO HARM

The Opioid Epidemic

Harry Wiland
with Peter Segall

Foreword by Georges Benjamin, MD
Preface by Andrew Kolodny, MD

TURNER
PUBLISHING COMPANY

TURNER PUBLISHING COMPANY
Nashville, Tennessee
www.turnerpublishing.com

Cover design: Pete Garceau
Book design: Karen Sheets de Gracia

Names: Wiland, Harry, author. | Segall, Peter, author. | Benjamin, Georges, writer of foreword.
Title: Do no harm : the opioid epidemic / by Harry Wiland, with Peter Segall ; foreword by Georges Benjamin.
Description: Nashville, Tennessee : Turner Publishing Company, [2019] | Includes bibliographical references and index. | Summary: "Do No Harm: The Opioid Epidemic follows author and director, Harry Wiland as he works to unearth the history and truth behind America's rampant opioid crises, and investigates how this crisis ballooned into an epidemic fueled by Big Pharma's ploys, the medical community's obliviousness, and policymakers lack of oversight"—Provided by publisher.
Identifiers: LCCN 2019025417 (print) | LCCN 2019025418 (ebook) | ISBN 9781684423231 (paperback) | ISBN 9781684423248 (hardcover) | ISBN 9781684423255 (ebook)
Subjects: LCSH: Opioid abuse—United States—History. | Opioids—Therapeutic use—United States. | Pain—Treatment—United States. | Pharmaceutical industry—United States. | Public health—United States.
Classification: LCC RC568.O45 W548 2019 (print) | LCC RC568.O45 (ebook) | DDC 362.29/30973—dc23
LC record available at https://lccn.loc.gov/2019025417
LC ebook record available at https://lccn.loc.gov/2019025418

PRINTED IN THE UNITED STATES OF AMERICA
19 20 21 22 23   10 9 8 7 6 5 4 3 2 1

This book is dedicated to my loving daughters, Winona and Julia. They continue to make a positive difference in this challenging world we live in. *Do No Harm* is especially dedicated to my loving and caring wife, Holly, who encouraged me to write this book in the hope of saving even one life from the scourge of opioid addiction. My sister-in-law Wilhelmina Wiland and my brother Michael Wiland were there for me since the beginning of the project. Dennis Marony is a friend both on and off the court. Mike Fallon keeps me honest.

I thank them all.

"primum non nocere"

("do no harm")

CONTENTS

FOREWORD

OUR NATION'S EPIDEMIC of opioid misuse is at the core of consecutive drops in US life expectancy in 2016 and 2017 (a decrease we have not seen since the great influenza pandemic of 1918). The epidemic is the result of a massive systems failure concerning every element of the health industrial complex, including certain pharmaceutical companies' deceptive marketing of the drugs, the complicity of a small number of clinicians who prescribed the drugs fraudulently, and a much larger number who prescribed them in an inappropriate way for pain therapy. Drug distributors, the pharmacy community, and regulators at both the federal and local levels failed to provide effective oversight for what we now know to be vast amounts of drugs being prescribed, delivered, and utilized by patients. Not surprisingly, the illegal drug market seized upon and leveraged these failures to make money by preying on vulnerable and desperate patients who then had both chronic pain and suffered from drug addiction. Like with many health problems, the complications did not stop there. For many of these patients, additional diseases like HIV/AIDS and other sexually transmitted diseases, mental health issues, and other chronic health conditions become comorbidities. Family strife, economic hardship, and other social challenges often followed. This real medical and societal mess was largely preventable had we followed that old medical adage to "first, do no harm."

So where do we go from here to address this epidemic and ensure it never happens again? Overall the focus needs to cover tools to aid prevention, efforts to improve treatment, and enhanced research. Prevention would be strengthened by having better surveillance systems to track drug production, distribution, and utilization to identify abnormal patterns of both illegal and legal drug use. This is especially important for pharmaceuticals with high addictive or abuse potential. Robust state and federal data systems need to be in place to accomplish improved surveillance. Enhanced systems to monitor morbidity and mortality from drug use must better support our nation's poison control systems. Upgrading the timeliness and accuracy of our death reporting systems is essential and should include better training and accountability.

Optimizing pharmacotherapy for pain must be a higher priority. Tragically, health providers who prescribe controlled substances remain woefully under-trained in pain management. Better education about pain management, especially on managing chronic pain, is essential and should continue throughout all levels of any health provider's professional education. Evidence-based prescription guidelines are a core component of ensuring sound prescribing practices, but continued research on how to ensure patients are properly managed is also required so patients are not denied needed pain therapy. People in administrative positions have a different need and thus must be appropriately trained in oversight, quality assurance, and administration. Regulators also need specialized training in how to provide effective regulatory oversight.

There needs to be a comprehensive strategy to address abuse and enhanced national efforts to place and enforce better controls on the amounts of opioids prescribed. Such a strategy would ensure the availability of medications for therapeutic purposes and minimize the availability of illegal drugs. One such strategy already in place: prescription drug management programs that monitor dispensed drugs that contain controlled dangerous substances. These systems provide a mechanism for clinicians to verify the prescribed use of controlled substances by patients. While such monitoring programs are a good first step, more needs to be done to ensure cross state linkages, particularly in regional areas that share patient populations. Enforcement by regulatory authorities, health occupation boards, and, when necessary, law enforcement to identify, penalize, and prosecute those providers who are actively breaking the law needs to continue. More efforts to break up illegal drug distribution chains with a particular focus on online advertising and sales are needed. The health insurance industry can play an enhanced role through drug utilization monitoring, utilization review, and prior authorization. Insurer engagement with workers' compensation programs for patients with chronic pain and drug assistance programs can be a valuable tool for both prevention and treatment.

Consumer education is a major need. Consumers are generally unaware of the addictive potential of these medications, and there is evidence to show that these medications are often passed around between friends, family members, and neighbors to "help" with pain. Youth experimentation with drugs—sometimes via leftover pills in the family medicine cabinet—is also a pathway to addiction. More drug take-back and other safe drug disposal programs would allow people to more easily remove unneeded and unwanted medications from their homes to reduce the risk of inappropriate drug usage.

Substance misuse must be medicalized and decriminalized. Treatment should become a first option for addiction, with treatment availability expanded to meet the need. Evidence-based treatment for substance misuse must become the norm. For example, medication-assisted treatment is very effective and should be more widely available. Research into new nonaddictive pain medications is ongoing, and the investment in this form of innovation both to improve pain therapy as well as reduce the number of overdoses must continue. Overdose management research is now experiencing a renaissance, having not been a research priority for several years. New antidotes are needed to combat the new, more potent synthetic opioids like fentanyl, a drug that is up to 100 times more potent than morphine.

Naloxone, which has been around for many years to treat narcotic overdoses, is a lifesaving treatment for opioid overdose. Naloxone is an opioid antagonist that binds to the opioid receptors, both blocking and reversing the effects of the drug. Its use is well known to emergency and critical care providers and is now a known entity for patients and consumers at risk for overdose. Previously its availability was limited, but recent efforts have made it more widely available. Many local jurisdictions have found new and innovative ways to get naloxone into the hands of patients, family members, and first responders. These efforts must be scaled up so no one dies of opioid overdose. And we have to address cost, because paying for substance misuse care and antidotes like naloxone are a barrier as well. Finally, the pharmaceutical industry is at it again, markedly increasing the price for naloxone to make a profit. Let's hope the system does not repeatedly fail us. If it does, it will be a sad commentary to the lesson this book hopes to promote.

Georges C. Benjamin
MD, MACP, FACEP (E), FNAPA
Executive Director
American Public Health
Association (APHA)

PREFACE

I MET HARRY WILAND in 2014. I agreed to become involved as an unofficial advisor to *Do No Harm* because I was impressed by his comprehensive approach to presenting the full impact of the opioid addiction epidemic. I introduced him to like-minded colleagues that appear in this book. I believe that getting the truth out about opioid analgesics and opioid addiction can save lives and *Do No Harm* does just that. Ultimately, Americans will need to think twice before taking a highly addictive drug. Prevention through education.

Do No Harm offers far more than a history of the opioid crisis. It details the pharmacological effects of opioids and why addiction should be understood as a disease of the brain. The book provides background on the role of opioid manufacturers and how their corrupt marketing practices led to millions of cases of addiction and hundreds of thousands of deaths. *Do No Harm* details the enormous profits drug companies continue to amass.

The book and documentary profile opioid addiction survivors and their families. It introduces us to local and national organizations on the front line of the crisis. The book explores regulatory and legal approaches to combating Big Pharma's voracious greed. It introduces the reader to successful treatment programs and the need for sustained financial commitments to ensure access to treatment for all those who need it. It urges local, state, and the federal governments to fund and support these programs. It visits with scientists and doctors in their laboratories to find out what future remedies are on the horizon.

I first became aware of the growing problem of opioid addiction in the early 2000s while working for New York City's health department. I was plugged into federal databases showing a sharp rise in visits to emergency rooms and sharp increase in overdose deaths involving prescription opioids. The data was so striking I recall wondering if a mistake had been made. As it turned out, it wasn't a mistake. The crisis was severe and getting worse rapidly, especially in Appalachia and New England. Soon, the rest of the country would experience the devasting impact of opioid addiction and death. We were in the midst of a serious new public health problem.

In 2006, when Len Paulozzi, a medical director at the Center for Disease Control (CDC), published a paper showing that the sharp increase in overdose deaths involving prescription opioids had paralleled an enormous increase in prescribing, the etiology of the crisis became clear. The epidemic was caused by a dramatic change in the culture of opioid prescribing. And the policy implications were also clear: the medical community needed to prescribe more cautiously or the crisis would continue to worsen.

After Dr. Paulozzi's paper was published, the response from industry-funded pain organizations was swift. They attacked Len Paulozzi's paper. The opioid lobby was going to do everything it could to preserve the status quo of aggressive prescribing.

The rise in prescribing that led to an epidemic of addiction was not driven by new evidence that opioids were safe for long-term use. It was caused by a multi-faceted industry-funded campaign that downplayed opioid risks, exaggerated the benefits and convinced the medical community that patients were suffering needlessly because of an overblown fear of addiction. We were taught that the compassionate way to treat just about any complaint of pain was with an opioid. We heard this from eminent pain specialists, from professional societies, from hospitals, and from state medical boards. From every different direction we were hearing that if you were a an enlightened physician then you would be different from those stingy doctors of the past that let patients suffer needlessly. You would know that opioids can be prescribed liberally and that the risk of addiction was very low. As we responded to a marketing campaign disguised as education, the opioid prescribing took off.

Do No Harm: The Opioid Epidemic is a wakeup call for the public and policymakers about the role opioid makers played in causing and fueling an epidemic of addiction.

When we talk about semi-synthetic opioids like oxycodone, which is in OxyContin, or hydrocodone, which is in Vicodin, it is important to recognize that these drugs are literally made from opium and that their effects are indistinguishable from the effects produced by the semi-synthetic opioid called heroin. Even an experienced heroin user can't distinguish the effects of oxycodone from heroin. So, when we talk about opioid analgesics, we are essentially talking about heroin pills.

By year four or five after the release of OxyContin, Purdue Pharma was spending thirty million dollars a year promoting opioids and not just OxyContin, but opioids as a class of drug. Other opioid makers were also promoting opioids. Prescribing of oxycodone, hydrocodone, fentanyl and morphine begins to soar.

From 1999 to 2018, nearly five hundred thousand Americans died from an opioid overdose. We have seen heroin flood into communities across the country. We have experienced increases in infants born opioid-dependent, children winding up in the foster care system because of their parents' addiction, and outbreaks of infectious diseases. This is the worst drug addiction epidemic in United States history.

Two things have to happen to bring the crisis to an end. We must prevent new cases of opioid addiction. And we must ensure easy access to effective treatment for those already opioid addicted.

The crisis remains severe but there are glimmers of hope. The CDC is reporting the first decline in overdose deaths in twenty-five years. The public is starting to recognize the dangers of opioid use and more opioid-addicted Americans are accessing treatment. But we still have a long way to go. Despite a recent trend in more cautious prescribing, there is still no other country on earth that comes close to our per capita opioid consumption.

Andrew Kolodny, MD

Brandeis University

July 2019

INTRODUCTION

DO NO HARM: THE OPIOID EPIDEMIC is a media project that includes the soon-to-be-released book, a theatrical length documentary (2018) and a 3-part, 3-hour series for public television that began national broadcasting in 2018.

Several years ago, I opened my print copy of the *New York Times* and started to read what turned out to be the first in a series of articles about the burgeoning opioid abuse crisis that was invading all parts of the country. This particular article told the harrowing story of a 21-year-old girl from Hudson, Wisconsin, Alysa, who had her wisdom teeth removed by her family dentist. She was given a 30-day prescription of OxyContin for pain. It was just enough for her to become addicted. Alysa needed money to support her habit. She started by stealing money from her mother's purse to buy more drugs. Eventually Alysa's mother called the police on her own daughter. She was sent to detox, but the family had no money to pay for an extended drug treatment program. After a year on the streets, doing everything she could to survive, the story ended with Alysa's body being found in a cheap transient motel, having overdosed from a combination of drugs.[1] Her tragic story haunted and obsessed me. *Do No Harm* honors Alysa's short life. Sadly, Alysa is not alone.

The more I dug, the more compelled I was to try to understand the ramifications of what many physicians were calling "the greatest man-made public health epidemic" in our nation's history, caused not by disease but by greed. I found myself reading everything I could on the subject. Liftoff came when I picked up the November 21, 2011, edition of *Fortune* magazine with an article by award-winning journalist Katherine Eban. Her piece, "OxyContin: Purdue Pharma's Painful Medicine," was about the deceptive and fraudulent marketing practices initiated by Purdue Pharma in their promotion of their new designer opioid drug, OxyContin two decades ago. The article introduced me to Andrew Kolodny, MD, and his organization called Physicians for Responsible Opioid Prescribing, or PROP. Over dinner in New York City, where Dr. Kolodny was then based, we agreed to work together to create a media package that would eventually include a television series, a 90-minute documentary, and this book. I could not have made the documentary, or written this book, without the freely given knowledge and support of the PROP membership. These physicians found each other out of a mutual recognition of the damage being done by the unrestricted use of opioid painkillers. The goal of *Do No Harm: The Opioid Epidemic* media project is to save lives through prevention and greater education about the scourge of opioid addiction and its root cause: greed (or lust for profit).

In this book I go deeper into the issues of addiction and its treatment by including longer passages from the in-depth interviews of over a hundred key individuals that appear as shorter segments in the 90-minute documentary and 3-hour public television series, largely due to broadcast scheduling limitations. Over a two-year period, as filmmakers and investigative journalists, we met with therapists, physicians, scientists, those in recovery, their families, reporters, academics, and financial experts in 18 locations across the country. I want to especially thank Doctors Andrew Kolodny, MD and Georges Benjamin, MD, the book's medical advisors, and Mike Moore, our legal expert and advisor.

Do No Harm describes the avarice that overtook many in the health-care community, spearheaded by such powerful drug companies as Purdue Pharma, Johnson & Johnson, McKesson, Insys, and Rochester Drug Cooperative. The book's appendix includes key documents and a 10-page excerpt from the State of Massachusetts brief against Purdue and other health-care companies. The excerpt from the Massachusetts brief is a damning legal and journalistic document. Brushing aside what is best for the patient, we read the calculating and nefarious emails from a former president of Purdue urging his sales team to pressure their clients to double and triple the prescription strengths of OxyContin because the higher its prescription strength, the more profit was to be made.

Many of the people I encountered naturally assumed I had had a problem with drugs or was close to someone who was struggling with dependency or addictive opioid abuse disorder. Was I, or a loved one, in recovery? Others asked what kind of recovery program I was involved with. My response was that I didn't have to be directly affected by opioids to want to inform and protect others through the power of media. It was the enormity and senselessness of the epidemic that compelled me to get involved.

Our characters are real people. Our stories are taken from real-life experiences. Lives lost change those who are left to carry on. Survivors struggle to make sense of the overdose death of a son or daughter, wife or husband, close personal friend, or classmate. Those in recovery celebrate the days, months, or years they remain sober. *Do No Harm* touches upon future alternate treatments and possible new medical solutions. We hope the class action legal suits being brought to courts across the country result in the allocation of sufficient funds for a comprehensive approach to treating the millions of Americans who are suffering—and will suffer—from opioid addiction. Hope can be elusive.

Harry Wiland

Santa Monica, California

October 2019

CHAPTER 1

Origins of a Crisis

"Drugs are chemicals. They work in the brain by tapping into the brain's communication system and interfering with the way nerve cells normally send, receive, and process information. Some drugs such as opioids, including heroin, can activate neurons because their chemical structure mimics that of a natural neurotransmitter. This similarity in structure 'fools' receptors and allows the drugs to lock onto and activate the nerve cells. Although these drugs mimic brain chemicals, they don't activate nerve cells in the same way as a natural neurotransmitter, and they lead to abnormal messages being transmuted through the network."

—*The National Institute on Drug Abuse (NIDA) Report, 2015*

ACCORDING TO THE Center for Disease Control and Prevention (CDC), at least 2.1 million Americans suffer from an opioid use disorder, commonly referred to as "addiction."[2] Every day in America roughly 130 overdose deaths are recorded. The majority are attributed to opioids. Beyond the facts and figures of this man-made epidemic are the revealing stories of both suffering and courage from all walks of life as the country struggles to find the solutions that will save lives. For those one-time addicts fortunate enough to survive, maintaining their sobriety becomes a lifelong challenge. Although a prodigious effort continues in university and corporate laboratories across the country, opioid abuse and addiction continues to ravage the country.

The origins of the opioid epidemic reveal a premeditated conspiracy and cover-up that have made a number of corporations and individuals extremely wealthy, including the extended Sackler family, the founders and private owners of Purdue Pharma.

THE OPIOID EPIDEMIC BY THE NUMBERS

 130+
People died every day from
opioid-related drug overdoses[3]
(estimated)

 10.3 m
People misused
prescription opioids in 2018[1]

 47,600
People died from
overdosing on opioids[2]

 2.0 million
People had an opioid
use disorder in 2018[1]

 81,000
People used heroin
for the first time[1]

 808,000
People used heroin
in 2018[1]

 2 million
People misused prescription
opioids for the first time[1]

 15,349
Deaths attributed to
overdosing on heroin
(in 12-month period
ending February 2019)[2]

 32,656
Deaths attributed to overdosing
on synthetic opioids other than
methadone (in 12-month period
ending February 2019)[2]

SOURCES
1. 2019 National Survey on Drug Use and Health. Mortality in the United States, 2018
2. NCHS Data Brief No. 329, November 2018
3. NCHS, National Vital Statistics System. Estimates for 2018 and 2019 are based on provisional data.

Updated October 2019. For more information, visit: http://www.hhs.gov/opioids/   HHS.GOV/OPIOIDS

Opioid Epidemic by the Numbers—hhs.gov/opioids
NATIONAL CENTER FOR HEALTH STATISTICS, CDC

Our health-care regulatory institutions failed to stop what they are now calling the worst man-made epidemic they have ever dealt with before it fully spun out of control. With opioid overdose deaths, beginning in 1996 to the present, estimated to be over 400,000 Americans and rising,[3] much more than a series of weak verbal reprimands and all

"I BELIEVE THAT in terms of the blame for our opioid addiction epidemic, Purdue Pharma's pursuit of financial profit showed they didn't care about the epidemic of addiction and overdose deaths that they were fueling. The fact that the Food and Drug Administration (FDA) failed to properly regulate the claims that Purdue was making. The failure of the medical establishment and the fact that it took money from opioid makers and promoted aggressive use. The fact that state medical boards failed to regulate the way doctors were prescribing. There is a lot of blame to go around." **—Dr. Andrew Kolodny, director of Opioid Policy Research, The Heller School for Social Policy and Management at Brandeis University, founder of Physicians for Responsible Opioid Prescribing (PROP)**

too easily affordable fines must be enacted to bring the guilty to justice and stop the carnage.

THE PLAYERS REVEALED

Ours is a David versus Goliath story. One side had all the money and power. But the other side had the truth. Dr. Andrew Kolodny and fellow PROP members questioned Purdue's claims that their time-release designer drug OxyContin was nonaddictive and safe to use for chronic pain. PROP members channeled their outrage by starting a resistance campaign against the overprescribing of opioids.

The Sackler brothers, Arthur, Mortimer, and Raymond, were born in the 1920s to Eastern European immigrants who ran a grocery store in Brooklyn. Their story was beyond the typical immigrant success story. The brothers' trajectory reached the pinnacle of the American Dream. All three brothers became prominent physicians. Arthur Sackler was honored by the Medical Advertising Hall of Fame. The fantastically successful marketing of OxyContin made Mortimer and Raymond and their descendants billionaires many times over. (Arthur died before OxyContin was released.) These men, the sons of Brooklyn immigrants, were soon firmly inside high society's inner circle. As philanthropists, they

"WE CAN'T SEE PURDUE'S FINANCIALS as easily as we can a publicly traded company because they're under no obligation to disclose their financial statements. But we do have third-party audit data that tracks prescriptions and estimates prescription sales. Those would imply that Purdue in the United States is making a little bit less than $700 million in gross sales, before discounts, *per quarter*, which is obviously a very significant number. They are somewhere south of three billion per year, at least. A reasonable working estimate for annual sales for Purdue in the United States would be somewhere between $2 and $3 billion."
—**Richard Evans, general manager, SSR Health**

became great patrons of the arts and generous academic benefactors. The Egyptian Temple of Dendur at New York's Metropolitan Museum of Art resides in the Sackler Wing. Galleries at the Smithsonian, Harvard, Oxford, and Peking University all bear the Sackler name. They endowed academic chairs in universities around the world. Their combined family fortune is worth more than $35 billion.[4] In 2018, Purdue Pharma's net valuation was estimated to be more than $14 billion. Because they are a private company, this is a best estimate calculation from USC professor of Pharmacuetical Economics and Policy Joel Hay, PhD.

Professor Hay continues: "Pain is one of the most common symptoms that patients will visit a doctor to deal with. All kinds of pain, back pain, knee pain, ankle pain, muscle pain. Opioids have a role, but for many types of pain, opioids are not the appropriate drug of choice. In particular, if you consider people with chronic pain issues, the evidence suggests that in most cases, opioids are not the right way to go, because they have many serious side effects. They can cause sedation that can sometimes be fatal. They're highly addictive and can cause overdose. When you have someone who has long-term chronic pain, the opioid treatment will, first of all, increase tolerance over time, so that actual pain benefit declines over time, plus you get all these additional side effects. The evidence suggests that perhaps between 20 and 50 percent

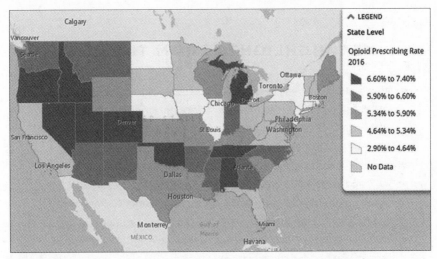

This state map displays the number of opioid prescriptions per 100 residents.
For more information, visit: cdc.gov/vitalsigns/opioids/

THE CENTER FOR DISEASE CONTROL (CDC), 2017

of people on long-term chronic pain relief with opioids will in fact go on to get some form of addiction that may require some type of treatment."

I asked Dr. Hay about the economics of the drug category. "Opioids are a major category of medical spending, according to the Centers for Disease Control (CDC). It's about $24 billion in direct costs for the medication. It's another $75 billion in health-care costs. This is a very significant category in terms of the economic costs. As with many classes of medications, most of the drugs that are taken, in terms of the opioid prescriptions, are not brand name. They are generic, and so the cost per pill is often quite low, but the brand name products account for most of the revenue. They're the ones that capture the vast majority of dollars of sales, and they're the ones that promote with advertising, with sales rep detailing, with journal placements, and with discount coupons. But I have to say, it's the brand name products that are really pushing the frontiers of getting more people into using these drugs."

In 1996, a year after receiving FDA approval for OxyContin, Purdue launched a $208 million marketing campaign that first focused on primary care doctors and their mostly blue-collar patients in the most

KEY HIGHLIGHTS FROM THE CDC

- After a steady increase in the overall national opioid prescribing rate starting in 2006, the total number of prescriptions dispensed peaked in 2012 at more than 255 million and a prescribing rate of 81.3 prescriptions per 100 persons.
- The overall national opioid prescribing rate declined from 2012 to 2017, and in 2017, the prescribing rate had fallen to the lowest it had been in more than 10 years at 58.7 prescriptions per 100 persons (total of more than 191 million total opioid prescriptions).
- However, in 2017, prescribing rates continue to remain very high in certain areas across the country.
  - In 16 percent of US counties, enough opioid prescriptions were dispensed for every person to have one.
  - While the overall opioid prescribing rate in 2017 was 58.7 prescriptions per 100 people, some counties had rates that were seven times higher than that.

vulnerable of American communities, starting in the coal-mining and steel-producing regions in West Virginia, Kentucky, and Ohio.[5]

Our research further revealed that Purdue created self-financed NGOs, such as the American Pain Society, to back their marketing claims that OxyContin was nonaddictive because of its time-release formula. These organizations claimed to be grassroots efforts by everyday sufferers of chronic pain who were helped by opioid painkillers. In reality, these were so-called "astroturf" organizations, created and funded by the pharmaceutical industry to roll out support for their misleading claims that opioids were "less than 1 percent addictive."[6]

According to Dr. Kolodny, it was easy for doctors and patients to overlook the risks of opioid dependence because the pills had been endorsed by the medical establishment and the FDA. Dr. Kolodny referred to this phenomenon as "invisible addiction." Countless

Americans ended up taking medication prescribed to them, only to discover months
later that they could not stop their dependence on opioids.

THE COVER-UP

American Pain Society

American Pain Society was largely funded by Purdue and other pharmaceutical companies.

Opioids have a long history in medical treatment. Before OxyContin, doctors viewed opi-
oids as dangerously addictive and primarily reserved them for cancer
patients and the terminally ill. But Purdue Pharma envisioned a much
larger market.

In a 2018 overview of the crisis, the National Institute on Drug
Abuse (NIDA) wrote: "In the late 1990's, pharmaceutical companies,
led by Purdue Pharma, reassured the medical community that patients
would not become addicted to prescription pain relievers, and health-
care providers began to prescribe them at greater rates."[7]

By the late 1980s, the patent on Purdue's main source of revenue,
a morphine pill for cancer called MS Contin, was running out. Executives anticipated a massive loss of revenue as generic versions came
onto the market, according to internal company correspondence from
that period. The company was focused on finding a new moneymaker. In
a 1990 memo, Robert F. Kaiko, vice president for clinical research, laid
out why it was important to develop a second painkiller. "MS Contin
may eventually face such serious generic competition that other controlled-release opioids must be considered," he wrote.[8]

Purdue had already developed a technique to extend the release
time of a drug over several hours by using special polymer coatings.
In MS Contin, the technique made morphine last 8 to 12 hours. Kaiko
and his colleagues decided to use it on an older narcotic—at least twice
as long as the generic competition. Over the next decade, Purdue sunk
more than $40 million into the development of OxyContin, according to
a 2003 court declaration by then vice president of scientific and medical

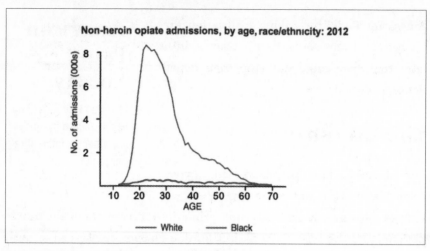

Dr. Andrew Kolodny's PPT Presentation, San Diego, 2014

affairs, Paul D. Goldenheim.[9] Purdue moved aggressively ahead on two paths: seeking patents for its new drug and running additional clinical trials to secure FDA approval.

The FDA approved OxyContin in 1995. Dr. Curtis Wright led the FDA's medical review of the drug. Shortly after OxyContin's approval, he left the FDA and within two years was working for Purdue in new product development. He has refused comment on the FDA's review findings that led to OxyContin's approval.

Despite test results that showed only about 50 percent of patients experienced 12-hour relief, Purdue continued to represent to doctors that OxyContin was a 12-hour drug. In spite of these mixed results, the FDA continued to allow them to make this claim. This was important to Purdue because it gave them the competitive edge they needed to successfully market OxyContin. Twelve-hour dosing was more convenient for patients. It was also far better for business.

PAIN AS THE FIFTH VITAL SIGN

In 1990, Dr. Mitchell Max, the president of the American Pain Society (APS), claimed patients were not being asked by their doctors and nurses about their pain. Nurses were not able to adjust doses, and physicians were reluctant to use opioids. Pain was often invisible, APS argued. Physicians were "rarely held accountable" for inadequate pain control. "Pain relief has been nobody's job," Dr. Max said in a speech before the APS.

Dr. Max recommended that patients be brought into the communication loop. He wanted to increase clinician accountability by developing assurance guidelines and measuring patient satisfaction. He cited a study that claimed "therapeutic use of opiate analgesics rarely results in addiction." However, this study was not a study at all, but rather an observational letter to the editor of the *New England Journal of Medicine*.[10] Dr. James Campbell, APS's president after Dr. Max, proclaimed in 1995 that clinicians should track pain as the "fifth vital sign," along with the four established vital signs of pulse, temperature, blood pressure, and respiratory rate.[11]

LIES TAKE THEIR TOLL

In 1995, the FDA approved OxyContin for sale. FDA officials, headed by Dr. Curtis Wright, allowed the company to state that the time-release version of OxyContin "is believed to reduce its potential to be abused."[12]

The following year, 1996, was pivotal for the opioid treatment of pain. Purdue introduced its graduated time-release version of OxyContin and kicked off a $208 million multipronged marketing blitz for OxyContin.

In 1997, the Joint Commission on Accreditation of Healthcare Organizations—the organization that gives accreditation to hospitals—developed a report for new pain standards. The American Pain Society, largely funded by Purdue, and the Robert Wood Johnson Foundation financed the report.

Also in 1997, OxyContin users began to voice their concerns outside of the medical community. A court testimony revealed that an overflow of messages concerning OxyContin's addictive side effects surged into Purdue's online chat rooms. *New York Times* journalist Barry Meier remarked that Purdue's response was to bury this information.[13]

In 2000, Dr. Dennis O'Leary, president of the Joint Commission, announced new standards for health-care organizations to improve pain management.[14] "The pain management paradigm is about to shift," he said. He emphasized the need for organizations to do systematic assessments and use quantitative measures of pain. The commission wrote that "the inadequate treatment of pain was recognized in the 1990s as a growing public health issue." This policy shift led the Joint Commission to rewrite its accreditation standards in 2001.[15]

Even though pain is not a sign that can be objectively measured, these successful lobbying efforts established pain as the fifth vital sign. The new Joint Commission guidelines required health-care providers to ask every patient about their pain. They also began using a patient survey to determine hospital reimbursement rates and instigated the creation of physician surveys and reviews.[16] It linked hospital reimbursement rates to patient satisfaction with pain treatment and the requirement that physicians submit to a patient survey regarding their pain treatment with opioids.[17]

Patients were given charts to rate their pain. As you can see, this chart offers no objective measurement.

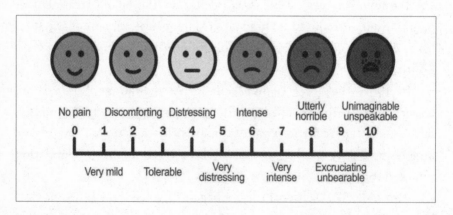

The Pain Chart
COURTESY OF PROHEALTH.COM

The Joint Commission is a not-for-profit organization that certifies nearly 21,000 health-care organizations and programs in the United States. In 2001, the Joint Commission published its official standards report to improve their care for patients with pain. Their new standards approved the treatment of both acute and chronic pain with prescription opioids. According to Dr. Richard Ries, "When the Joint Commission established pain as a vital sign, it just added lighter fluid to the fire."[18]

Pharmaceutical industry lobbyists were able to convince the Joint Commission to adopt guidelines written by industry-funded think tanks such as the American Pain Society (APS). Those guidelines provided a simple numbered scale (or a chart like the one on page 32), which asked patients to rate their pain from 1 to 10. Doctors, now under more pressure to produce short-term patient satisfaction, would then prescribe opioid painkillers. Having read new literature, also written by pharma-industry doctors and think tanks, primary care doctors would prescribe these painkillers they were being told were not as addictive as once believed.

The Joint Commission's new standards were hailed by pain-management specialists and called "a rare and important opportunity for widespread and sustainable improvement in how pain is managed in the United States."[19] The standards recommended using patients' self-reported pain using numerical scales. This was supported by a study that found emergency department nurses significantly underestimated patients' pain compared to what patients self-reported (4.2 versus 7.7 on a 10-point scale). However, no large national studies were conducted to examine whether implementation of the standards improved pain assessment or control.[20] "Pain is whatever the experiencing person says it is, existing whenever the experiencing person says it does,"[21] according to the book *Textbook of Basic Nursing* by Caroline Bunker Rosdahl and Mary T. Kowalski. "Pain is a subjective experience, and self-report of pain is the most reliable indicator of a patient's experience. Determining pain is an important component of a physical assessment."[22]

Purdue, one of two drug companies providing money for the Joint Commission's pain-management education programs, was allowed to distribute educational videos and a book about pain management. These products were available to buy on the Joint Commission's website.[23] From 1996 to 2002, Purdue paid for 20,000 pain-related education programs through which doctors could earn continuing education credits, referred to as CEUs, required for maintaining their medical license, according to the General Accounting Office (GAO).[24] Without reliable scientific proof, these so-called findings stated that under a physician's proper care, opioids were proven to be nonaddictive.

OxyContin sales rose from $45 million in 1996 to more than $1.5 billion in 2002. But the drug's huge success as a treatment for long-term chronic pain—and much of the marketing that drove it—had no basis in meaningful science, according to the CDC in its 2016 Guidelines.[25] There was no controlled, double-blind research—and there still hasn't been—that supports the notion that opioids are effective for treating chronic pain over a period of many months, let alone years. "For the vast majority of patients, the known, serious, and too-often-fatal risks far outweigh the unproven and transient benefits," said Dr. Thomas Frieden, former head of the CDC.[26]

Lack of oversight has cost our country dearly. The United States is in a health-care crisis that has taken hundreds of thousands of lives, fractured families, and devastated communities across the country. National Public Radio (NPR reported in 2018 that the opioid epidemic has cost the United States more than a trillion dollars since 2001 in lost earnings and productivity.[27] Early deaths and the inability to work due to substance abuse disorders have cost additional billions in lost tax revenue.

Since 2000, the following statistics have been reported from the CDC:

- In 2016, according to the CDC's National Center for Health Statistics, across demographic categories, the largest increase in opioid overdose death rates was in males between the ages of 25 and 44.
- According to the CDC, the number of opioid overdose deaths

in 2017 is six times higher than the number of opioid deaths in 1999.[28] According to the *Journal of the American Medical Association* (September 2017), for the first time since 1993 American life expectancy actually dropped. The driving factor in this trend was opioid overdose deaths. The drop continued in 2018.

■ The *New York Times* in December 2017 reported on the increasing numbers of children being placed into foster care because their addicted parents could no longer take adequate care of them, labeling them "the opioid plague's youngest victims." In 2017, 440,000 children were in foster care, a 10 percent increase since 2010.

"Opportunities to Prevent Overdose Deaths Involving Prescription and Illicit Opioids" are examined in the CDC's Morbidity and Mortality Weekly Report:

■ Overall drug overdose death rates increased by 21.5 percent.

- The overdose death rate from synthetic opioids (other than methadone) more than doubled, likely driven by illicitly manufactured fentanyl (IMF).
- The prescription opioid-related overdose death rate increased by 10.6 percent.
- The heroin-related overdose death rate increased by 19.5 percent.

■ Death rates from overdoses involving synthetic opioids increased in 21 states, with 10 states doubling their rates from 2015 to 2016.

- New Hampshire, West Virginia, and Massachusetts had the highest death rates from synthetic opioids.

■ Fourteen states had significant increases in death rates

involving heroin, with West Virginia, Ohio, and Washington, DC, having the highest rates.

- Eight states had significant increases in death rates involving prescription opioids. West Virginia, Maryland, Maine, and Utah had the highest rates.
- Sixteen states had significant increases in death rates involving cocaine, with Rhode Island and Ohio having the highest rates.
- Fourteen states had significant increases in death rates involving psychostimulants; the highest death rates occurred primarily in the Midwest and Western regions.[29]

"Effective, synchronized programs to prevent drug overdoses will require coordination of law enforcement, first responders, mental health/substance-abuse providers, public health agencies, and community partners," said the report's lead author, Puja Seth, PhD.[30]

As we have seen, the flagrant mistruths about OxyContin and other opioids have taken their devastating toll. If these prescription drugs are not addictive, then why have so many Americans died of overdoses? Purdue's false marketing campaign—with no real scientific data—was responsible for the deaths of hundreds of thousands of American lives.

THE COUNTERATTACK

In 2003, Dr. Gary Franklin and his Washington State colleagues reported a jump in opioid-related overdose deaths among workers covered by the Washington State workers' compensation system. Researchers linked these deaths to the relaxation of prescribing laws in the late 1990s. In response to the epidemic, the state drafted new guidelines that went into effect in 2007 and were updated in 2010 and 2015. Countering the marketing thrust of Purdue, the Washington State guidelines directed physicians to use opioids more conservatively and at lower doses. It suggested other strategies such as graded exercise and cognitive-behavioral therapy as a preferable alternative to medication.

In 2006, Dr. Len Palouzzi, a CDC research scientist, published a graph that showed the increase in opioid overdose deaths was parallel to the increase in sales of opioids. In 2007, the federal government won a $634 million settlement against Purdue. The company's legal team, led by former mayor and current White House counsel Rudy Giuliani, admitted to fraudulent advertising practices but maintained that they did nothing wrong. While this was one of the largest settlements ever won by the government against a corporation, it allowed Purdue and others to continue selling opioids. Though the settlement was the largest in American history, the amount Purdue paid was only a fraction of their earnings that ranged between $2 and $3 billion annually. Purdue had lost the battle but won the war. To date, it is still selling opioids.

For a brief moment in 2013, it seemed the problems with 12-hour dosing might get wider attention. The FDA had called for public input into how to improve labels for powerful pain medications. Dr. David Egilman, a Brown University clinical professor of family medicine, who had served as a plaintiff's expert witness in several unsuccessful suits against Purdue, saw this as an opportunity to alert agency officials to the problems with OxyContin's 12-hour claim. In a five-minute presentation, Egilman accused Purdue of ignoring its own science for financial reasons and sending patients on a dangerous roller coaster of addiction, withdrawal, relief, and possible overdose. "The [12-hour] dosing schedule is an addiction-producing machine," he said.[31]

The year 2016 can be looked upon as the big turn-around. The first major achievement was the issuing of the CDC's groundbreaking 2016 revised pain guidelines that came out against the use of opioids for the treatment of chronic pain. The guidelines ended months of arguments with opioid-supportive pain-management doctors and drug industry groups who had bitterly opposed the new CDC recommendations on the grounds that they would create unfair hurdles for patients who have legitimate long-term pain.[32]

"We lose sight of the fact that the prescription opioids are just as

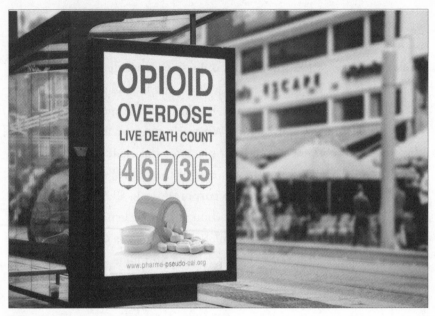

Opioid Overdose Live Death Count

GRAPHIC COURTESY OF MATT STEFL, CLINICAL PROFESSOR, MARKETING,
LOYOLA MARYMOUNT UNIVERSITY, LOS ANGELES, CALIFORNIA

addictive as heroin," said Dr. Frieden, the then head of the CDC. "Prescribing opioids is really a momentous decision, and I think that has been lost."

In 2016, the American Medical Association announced that it was dropping pain as the fifth vital sign. The AMA's main solution to the problem was to simply stop asking patients about their pain.[33]

"Just as we now know the earth is not flat, we know that pain is not a vital sign. Let's remove that from the lexicon," said AMA delegate Dr. James Milam. "Let's get rid of the whole concept and move on."[34]

Dropping pain as the fifth vital sign in March 2016 meant that the AMA, the country's largest medical society, essentially adopted the same policies advocated by Physicians for Responsible Opioid Prescribing (PROP). In a 2016 Senate hearing on opioid abuse, Dr. Kolodny testified that opioids such as OxyContin were nothing more than heroin pills.

In February 2018, over mounting pressure, Purdue announced that they would suspend the marketing of OxyContin to physicians until further notice. But that didn't mean they would suspend sales of their star performer, OxyContin.

FUTURE JUSTICE

Dozens of states, cities, and counties have sued companies including Purdue Pharma, Insys, Endo Pharmaceuticals, Janssen Pharmaceutica (owned by Johnson & Johnson), and Rochester Drug Cooperative. At the time of writing, hundreds of lawsuits are pending against these companies and others, from individuals affected by the crisis to a coalition of over 40 state attorneys general. The suits allege that the companies triggered the opioid epidemic by minimizing the risk of addiction and overdose from painkillers such as OxyContin, Percocet, and Duragesic. Opioids don't just cause problems when they're misused, the suits argue: They do so even when used as directed by a physician.

In 2017, Mike Moore, the lawyer who tried and bested Big Tobacco, began trying his hand against Big Pharma and their unproven marketing claims. In the Tobacco Master Settlement Agreement of 1974, the original participating manufacturers (OPM) agreed to pay a minimum of $206 billion over the first 25 years of the agreement. Now it is Big Pharma's turn to feel the weight of Moore's legal skills. "There are hundreds of lawyers working on this all across the country," he said. "I'm just trying to keep people focused on solving the problem rather than being focused on trying to make a bunch of money. And trying to say, 'Let's do something about the opioid epidemic.' We have an opportunity here to do some good. Let's do it. And I say that to the companies, too. I truthfully think there's folks in corporate America in this business that would probably want to be part of the solution rather than part of the problem. I think they'll be significant players too. It's just the lawyers sometimes on their side get in the way of making the right decisions." Moore adds, "Litigation is a blunt instrument; it's not a surgical tool. But it provokes interest quicker than anything I've ever seen."[35]

CONCLUSION

Providing the tools necessary for universal long-range recovery and rehabilitation is critical for those who cannot find or afford medical-assisted treatment (MAT) and professional intervention. Changing the *perception of addiction*—understanding that it is a disease of the brain and not a crime—is required before we can improve upon the currently inadequate system of treatment and support. We urge health-care professionals and their national network of community partners to take the lead and offer comprehensive long-term treatment to all those suffering from drug abuse, as well as emotional and psychological support to their families engaged in fighting this virulent epidemic.

CHAPTER 2

Ancient Times to Modern Medicine

WHY ARE OPIOIDS such a potent and dangerous drug? How do they work within our body's systems? How long have they been used by humans for the relief from pain? Why are so many people taken in by these drugs against their better judgment? These and other issues are keys to a greater understanding of the opioid epidemic.

A SHORT HISTORY ABOUT THE DEVELOPMENT AND USE OF OPIOIDS

The powerful effects of the poppy flower have been well known for centuries. Its uses, both medicinal and recreational, have been documented across cultures spanning the Eurasian continent. But along with the recognition of the plant's benefits was a clear understanding of its dangers. Opioid's addictive nature has led many societies to attempt to ban or at least curtail its use, yet it has remained almost ever-present throughout human history. Its ability to fight pain makes opioid products incredibly enticing for the medical community, and its euphoric effects draw people to it despite its dangers. Even now, after all the damage opioids have wrought across the globe, opioids remain a legitimate medical tool, especially with end-of-life and cancer patients, with few calling for the drug to be banned outright.

Opium poppy ready for harvesting.
COURTESY DEA MUSEUM

HOW OPIOIDS WORK

Since ancient times, the milky fluid that seeps from the unripe poppy seedpod has been scraped off and dried to produce what is known as opium. The seedpod is first cut with a bladed tool, which allows the opium "gum" to secrete. The semi-dried gum is harvested, and the resin is used for consumption.

One opiate by-product of the poppy is morphine. Heroin is a slight chemical variant of the morphine molecule called diacetylmorphine. An important difference between heroin and morphine is that heroin is far more fat-soluble. Because the brain is mostly fat, when someone uses heroin, it gets into the brain much faster than morphine, producing the rush that people experience when they use the drug.

Most other opioids are either synthetic or semisynthetic and are a manipulation of the morphine molecule. An example of a synthetic opioid would be oxycodone, the drug that is the basis of several opioid painkillers, including OxyContin. Oxycodone was developed in Germany

"WE NEED TO have a greater public awareness. We need to know ourselves better. There's nothing evil about seeking reward. It's just that you have to be careful because you can easily hijack that part of the human brain. And in hijacking it, drugs are a very, very special, easy route, especially the opioids, because they are so compelling. Once you begin to find that you like them, it isn't very long before you need them. Once you need them, you learn that you can't do without them. And that cycle keeps on going." —Peter Whybrow, MD, director of the Semel Institute at UCLA's School of Medicine and a psychiatrist

at the Goethe University Frankfurt in 1916. An array of synthetic opioids was created in the past hundred years. Some are less potent than morphine while others, such as fentanyl, are much more powerful. All of these chemical compounds act within a similar area of the brain, known as the nerve cell receptor site. Opioid receptors are also found on nerve cells outside of the brain, including on the glial cells along the spinal cord.

Nerve cells communicate with one another by producing electrical impulses down the length of the neuron, but the nerve cells don't completely touch. There is a narrow gap called the synaptic cleft between the nerve cells. The synaptic cleft is a saltwater gap that the electrical impulses cannot cross. A separate impulse is released and goes down the axon, or the length of the nerve cell. It triggers a chemical messenger that can cross the gap and bind to a receptor on the other side, directing the receiving nerve cell to either produce more electrical impulses or turn them off.

Visualize the messenger and receptor as a key and a lock that can open our brain to various stimuli. These chemical messengers, called neurotransmitters, have just the right shape to be able to unlock the receptor molecule. We have receptors in our brains for compounds chemically similar to opioids, which is what makes us so susceptible to addiction.

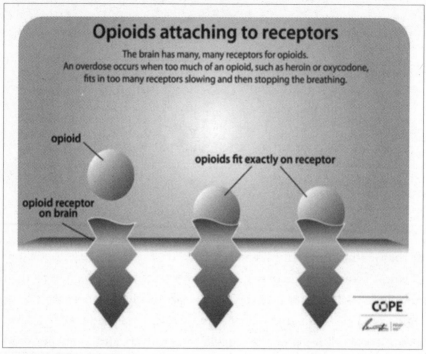

Opioids Attaching to Receptors
COURTESY OF SLIDEPLAYER.COM

Dr. Kelly Clark is the president of the American Society of Addiction Medicine. She is based in Louisville, Kentucky, the state arguably hardest hit by the opioid crisis. "We had a school with 300 kids and 30 dead parents," she said. "We had another school, 150 kids, 15 dead parents. We have entire communities that don't have parent-teacher days anymore because the parents are either incarcerated, away at a rehab, or dead." In 2000, the DEA identified 10 counties with the highest numbers of prescription opioids. Five of them were in Kentucky. As the government cracked down on prescription opioids, heroin filled the gap.

"Unlike alcohol or methamphetamine, we actually have opioid receptors in our brains," Dr. Clark said. "Being the clever species, we have managed to extract from a poppy flower, and then in labs, something that really targets those opioid receptors in our brains." The receptiveness of our brains to the opioid compound not only makes us highly

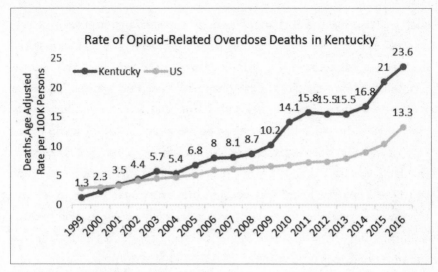

Opioid Overdose Deaths in Kentucky
CDC WONDER, 2017

susceptible to addiction but renders us vulnerable to dependency even after long periods of abstinence. "What happens when people have been using these very powerful opioids is that their brains change and don't change back," Dr. Clark continues. "They can go into a period of quiescence. This is how people can go for years once they're off all opioids. Their doctors and they think, 'Hey, I've gotten over this. I don't have a problem anymore. I've got a new life.' They have an accident, and they get started on an opioid. Their brain has been changed, and it kicks right back into the gear. Those receptors change right back. They're off and running again with their addictive disease."

PAINFUL WITHDRAWAL SYMPTOMS

Humans have known for millennia just how addictive the opium plant is, but it wasn't until recently that we truly understood its effects on the brain. Once someone is physically dependent on a drug, stopping use of that drug can cause withdrawal. With opioids, the symptoms of withdrawal can be extremely painful. "Synapsis will change, transmitters will change. Their brain will change," said Dr. Chris Evans, professor of Psychiatry and Biobehavioral Studies at the University of California, Los Angeles, and director of the Brain Research Institute. "They will become adapted to the drugs, so the drug has really become a normal state for them. Then when they take away the drug, that's when you have withdrawal. Withdrawal is usually the opposite effect of the drug. So in the case of opiates, opiate drugs cause constipation. When you take away the drug, you have diarrhea. They're anxiolytic; they stop anxiety. When you take away the drug, you become more anxious. This is true with the reward system as well. When you take away the drug, you become unhappy, depressed. If you're taking the drug for depression, then that symptom becomes much worse."

Opium's effects have been used for centuries as pain relief. The pain-fighting effects of opioids are precisely what attracted the medical community in the first place. But when opioids are taken away, one of the withdrawal symptoms is pain, regardless of any independent, preexisting pain. We will see in later chapters how this became a critical feature in the origins of the opioid crisis. Patients who were prescribed opioids to treat their pain would begin to experience withdrawal, which caused intense pain in and of itself. This would cause them to take more opioids, trapping patients in a worsening cycle of dependency, addiction, and pain.

THE HISTORY OF OPIUM

Historically, the use of opioids dates back to ancient times. The earliest references to opium come from Mesopotamia in 3400 BCE. The Sumerians called it the "joy plant."[36] Homer described its use in *The Odyssey*, and for thousands of years people have used the drug to relieve pain and turn anxiety into euphoria. The plant spread through trade and, with it, its reputation for potency and addiction.

As their empire grew, the British used the opium trade to expand their control over China and the Indian subcontinent. In the

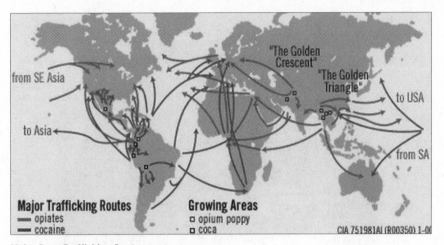

Major Drug Trafficking Routes

CENTRAL INTELLIGENCE AGENCY (CIA)

mid-nineteenth century, opium became a significant force in the international economy. Chinese merchants found it useful as a substitute for cash, and since poppies can be grown in almost any soil or weather, cultivation quickly spread throughout China and other parts of Asia. The imperial government of China tried to ban opium, but local officials often merely looked the other way, taking bribes and trying to avoid antagonizing local farmers who depended on the crop. One provincial governor observed that opium, once regarded as a poison, was now treated in the same way as tea or rice.

By the 1880s, governors in provincial China who had initially suppressed opium use and production depended on its taxes. In a stagnating economy, opium supplied fluid capital and created new sources of revenue. Smugglers, poor farmers, retail merchants, and officials all depended on opium for their livelihood. Much of the opium in China was produced or facilitated by the British Empire. When Chinese officials destroyed a shipment of opium aboard a British trade ship in 1839, the British Empire began a war that would bring China to its knees. This war would begin what the Chinese refer to as the "Century of Humiliation," as Britain, its European rivals, the Japanese, and the Americans divided China into veritable fiefdoms.[37]

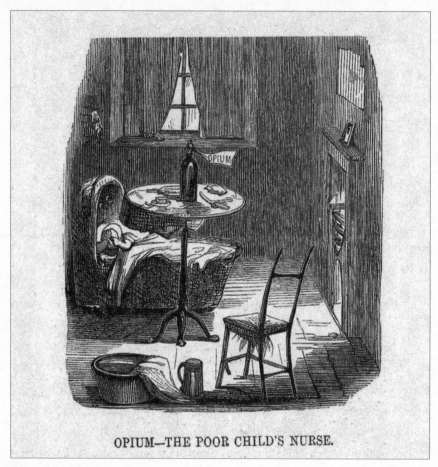

OPIUM—THE POOR CHILD'S NURSE.

Harper's Weekly, 1870
HARPWEEK.COM, ARTIST UNKNOWN

Opioid products have a long history in the United States. An opium tincture called laudanum dates back to the 1660s and was widely prescribed in the Victorian era for all kinds of pain.[38] Opium was used to treat wounded soldiers in both the American Revolution and Civil War. By the late-nineteenth century, opioids had found their way into a variety of household products, including tooth powders and headache medicines.[39] The drug's addictive effects didn't go unnoticed; as more and more people began to suffer from addiction, doctors and then the federal government began to respond.

The Pure Food and Drug Act was a landmark leg-
islation passed in 1906 under the administration of
President Theodore Roosevelt. It gave the government
the ability to regulate the contents of foods, alcohol,
and medicine. In 1914, the Harrison Narcotics Tax Act
put additional restrictions on the manufacture and
sale of opium products but still allowed for some medical use.[40] These laws were America's first efforts at
drug prohibition, particularly for recreational drugs.
These acts codified the idea that drug users and
addicts were criminals and moral deviants.[41]

Bayer heroin bottle,
originally containing
5 grams of Heroin
substance.

In World War I, the German military introduced heroin to its soldiers to alleviate pain and reduce the need for sleep. Oxycodone was
synthesized in a German laboratory after the Bayer pharmaceutical company stopped the mass production of heroin due to addiction
and abuse problems. It was hoped that the drug would retain the pain-

Current legal production of opium.
COURTESY DEA MUSEUM

killing effects of morphine and heroin with less of the euphoric effect. This was achieved to a certain extent as oxycodone does not "hit" the central nervous system with the same potency as heroin or morphine and doesn't last as long.

In twentieth-century medicine, opioids were used with great caution and mostly in the treatment of intense cancer pain, end-of-life care, or emergency pain relief from traumatic injury or surgery. It was understood that these drugs were highly addictive and should be used only in special circumstances and under strict supervision. According to the DEA, the growing of opium for medicinal use currently takes place in India, Turkey, and Australia. Two thousand tons of legal opium are produced annually, and this supplies the world with the raw materials needed to make medicinal products.

THE ILLEGAL OPIUM TRADE

Traditionally, there were at least three main sources for illegal opium: Burma, Afghanistan, and Colombia. Opium and heroin are ideal trade products—they are in great demand, incredibly profitable, and relatively easy to produce. Production of black-market opium requires no modern machinery or advanced technical knowledge. Modern transportation allows opium and heroin to be smuggled around the globe in days, and the products have long and stable shelf lives. As the opioid crisis in the United States grew and the demand for black-market opiates soared, Mexican drug cartels, which had traditionally trafficked in cocaine, shifted their focus to the production and sale of heroin. In 2015, the DEA reported that 93 percent of the heroin it seized came from Mexico, particularly the southern state of Guerrero.[42] Guerrero is a mountainous state, and its rugged terrain makes it conducive to both the growing of poppies for heroin and hiding from the authorities. The plant's high resilience and lucrative returns make it an attractive proposition for the poor farmers of the region.

HOW OXYCODONE ABUSE ALSO LED TO HEROIN USE

In the United States, oxycodone is a Schedule II controlled substance, both by itself and in combination with non-opioid pain relievers such as acetaminophen, ibuprofen, or aspirin. Oxycodone was first introduced into the US market in 1939 and is the active ingredient in a number of pain medications commonly prescribed for the relief of moderate to heavy pain.

Oxycodone is a drug subject to abuse and is included in the sections of the law for the most strongly controlled substances that have a commonly accepted medical use. It is also subject to international treaties controlling psychoactive drugs subject to abuse or dependence.[43] Oxycodone is sold in a sustained-release formula in the US by Purdue Pharma under the trade name OxyContin, short for oxycodone continuous release. OxyContin is made of pure oxycodone and the inert filler hydrochloride. As with OxyContin, hydrochloride makes it soluble and easier for our bodies to ingest. OxyContin has similar euphoric effects to morphine and heroin. Nausea, drowsiness, constipation, lightheadedness, rash or itchiness, dizziness, and emotional mood disorders are the most frequently reported side effects.

Since the original formulation of OxyContin contains only oxycodone and an inert filler, abusers were able to simply crush the tablets. They then either ingested the resulting powder orally, intranasally, intravenously, intramuscularly, or subcutaneously injection by dissolving the powder. Some abusers even used the drug rectally to achieve rapid absorption into the bloodstream. Injection of OxyContin is particularly dangerous. The oxycodone contained in OxyContin produces typical opioid effects and is considered to be a reasonable substitute for heroin. It is known in many parts of the country, including Appalachia, as "heroin pills."[44]

The vast majority of OxyContin-related deaths are attributed to ingesting substantial quantities of oxycodone in combination with

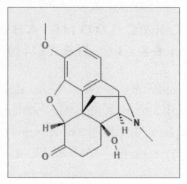

Comparison of the oxycodone molecule and the heroin molecule

COURTESY OF THE NIH MEDICAL LIBRARY,
HTTPS://PUBCHEM.NCBI.NLM.NIH.GOV/COMPOUND/HEROIN

another depressant of the central nervous system such as alcohol or benzodiazepines.[45] When taken in large quantities, opioids can cause respiratory depression, the failure of the respiratory system, which leads to suffocation and death. In 2010, in response to growing concern about the abuse of OxyContin, Purdue Pharma released a reformulated version, which was harder to snort or inject. Previously, OxyContin pills could be crushed into a powder that could be snorted or mixed with water and injected. The new formulation instead produced a gummy substance that was difficult to snort or inject.

In a 2018 working paper for the National Bureau of Economic Research, the authors detail how the reformulation of OxyContin caused a shift from the abuse of that drug to the use of heroin. "We attribute the recent quadrupling of heroin death rates to the 2010 reformulation of an oft-abused prescription opioid, OxyContin. The new abuse-deterrent formulation led many consumers to substitute to an inexpensive alternative, heroin," the authors wrote.[46]

This transfer between prescription opioids and black-market drugs has been a crucial feature of the opioid crisis. While official numbers vary, it is widely recognized that a majority of those in treatment, or who have died from heroin, began by abusing prescription opioids.[47] (In 2018, Attorney General Jeff Sessions said the number was as high as 80 percent.[48]) Though not all heroin users began with prescription drugs, it is widely believed that the demand for illicit opioids was bolstered by the widespread abuse of prescription opioids. The demand fueled the production of opium in Mexico and significantly drove down the price of heroin on the street.[49]

THE THIRD WAVE OF OPIOID EPIDEMIC: WHITE MEN

The current opioid epidemic is the largest in America's history but is by no means its first. As we learn earlier in the chapter, opioids have been in the United States since the country's founding, but it is only in the current crisis that heroin has been associated with white communities. In the past, drugs like opium and heroin were associated with communities of color, Chinese immigrants, or black people in the inner city. "This is actually the third wave of opioid epidemic for the country," Dr. Clark said. "The first wave was with opium. That actually followed the railroads built by the Chinese. The second wave was back in the 1970s, which was when many in the urban, inner city, minority population was abusing heroin and crack cocaine. We're in this third wave of opioid epidemic. The epidemic that we're dealing with right now is different than any other epidemic we've dealt with in this country. Like infectious diseases, it knows no class or race or cultural boundaries. It impacts every one of every demographic group. Unlike other diseases, it's now really entrenched into our society. Forty-four percent of Americans know someone personally who's suffering with opioid addiction." While it's true that opioid addiction knows no boundaries, the current epidemic is largely associated with white, working-class males. Coincidentally, we're starting to hear a more compassionate approach to solving the crisis. Previous efforts deliberately portrayed drug use as delinquent behavior, and heroin as a specifically black problem.[50]

In 1972, President Richard Nixon inaugurated the "War on Drugs" to combat the increasing drug problem in the United States. Nixon's War on Drugs focused not on treatment but on punishment. In 1994, a former aide to Richard Nixon, John Ehrlichman, told *Harper's Magazine* writer Dan Baum about the motivation behind the War on Drugs. "You want to know what this was really all about?" Ehrlichman asked Baum. "The Nixon campaign in 1968, and the Nixon White House after that, had two enemies: the antiwar left and black people. You understand what I'm saying? We knew we couldn't make it illegal to be either against the war or black, but by getting the public to associate the hippies with marijuana and blacks with heroin, and then criminalizing both heavily, we could disrupt those communities. We could arrest their leaders, raid their homes, break up their meetings, and vilify them night after night on the evening news. Did we know we were lying about the drugs? Of course we did."[51] Ehrlichman spent 18 months in prison for crimes related to the Watergate scandal and in his later life became a radio host and TV pundit.[52]

The association of drugs with people of color facilitated a knee-jerk "tough on crime" approach. Mandatory minimum sentences were instituted for low-level drug offense and created a police surveillance system that routinely and flagrantly violated the rights of countless people. It was during this time that the prison population exploded.[53]

The United States quickly became the country with the most incarcerated people, with more than two million people in prison.[54] America has only 5 percent of the world's population but 25 percent of the world's prisoners.[55] Eighty percent of inmates in federal prison are black or Latino, and in state prisons that number is 60 percent.[56] Today, 80 percent of opioid overdose deaths are white people, while only 10 percent are black and 8 percent Latino. It is no coincidence then that the institutional approach to combating this current drug epidemic has become one of compassion and treatment rather than punishment and vilification.

In an interview with National Public Radio's Noel King, Dr. Andrew Kolodny of PROP had this to say: "What we got from policymakers was a message that we could potentially arrest our way out of the problem. What we got was a war on drugs and a crackdown on crime. What we're

"OUR PREVENTION AND TREATMENT in this country are archaic at best. We have evidence-based prevention. We have evidence-based treatments, but we don't use them. We've known for years that D.A.R.E. to keep kids off drugs not only doesn't work to keep kids off drugs, but in some cases, actually increases the chances that kids are on drugs. But we use it in 75 percent of our communities instead of using evidence-based practices." **—Dr. Kelly Clark, MD, president of the American Society of Addiction Medicine**

seeing now is a very different response now that we've got an addiction epidemic that's disproportionately white. We're hearing from policymakers, even conservative Republican politicians, when they talk about the opioid crisis, many begin by saying we can't arrest our way out of this. We have to see that people who are addicted can access effective treatment. We didn't hear that during the crack cocaine epidemic. It's good that we're hearing it now. It's too bad we didn't hear it then."[57]

THE RISE OF FENTANYL

Even as positive changes in the treatment of addicts take hold, the current crisis is constantly changing and creating new challenges every day. In a similar vein to how the use of prescription opioids led to a boom in the market for cheaper heroin, the demand for heroin has in turn fueled the rise of fentanyl as an even cheaper, and more dangerous, street drug. Fentanyl is a synthetic opioid much like oxycodone and is similarly used in medicine to treat very specific kinds of extreme pain.

As the heroin epidemic grew, illegal drug manufacturers began mixing fentanyl into their heroin and selling it to unsuspecting addicts. Fentanyl, according to the *Washington Post*, is 50 times more powerful than heroin and indistinguishable to the naked eye.[58] According to the *Post*, fentanyl-related overdose deaths in the 24 largest cities in the US rose nearly 600 percent from 2014 to 2016. Fentanyl is manufactured in

"I HOPE WE BEGIN to focus on prevention because we can't incarcerate our way out of this problem. All of the systems that I'm aware of are just completely saturated and just strapped for resources. Funding is difficult, and we do very little prevention around these issues. I don't think we can build big treatment centers. I don't think we can build big prisons. It seems to me that prevention does work and has worked in other situations like heart disease, prostate cancer, and smoking. I think it is time to really focus seriously on prevention." —Karyn Hascal, president of The Healing Place, Louisville, Kentucky

Mexico and China and mixed into heroin and even cocaine. Some long-time addicts are said to even prefer their drugs to be mixed with fentanyl because of its extreme potency.

These numbers are thought to be far below the actual number because many authorities were not looking for fentanyl and therefore missed some of its impact. Postmortem analyses did not test for the drug in many cases, and drug-sniffing dogs have had to be trained to find fentanyl among the myriad of other drugs authorities search for.[59]

In the past few years, authorities have had to scramble to control fentanyl as yet another deadly element in an ever-widening epidemic. Fentanyl's appearance in recent years underscores the complexity of dealing with a crisis now fueled in large part by black-market actors and the almost casual ability to score opioids on downtown street corners across the country. What began with patients abusing prescription opioids quickly bolstered the heroin trade and expanded the number of people using that drug. Now heroin and other drugs are being mixed with a cheaper and more powerful drug by shadowy cartels in the international drug trade.

■ ■ ■

The opioid epidemic in many ways stems from society's inability to address yet another crisis—that of chronic pain. The gravity of chronic

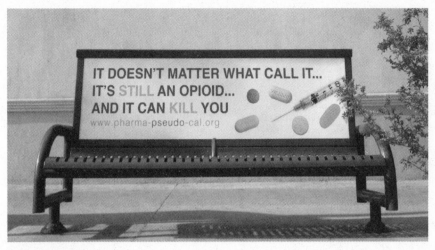

Opioids Can Kill You

COURTESY OF PROFESSOR MATT STEFL, MARKETING, LOYOLA MARYMOUNT UNIVERSITY, LOS ANGELES, CALIFORNIA

pain's effect on society has only recently begun to be truly understood and managed. OxyContin and other opioids were developed as a remedy for the millions of people suffering from chronic pain. What began as an effort to promote the use of opioids for everyday pain soon spiraled out of control and into the national epidemic we have today. In the next chapter we will take a closer look at the science of pain and the evolution of pain medicine and treatment.

CHAPTER 3

The Science of Pain and Pain Management

"The opioid makers never fooled pain-management doctors. They knew that opioids could be addictive. But there are only 5,000 of them. They fooled primary care doctors. There are 500,000 of them."

—*Gerald Sacks, MD, anesthesiologist,*
Pain Institute of Santa Monica, California,
May 10, 2019

PAIN, AS IT is most commonly understood, is the sensory response to a negative influence on the body. It's nature's way of telling us something is wrong. Pain as a medical condition has been little understood until quite recently. We automatically accept pain as a purely physical sensation. Yet when we dig deeper, we find that the sensation of pain is much more complex. Unfortunately for us, pain is made worse by our ability to comprehend the gravity of its consequences.

Pain is now understood by doctors as a biopsychosocial phenomenon. It is affected not only by our physical condition but also the context in which we experience pain. Elements such as our surroundings and our mental health can affect how much pain we actually feel. In

"ONE QUESTION WOULD be why are we in the midst of this opioid epidemic? Another: Why did it start or why is it so bad right now? There are a number of factors. Bad research happened in the early '90s around whether you could treat pain with opiates that was not just terminal pain or acute trauma pain. Many doctors were hesitant. Somehow, in response the research got read that if somebody bumped their knee and had a little pain you should give them a bottle of opiates. What happened with primary care doctors and pain clinics is when they gave lots of pills, their patients kept coming back and saying it was working. Then after a while, they came back and said, 'Now my pain is worse. I think I need more.' And up you go, up on the dose." —Dr. Richard Ries, University of Washington, School of Medicine

his book *Why We Hurt*, Dr. Frank Vertosick Jr. pointed out that while many organisms experience the physical aspect of pain and interpret it as a warning, humans alone understand its full breadth and scope. Understanding the repercussions of pain affects our experience of pain. "When a dog breaks his leg, he feels physical pain," Dr. Vertosick writes, "but when a man breaks a leg, he will experience both physical and psychic pain." The man understands that his injury might affect his work, his personal life, that it may follow him for years to come. "The terrible pain of a broken leg soon merges with the psychic agonies of anger, frustration, worry, and despair. The dog is in pain; the man suffers."[60]

Pain is inescapable. Some philosophers have even regarded it as synonymous with human life itself. Yet according to many medical professionals, pain has been tragically misunderstood for centuries. As Dr. Vertosick wrote, "Pain isn't synonymous with life; it's synonymous with intelligence." It is precisely because we failed to recognize the psychic aspect of pain that past treatments fell short. Only recently have we begun to properly understand pain. Acute versus chronic pain is one of the major themes of the book.

THE TWO TYPES OF PAIN: ACUTE AND CHRONIC

There are two types of pain: acute and chronic. Acute pain is caused by a direct and often identifiable source, such as a disease or an injury. Treating acute pain is often short term and is done by treating the condition that causes it: Treat the cancer, treat the pain. Treat the toothache, eliminate the pain. Chronic pain is far more complex and elusive. Chronic pain is reoccurring pain, the origins of which can be a mystery to both patients and medical professionals. What makes chronic pain so difficult to diagnose is that its causes are incredibly diverse. There are any number of conditions that can produce pain. Discovering the source of the condition can be a challenge. A person's genetic makeup and their mental condition can contribute to chronic pain.

There are four subcategories of chronic pain: nociceptive, inflammatory, dysfunctional, and neuropathic. Nociception is the body's response to a negative stimulus, the kind caused by, say, stubbing one's toe. Conditions like osteoarthritis, the grinding of socket bones due to eroded cartilage, is also a kind of nociceptive pain.

Inflammatory pain is the kind caused by damaged tissue, for example the kind resulting from a sports injury. Inflammatory pain often follows nociceptive pain. When you sprain your ankle, your body sends signals to the brain that this was bad (nociceptive pain). Afterward the damaged tissue in the ankle area feels tender to the touch and lasts until the tissue is repaired (inflammatory pain).

Dysfunctional pain can be set off without any outside stimulus as far as we can tell. This kind of pain results from conditions like fibromyalgia, a musculoskeletal disease causing pain throughout the body, or irritable bowel syndrome (IBS). Dysfunctional pain, as the name suggests, is the result of the nervous system not functioning properly, often for genetic or environmental reasons.

Last, there is neuropathic pain. Neuropathic pain results from damage to the nervous system, and like dysfunctional pain, it can be

> **"PAIN MANAGEMENT IS** a discipline in the field of medicine that doesn't have a clear home because there is a multidisciplinary component to this specialty. It involves anesthesiologists, primary care providers such as family medicine internists, rehabilitation physicians, psychiatrists, addiction specialists, occupational therapy, physical therapy, nursing, pharmacy, and chaplaincy work as well. It is a polyglot of medical specialties." —**Andrew Saxon, MD, VA Puget Sound Health Care System**

triggered without any outside stimulus. Judy Foreman, former health columnist for the *Boston Globe* and author of two books about pain, likens neuropathic pain to the AIDS virus. In the way that AIDS attacks the immune system—the very system meant to fight back against such conditions—neuropathic pain "attacks the nervous system itself, altering the way nerves function."[61]

To add to the complications, one's own mental and social conditions can both trigger and exacerbate pain symptoms. This is why doctors refer to pain as a biopsychosocial phenomenon. Treating people's pain is as much about treating their mental condition as it is about treating their physical pain.

THE BEGINNING OF PAIN MEDICINE

Only fairly recently have doctors received much training at all in treating pain. It wasn't until the middle of the twentieth century that a revolution in pain medicine occurred, largely due to the work of one man. Born in Sicily in 1917, John Bonica would become a pioneer of pain medicine. He was the first to promote a multidisciplinary treatment for pain, which he developed after treating soldiers returning from the Second World War. He published the world's first comprehensive book on treating pain, *The Management of Pain*, in 1953, and in 1960, he joined the University of Washington, where he started the country's first multidisciplinary pain clinic. Dr. Bonica helped put himself through medical school working as a professional wrestler known as "The Masked Marvel."[62]

According to Dr. Andrew Saxon, "Dr. Bonica provided anesthetic blocks, what we now call regional anesthesia, to injured combatants and was able to eliminate sensation in the body part that was causing the pain. Because pain can emanate from different organs with different injuries, Bonica recognized the necessity of developing more than a single specialty in the complex field of pain management."

Just a few decades ago, chronic pain wasn't even thought of as a condition doctors would treat. "They would have just dismissed it as not a valid medical condition," said Dr. David Tauben.

Dr. Tauben is chief of Pain Medicine for the University of Washington, heading the department started by Dr. Bonica. Dr. Tauben recalled that as a medical student at UW in 1980, "We had 3 hours of pain education. Now we have 26." According to Tauben, chronic pain was often stigmatized in the medical community. There was a belief then that sufferers of chronic pain had somehow brought it on themselves, that their pain resulted from poor lifestyle choices. He continued in our interview, "Psychologists thought like my medical students [thought], that these people [were] awful. Why would you want to see these patients? And to make matters worse, there's nothing you [could] do for them. There's a move afoot now to make a change on that, but this is recent."

"AS A PROFESSION, physicians are really under-trained in dealing with both pain and with addiction. I'm a psychiatrist; I had four years of training in medical school and four years of training for psychiatry. I got two months of training in addiction as a psychiatrist. And we have almost no training in dealing with pain. Physicians were marketed to that pain is something that people shouldn't have to suffer. We don't like it when our patients have to suffer." —Dr. Kelly Clark, MD, president of the American Society of Addiction Medicine

A MULTIDISCIPLINARY APPROACH TO TREATING PAIN

People in chronic pain suffered silently and became limited in what they could do. Pain was thought of as simply a part of life and there was nothing to be done about that. At least that was the thinking up until only a few decades ago. As a student, Tauben decided to take advantage of UW's pain clinic, thinking that treating pain would naturally be a large part of his practice. "I was taught that we shouldn't, not only not be using opioids, but we probably shouldn't be using any drugs at all," Tauben said. "Behavioral counseling and physical rehabilitation was the preferred way to go." The University of Washington taught a multidisciplinary approach to treating pain, one that recognized the profound impact one's mental health had on his or her experience of physical pain.

"The old saying was 'recover their locus of control,'" and Dr. Tauben added, "and their locus of control is in themselves. They have to find it. We do the same thing with blood pressure, cardiac disease, and cancer. We tell people to maintain these problems themselves by not gaining weight, by maintaining fitness, by avoiding tobacco. Using self-management has a far greater impact not just on cost but on total health-care outcomes."

But while this multidisciplinary approach may be the best way to treat sufferers of chronic pain, it can also be the most difficult to deliver. When he moved into private practice, Dr. Tauben discovered it was quite difficult to find other specialists necessary for providing a multidisciplinary treatment. This was in Seattle in the early 1980s, a major American city with a highly educated population of medical professionals. But some of the areas hardest hit by the opioid crisis were rural, working-class towns in Rust Belt states like Ohio, West Virginia, and Kentucky. If physical therapists were hard to come by in 1980s Seattle, finding one in Hazard, Kentucky, was nearly impossible.

Finding a team of specialists to provide treatment can be a challenge in and of itself, but getting busy people to adhere to a multifaceted

and long-term program can be a real challenge. One of the most difficult aspects of treating pain with such an approach is the demands it
places on the patient. Not only is the pain sufferer asked to submit to
a potentially months-long regimen of physical and mental therapy, but
those treatments are also likely to involve major life changes that can
be difficult for some people to make. Many people experience chronic
pain as a result of their jobs. Both carrying and lifting things or sitting
in an office chair all day can cause chronic pain. But asking someone to
avoid such behavior may not be possible if those are the requirements of
a person's livelihood.

People often live in social situations where bad habits that contribute to pain can be difficult to change. Take, for example, a poor diet.
Many people are constrained in their eating habits by time, place, and
money. A working-class parent of small children in a proverbial "food
desert" (a place with poor access to nutritious food) might be hard-
pressed to find the time to shop for and cook healthier foods. These
foods are often more expensive than the highly processed, quick-made
meals many working families rely on.

It can be hard to break old habits, especially habits that make
people feel good in the moment, such as eating or watching TV. Particularly if those habits are an individual's coping mechanism in an otherwise stressful environment. After working all day, running errands, and
caring for family, many people simply do not want to, or cannot find the

"**WE KNEW WE** had a problem because of our issues in the eastern
part of [Kentucky]. In our mining communities, areas that had no health
insurance, people who were living paycheck to paycheck needed to deal
with their pain to get into the mines. Given their lack of access to health
care and some of the grueling work that occurs in the mines, they would
start taking pain pills to get to work." —**Dr. Kelly Clark, MD, president of the
American Society of Addiction Medicine**

"**PEOPLE HAVE IT** in their head that there's a pill for something. Regardless of whatever their pain is, there's something out there that's going to help them. We saw a lot of people that were always complaining about either injury from an accident or one that was work-related. Then there is this new miracle drug that's going to eliminate all your pain. Then once they start taking that, they're addicted, and they don't say, 'I'm going to stop this stuff.' It's going to continue on to the point that their bodies can't physically take it anymore.

"There's probably not anybody in this county, or this region, rather, that's not been affected in some way or [doesn't] have somebody in their family that's been addicted at one time. I've had a lot of close personal friends . . . I've had officers that used to work with me years ago that [are] no longer police officers, addicted to narcotics of some form or another.

It's just heartbreaking to see the families that I've talked to and dealt with that [are] dealing with children that [have] basically stolen everything in their homes to sell to get prescription medication. I've had people in here before that said I've got a $500 or $600 [a] day habit, that I've got to get that money somewhere. The majority of the cases that we work, criminal cases, are all related to narcotics in some way or another. They were either stealing to obtain money or stealing pills themselves if they can. Some way or another, it always goes back to drugs."

—Chief Minor Allen, Hazard Kentucky Police Department

time, to exercise or meditate or perform any of the other recommended activities that can reduce stress and improve overall health and thus their ability to better cope with chronic pain.

NO QUICK-FIX SOLUTION TO CHRONIC PAIN

The idea that there is no easy solution for chronic pain goes against our culture's insistence that there in fact must be a quick fix for everything. To suggest that there isn't in an era where technology often does provide a solution doesn't quite fit with our expectations. The constant reinforcement of the quick-fix ideology conspires to make us believe that everything, pain included, can be solved quickly and easily.

Dr. Anna Lembke is a psychiatrist and chief of the Addiction Medicine Dual Diagnosis Clinic at Stanford Medicine. She is the author of *Drug Dealer, MD: How Doctors Were Duped, Patients Got Hooked, and Why It's So Hard to Stop*. She found herself as a doctor behaving more like a drug dealer. Her interactions with patients were not the deep, interpersonal interactions necessary to understand and treat a patient but more a curator and provider of various prescription drugs. "Doctors today are expected to handle all of these complex issues in a 10-minute visit," she said. "It's impossible. It would be difficult to do in a 5-hour visit, but at least there would be some hope there." Medicine should be about helping people find real and lasting solutions to their health problems, but the way the American health-care system has operated provides little resources for solving those issues in a meaningful way, "instead, what we're doing is providing doctors with a prescription pad."

For Dr. Lembke, this is the result of several issues, not least among them is what she called "a crisis of modernity." In a highly developed nation like the United States, we seem to have everything at our fingertips. Even people in poverty have access to running water, electricity, and heat. These technologies freed people from the endless cycle of chopping wood, building fires, boiling water, and all the other supplementary tasks necessary for everyday activities like cooking and cleaning. Yet, as Dr. Lemke pointed out, "It's amazing when you think we're living in a time when all of our creature comforts are accounted for. Even the poorest of the poor have leisure time they didn't have a hundred years ago, have extra income to spend on recreation that they didn't have a hundred years ago, and yet despite the increased comfort level in our lives, we're all more miserable than ever."

"More miserable than ever" may be rhetorical flourish, but according to the CDC, more Americans than ever before are taking antidepressants, and a report published in 2017 showed that number to have grown by 65 percent in 15 years.[63] Admittedly, this may be an issue of

"THE RESEARCH IS pretty clear now—about as clear as a lot of things in medicine. If somebody has a confirmed serious opiate addiction and it's been around for a year or two at least, they've developed an opiate-use lifestyle, built their life around using and getting, often with crime involved, and a lot of money is involved. The chances of somebody getting sober using just abstinence, even if they go to tons of meetings, even if they do lots of talking, even if they go to residential care, are extremely low—they've got about a 5 percent chance of not relapsing within the next three months.

"I think the most challenging are my opiate-addiction patients. Because when people are dependent on opiates, and when it's still controlling their life, you're not just dealing with that person there. You're dealing with this monster the size of my office wall. When [the monster] is in control, there's just you and that little patient, and we're about this big, and there's this opiate addiction thing that's changing [the patient's] thinking." —**Dr. Richard Ries, University of Washington, School of Medicine**

self-reporting. Are we taking more antidepressants now because we are in fact more depressed and because medical science now understands mental health better than ever? Or is it because our culture of instant gratification tells us that we don't have to feel anything negative, and if we do, there's something wrong with us? And if there is something wrong with us, our advanced society must be able to provide us with an easy solution.

We live in a culture where there seems to be a product for everything. Even fundamental aspects of human nature like pain and sorrow have been reimagined as superfluous inconveniences easily corrected by the right consumer choice. "My belief is the great challenge of the twenty-first century is going to be able to figure out how can we limit our consumption of recreational goods and services," Dr. Lembke said. "What really is the good life? What does it mean to live a meaningful life? It's certainly not pleasuring yourself at all costs. We're all engaging in that and we're trying for that, and it's not really working. I also feel that the isolation, alienation that people experience is a huge contributor [to the addiction crisis]. How do you build community in a largely secular society?" What will ultimately win out: instant gratification or individual fulfillment?

Some have pointed to the large numbers of deaths among the white working class of rural America and called them "deaths of despair."[64] A kind of slow suicide propelled by a disaffection with current conditions and a deep sense of alienation. "I really see the opioid epidemic as the canary in the coal mine when it comes to problems in the health-care system, but I also see the rising rates of addiction more broadly as illustrative of a crisis in our society," Dr. Lembke explained in our interview. At Stanford, Dr. Lembke focuses as much on the spiritual as she does the medical. For many in addiction recovery, that line is also blurred.

FOCUSING ON MENTAL HEALTH, SPIRITUALITY, AND CONNECTION FOR RECOVERY

Harriet Rossetto and Rabbi Mark Borovitz are a husband and wife team who run the Beit T'Shuvah recovery center in Los Angeles. "We see addiction to all substances and activities as primarily a spiritual emptiness that people try to fill," Ms. Rossetto said. "With opioids, with alcohol, [and] with [other] high-risk behaviors, because they are seeking connection." Beit T'Shuvah, like many addiction recovery programs, practices the 12-step program developed by Alcoholics Anonymous. Their program focuses on spiritual healing as the only real means of achieving sobriety. The twelfth step states, "Having had a spiritual awakening as the result of these steps, we tried to carry this message to alcoholics, and to practice these principles in all our affairs."[65]

Recovery programs, religious or secular, 12-step or otherwise, almost universally acknowledge that the foundation of a healthy and lasting sobriety is fundamentally grounded in mental health. "There was a book published recently called *Chasing the Scream* by Johann Hari,"

Rossetto said, "in which he says that the opposite of addiction is not sobriety, it's connection. I think that's true. I think all addicts are craving connection between themselves with other people, with families, with community, and with belonging. I think it's no accident that the person from whom one buys one's drugs is called the connection." Rabbi Borovitz added, "The problem is we keep trying to fit in, and this pill or that pill will help you feel better to fit in. The truth is we shouldn't try [to] fit in. We're not a jigsaw puzzle. We belong. We're entitled to be who we are. We're entitled to feel our own pain and learn from it. We're entitled to fail forward. We're entitled to live, and to be part of something. Not because we fit in or we change ourselves or because we really become our true selves. Because of the prescription of opioids and the cheap prices of heroin, we are stopping people [from discovering] who they are. We're helping people not live fully, completely, and wholly in their lives."

Rabbi Borovitz continued, "The most dangerous place for an addict to be these days is in his doctor's office, and that pain and suffering are necessary to the process of recovery and healing. You cannot take away pain or suffering because that is part of what it takes to grow as a human being. We believe that people can live better through abstinence, through spirit, through our integrative treatment, through dealing with the issues that got them to use. Because remember, using is a solution to the inner psychic pain and the emotional distress. If we deal with those, then we don't have to keep them medicated.

"In recovery, success and failure, they get mixed up. If somebody keeps coming back after they slip or relapse, then that, to us, is success. Everybody here has a spiritual counselor, a therapist, and an addiction counselor. There's a team approach, and they're part of the team, and the community is part of the team. Anytime someone relapses, it's a blow. What we do is we hold on. Because we believe in *teshuvah*, Hebrew for repentance, return, and new responses, and repair, change, and hope, we're always open for somebody to return. And sometimes, if we're not the right place for them, we help them get to the right place.

It's not one-size-fits-all for anybody, and even here it's an individualized program."

Rossetto and Borovitz's views on community-based recovery are shared by many medical professionals. Dr. Lembke called it a "poverty of alternative rewards." When addressing the addiction crisis, "it's very important that we make sure that we offer something else to people who have nothing to do all day," she said. "Who have no employment, who have no comforting or meaningful relationships in their lives. Those are the people that we have to find a way to give them a life worth living that doesn't involve substances."

WHY A MORE HOLISTIC TREATMENT FOR PAIN FAILED

The problem is that neither our health-care system nor our overall culture is structured to provide such things to people who need them. "Health-care providers often try to solve these greater cultural issues by addressing them as a medical condition by, for example, covering the costs for antidepressant medications, but not for talk therapy." Doctor Lembke continued, "If you talk to any doctor who does chronic care, or who does outpatient ambulatory care, what they will tell you is, sure, their patients have diabetes. Sure, their patients have hypertension, but their patients are also unemployed. They're homeless. They have multigenerational trauma. They have nothing to do all day."

She took a moment to put all of her thoughts together and then went deeper. "I don't think that's working very well. Opioids are like this proxy for the missing doctor-patient relationship," she said. "I really feel like it's like a transitional object. I write you a prescription, I only have 10 minutes, but you take it home, you ingest the opioid, you get a warm feeling. It's a like a warm blanket coming over you. Your mood is lifted. You feel almost cradled. It's almost like I'm there, I'm holding you. I'm caring for you in a way that I'm not really doing, but it's sort of the best that we have. Then you come back three months later, and you say,

'Doctor, thank you so much. You've helped me.' Of course, I feel gratified. That's why I went into medicine in the first place, and I write you a refill."

But opioids were not always this sort of proxy Dr. Lembke described. As a student at the University of Washington's pain clinic, Dr. Tauben was told not to use drugs of any kind. Perhaps some antidepressants if the patient needed them, but overall the best way to treat chronic pain, both in terms of health-care outcomes and cost, was through behavioral counseling and physical therapy.

So what happened? As noted above, there were certainly issues with providing long-term, multidisciplinary care. Access to health-care facilities being a significant one. There were also changes to medical reimbursement. Health insurance providers in the 1980s started to move away from covering long-term pain treatments. "Health insurance is a short-term venture," Dr. Tauben said. "People changes jobs; they change their insurance. People get sick; they lose their insurance. The shortest-term gain is getting people moved through, and the fastest way to do that was giving them drugs." Dr. Tauben was prescribing, not drugs, but physical and psychological therapy, treatments that could take several weeks or even months. "They stopped referring us patients . . . 'You're too nice,' they said, 'we don't want to do those things.'" The exact phrasing, he recalls, was, "we don't see the value of spending this money on these patients." Dr. Tauben said that "[health insurers] couldn't see the pain, It was invisible to our state-of-the-art imaging and therefore it was not considered a 'medical problem.' And they weren't interested in paying for things that weren't strictly biomedical.

"The space and time to provide thoughtful listening and understanding of the patient's circumstance and clearly understanding the diagnosis beyond the biomedical became impossible for the primary care clinicians alone to deliver. This was complicated by the recognition that pain is often not acknowledged in patients initially in hospitals where it was most widely focused, and the move to patient-centered care where needing to listen and care for patients' symptoms was valid and appropriate but difficult to accomplish," Tauben said.

But more crucially, there was also a shift in the thinking about opioid treatment for chronic pain. We saw in the previous chapter how opioids have long been used in medicine, but only in extreme circumstances: cancer, end-of-life care, or traumatic injury. But in the 1980s, some began to argue that opioids were not as addictive as once believed, and there was a sense that through technology and proper oversight we could control what was long thought of as an inherently dangerous drug.

Dr. Tauben reflected on this course change. "At that time, [the late 1970s and '80s], there was a pervasive spirit of hope, of optimism and power over our environment. We're going to tackle these health catastrophes and tragedies by means of technology and other fixes that would come out of a pill bottle or out of some new infusion of some yet-to-be-discovered but soon-to-be-at-hand treatment." It all made a certain amount of sense. Man had walked on the moon just years earlier, so why couldn't we tamp down the effects of a narcotic plant? We like to think of ourselves as masters of the universe, that we can truly make the impossible possible if only we have enough determination. "The perception was that doctors could fix everything, if only they were smart enough or interested enough or willing to take it on," Tauben said. "They have, well, the magical capabilities that physicians had, and physicians didn't mind [hearing] that."

The belief and trust in doctors and science played an important role in the growth of the crisis. When the crisis gets talked about now, we often talk about the large numbers of people addicted to heroin and the deaths stemming from opioid abuse. But it's important to remember that many people became addicted to opioids through legitimate prescriptions given to them by medical professionals. The public trusted doctors who had in turn trusted their network of peers and institutions that had told them opioids were safe.

Dr. Andrew Saxon works in the Seattle area, primarily at the VA Puget Sound Health Care System. He has worked in addiction medicine for more than 30 years, primarily working with veterans. Many of his patients became addicted to heroin during their time in Vietnam. He, like Dr. Tauben and others, watched this crisis unfold throughout his career and has given thought to how it arose. "I think there are a number of factors about how it happened, and clearly one of the factors has to do with misguided advice in terms of how to treat people with chronic pain," he said. "That is all now well known." The misguided advice Dr. Saxon is referring to is a number of studies that said that opioids were not as addictive and that they could be used to treat chronic pain. Twenty to 25 years ago, there was a paradigm shift. Physicians were taught originally that opioids were to be reserved for very short periods to address serious conditions like severe injury or terminal illnesses such as later-stage cancer. Dr. Saxon continued, "Then there was the shift to anyone who has pain should have that pain taken care of, which is unrealistic because pain is a part of life," he said. "Pain is very important from an evolutionary perspective. It keeps us from doing things that are dangerous to us. It is unrealistic to think that we can get rid of all pain."

Physicians were targeted by opioid manufacturers and told that these powerful drugs could be used in a controlled way to help people with their everyday pain. That was a sentiment that both doctors and their patients were receptive to. Who doesn't suffer from some sort of pain? How much relief could be found if there was a way to treat the aches and pains that keep people from doing the many things they would like or need to do?

"I love seeing patients. I do feel that I can help them," Dr. Lembke said. "But in order to feel that way, I had to make a major shift in my practice about 15 years ago because I was becoming very frustrated. I was becoming angry with my patients, angry with myself. Angry with them because they were coming to me with all of these complicated issues and expecting me to deal with [them] without the resources required. Angry with myself because I knew what I was doing was inadequate to really help them. I was feeling totally overwhelmed in the face of their complex problems." Opioids seemed to provide a way out of this predicament. "Wouldn't it be nice if we could treat our patients with pain even if they weren't dying from cancer?"

Dr. Tauben recalled that many "patient's families would say, 'My grandma was dying of horrible cancer, and I've got the same pain she has. It's clearly different, but do I have to be dying of cancer to deal with pain relief?' Now, that sticks in your craw, then you say, 'Well, maybe we could use these drugs.' At the time there seemed to be good medical evidence that suggested that this was possible. It was only until the so-called genie was out of the bottle that doctors discovered that there wasn't fact-based scientific evidence, and what had been presented as studies were rather untested observations than conclusions or recommendations.

"That was compounded by the fact that the Joint Commission on Accreditation of Health-Care Systems in 2000 came out with this requirement that pain become the fifth vital sign," Dr. Saxon said. "So, before there were four vital signs: heart rate, blood pressure, respiratory rate, and body temperature, which clearly are vital signs critical to life. And they suddenly came around and said, 'Well, you've got to ask every single person about their level of pain, and that's a vital sign.' Now, that's quite ironic, because in medicine we acquire two different classes of information about patients. One is symptoms, which is subjective to how the patient's feeling and the other is signs, which are things we can objectively observe or measure. Pain is not even a sign. It's a symptom. There's no way objectively to determine pain."

THE INTRODUCTION OF THE PAIN SCALE

Patients were to rate their pain on a scale of 1 to 10, but it soon became the case that any number on that scale was an excuse for the prescription of opioids.

"Doctors began to chase a pain score, which is very difficult to quantify and substantiate, particularly in chronic pain," Dr. Tauben said. But

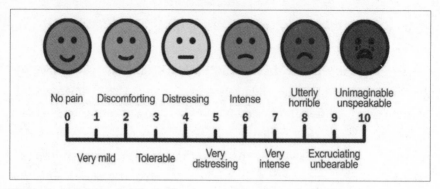

No pain   Discomforting Distressing   Intense   Utterly   Unimaginable
                                                      horrible unspeakable

0   1   2   3   4   5   6   7   8   9   10

     Very mild   Tolerable   Very   Very   Excruciating
                               distressing intense   unbearable

"[It] just added lighter fluid to the fire, because it became equivalent to say, 'If you have pain, you need opioids.'"

—Dr. Richard Ries, professor and director of Addictions at the University of Washington School of Medicine

COURTESY OF PROHEALTH.COM

that scale, in addition to being a poor metric for measuring pain, turned out to be the brainchild of the very people who were selling opioid pain-killers: Purdue Pharma.

"It's also important to realize that the Joint Commission developed this 'pain as the fifth vital sign' as part of a grant that was provided to them by the pharmaceutical company, Purdue Pharma," Saxon continued, "which was the company that introduced OxyContin into the market." The organization tasked with accrediting health-care systems "is taking money from a pharmaceutical company to make sure every patient gets asked about pain, and that pharmaceutical company's product might be used more frequently. It became a situation where every physician, every health-care provider, any type, had to ask patients about their pain level, and if their pain was above seven and let's say, ibuprofen didn't take care of it or Tylenol didn't take care of it, 'Oh well, then we've got to give them something else,' which will be opioids. And that led to a real over-expansion of the prescribing of opioids for chronic pain. And we now know that they're not terribly effective for many patients with chronic pain. And we know that the best treatments for chronic pain probably aren't even medications," Dr. Saxon said. In fact, what we now know is that this kind of freewheeling over-prescribing led to our current opioid epidemic.

THE ILLEGITIMATE "ARTICLES"

We will see in the next two chapters how Purdue Pharma, using techniques pioneered by one of its founders, Arthur Sackler, used their influence to corrupt legitimate systems of research and review to make it appear that there was good science to support using their drugs. "Without good evidence," Dr. Tauben said, thinking back, "it was definitely a prospective trial without an institutional review board approval and without ongoing analysis. I think it was, frankly, an experiment done on the American people." When asked how exactly this was allowed to happen when doctors are the very people we assume would avoid doing such things, Dr. Tauben said that a few articles had appeared in medical publications that argued that opioids were not as dangerous as once believed, and there was a certain amount of success with opioid patients. "Enough patients would stabilize on a pretty low dose," he said. "They wouldn't develop tolerance; they would function fine and do well. That was a reinforcing observation."

One such "article" was "Porter and Jick," a study cited many times over for the promotion of opioid painkillers. "Porter and Jick," however, was not an article about a study, but a letter to the editor of the *New England Journal of Medicine*. No more than five sentences, the letter from Dr. Herschel Jick and one of his graduate students, Jane Porter, stated, "We conclude that despite widespread use of narcotic drugs in hospitals, the development of addiction is rare in medical patients with no history of addiction."[66] Their conclusion was not based on any test Porter and Jick conducted on their own but from the review of thousands of hospital records.

"And then Dr. Russell Portenoy's article endorsing the use of opioids came out," Dr. Tauben said. "If you read it carefully, it was [evaluating] a pretty low dose, and these were super selected patients. And a subset of the patients had modest relief, and it was certainly no panacea, nor did it claim to say [so] in the article, although they'd been brutally accused of wildly promoting opioids. I think neither [doctor] actually did that,

ADDICTION RARE IN PATIENTS TREATED WITH NARCOTICS

To the Editor: Recently, we examined our current files to determine the incidence of narcotic addiction in 39,946 hospitalized medical patients[1] who were monitored consecutively. Although there were 11,882 patients who received at least one narcotic preparation, there were only four cases of reasonably well documented addiction in patients who had no history of addiction. The addiction was considered major in only one instance. The drugs implicated were meperidine in two patients,[2] Percodan in one, and hydromorphone in one. We conclude that despite widespread use of narcotic drugs in hospitals, the development of addiction is rare in medical patients with no history of addiction.

JANE PORTER
HERSHEL JICK, M.D.
Boston Collaborative Drug
Surveillance Program
Waltham, MA 02154   Boston University Medical Center

1. Jick H, Miettinen OS, Shapiro S, Lewis GP, Siskind Y, Slone D. Comprehensive drug surveillance. JAMA. 1970; 213:1455-60.
2. Miller RR, Jick H. Clinical effects of meperidine in hospitalized medical patients. J Clin Pharmacol. 1978; 18:180-8.

New England Journal of Medicine, Letter to the Editor, January 10, 1980

NEW ENGLAND JOURNAL OF MEDICINE

but with reading and rereading and just the telling of the story again and again, it caught on."

Dr. Russell Portenoy, director of the MJHS Institute for Innovation in Palliative Care and chief medical officer of MJHS Hospice and Palliative Care, edited a number of papers about opioid painkillers. He also received funding from Purdue Pharma for speaking engagements. In 2012, Portenoy told the *Wall Street Journal,* "Did I teach about pain management, specifically about opioid therapy, in a way that reflects misinformation? I guess I did."[67] In a statement to the *New Yorker* writer Patrick Radden Keefe, Portenoy said he has "refocused" his approach to pain management and that "no funder has had any undue influence over my thinking."[68] We will return to the topic of funder's influence on doctors, conscious or unconscious, in a later chapter. As Dr. Tauben said, neither "so-called findings" were clear-cut declarations of a perfect drug.

Many factors contributed to rather scant evidence being inflated into sound medical doctrine. Promotion on the part of the pharmaceutical industry certainly played a large part, but there was a willingness on the part of all of us—doctors, patients, health-care professionals, pharma—to believe it was true.

Furthermore, medicine isn't always as based in grounded research as we might like to believe. "Evidence-based medicine should not rule out above medicine-based evidence," Dr. Tauben said. "You don't have to do an experiment on the safety of parachutes to know that if you jump out of an airplane without a parachute, you will not survive." Dr. Tauben pointed out that it wasn't until recently that we truly understood how Tylenol works, or even aspirin, but these drugs are common because they are known to work with little side effects. "Seeing things in practice repeatedly based on a belief that wasn't grounded in careful science, that's the fault, but it wasn't an outright lie," he said. "It was just a lack of attention to the fact that evidence of harm wasn't yet seen, wasn't obvious."

THE THREAT OF ADDICTION— OR PATIENTS TURNING TO HEROIN

For a time there seemed to be evidence that opioids could be used to treat chronic pain. But there was little oversight to test these assumptions. The effects of addiction weren't readily apparent in the beginning. However, as we have belatedly come to realize, opioids are dangerously addictive, and even limited exposure can trigger physical and mental dependency.

Once someone is physically dependent on opioids, the withdrawal symptoms themselves can be extremely painful, causing people to crave the drug even more. "There are patients who'd tell me, 'If you take away my opioids, I'm just going to go get heroin,' Dr. Tauben said. In many cases that's exactly what happened. "The drug dealers out there," University of Washington professor Dr. Ries said, "who have their

"THE AMERICAN MEDICAL ASSOCIATION and the Centers for Disease Control (CDC) have to get together and figure it out. It's ultimately going to be a decision that physicians make. The CDC has tried to lead them on the right path. But patients don't have a relationship with the CDC. They don't have that kind of relationship with the federal government. They have a relationship with their family doctor who they're going to. What that doctor tells them—'Here's what we're going to try for you'—is what they're going to listen to. The CDC wants those doctors to start saying to those patients who come in with the back pain, 'Look, I can't give you a pill that's going to help. What we can do is start you on physical therapy, try to get your insurance company to pay for acupuncture, and get you into a meditation class.' And it's going to be a challenge to get doctors to that state." —Jeanmarie Perrone, MD, emergency room physician and medical toxicologist, University of Pennsylvania

methamphetamine, their cocaine, their various pills, et cetera, started saying, 'Hey, more people are showing up asking for this stuff because they're in withdrawal and they don't know where to go.' And then cheap heroin started showing up, and good American capitalism and creativity filled in the gaps. I can remember this 15 years ago, my patients coming in here for buprenorphine treatment were saying, 'You know, heroin is a lot cheaper than those pills and it works better.'"

The doctor is then faced with the proposition of cutting off their patient when that patient has explicitly told them they will use heroin instead. So the only choices are heroin, which can be mixed with any number of toxic chemicals, or continuing their patients on a prescribed opioid drug they know to be harming them. In some cases doctors were even compelled by law to provide opioids. "If you didn't [provide opioids], you would be under penalty of censure by the medical society, censure by lawyers. I was part of a lawsuit," Dr. Tauben said. "We were being sued by a patient advocacy group that said we were going to be depriving people of their opioids."

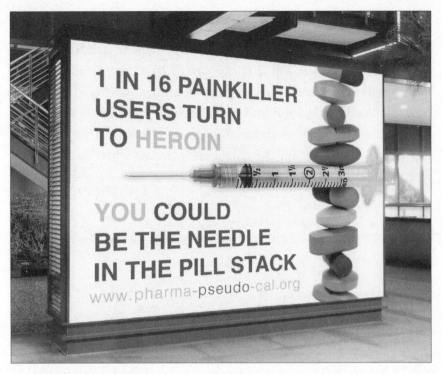

Painkiller Users Turn to Heroin
COURTESY OF PROFESSOR MATT STEFL, MARKETING,
LOYOLA MARYMOUNT UNIVERSITY, LOS ANGELES, CALIFORNIA

According to the National Institute on Drug Abuse (NIDA), more than 130 people die every day from opioid overdose.[69] The CDC states that "the total 'economic burden' of prescription opioid misuse alone in the United States is $78.5 billion a year, including the costs of health care, lost productivity, addiction treatment, and criminal justice involvement." All of this the result of an attempt to treat people's everyday pain.

■ ■ ■

IF THERE IS a silver lining to be taken from all of this, it's that this crisis has opened our eyes in many ways. We know now that pain is not simply just a physical phenomenon and that mental and social problems cannot simply be medicated away.

It was, as Dr. Tauben pointed out, a kind of experiment on the American people to try to find an easier, perhaps better, way to treat pain. All kinds of pain. But that experiment failed spectacularly. In the next chapter we'll see how the pharmaceutical industry "cooked the books" in a way to make it look as if the experiment would work, even when there was ample evidence to suggest otherwise. That story, like many of the stories from the opioid crisis, is one where making more money far outweighed the public good.

CHAPTER 4

Arthur Sackler's Marketing Tactics

"NO AMOUNT OF charity in spending such fortunes can compensate in any way for the misconduct in acquiring them," Theodore Roosevelt said after John D. Rockefeller proposed to start a foundation in 1909. It was not an isolated thought at the time.[70]

The story of the opioid crisis is one of misinformation, sometimes deliberate, sometimes accidental. In the previous chapter we saw how there were intentional lies on the part of the pharmaceutical industry. Yet at the same time there was some evidence to believe that what was being said about opioids might hopefully be true. There was, and still remains, some evidence that opioids can be used for chronic pain under close supervision. But in this chapter we're going to look at medical advertising and the line between creative license and outright lies.

In 2007, executives from Purdue Pharma and the company itself were collectively fined $634 million for falsely marketing OxyContin and understating its risk of addiction.[71] This was a case of outright and knowing deception. But what about instances of more subtle misrepresentation? Deception is part and parcel to advertising as we know it today. Beer advertisements with beautiful women and clothing brands featuring celebrities

Arthur Sackler, MD
MEDICAL MARKETING
HALL OF FAME

broadcast a very clear, if unspoken, message about power, wealth, and sex. Prices are regularly listed ending in ".99" rather than an even dollar amount because marketing experts know that this tricks the mind into seeing a lower price. Neither of these or other common tactics are illegal. Defenders of such practices would argue that these methods are so transparent that if a person were to believe that drinking X brand of beer will inherently make him successful with women, then that person has only himself to blame. But if these methods have little or no effect, if we all see past them, then why do they dominate the advertising industry? Advertisements do affect us, often in ways we don't notice or cannot help. They are designed to evoke certain emotions and have us believe that a particular consumer product is the precise answer we had been looking for. And this is exactly why OxyContin had such dangerous ramifications—because people in pain were desperate for a solution.

ARTHUR SACKLER'S MEDICAL MARKETING TECHNIQUES

In 1997, 10 years after his death, Arthur Sackler was inducted into the Medical Advertising Hall of Fame (MAHF). "Dr. Sackler saw the important role nonpersonal selling could play in this environment and became an advocate for the full-blown marketing programs (field force plus multimedia promotional activities) employed today," his page on the MAHF website reads. The page adds that his career "profoundly influenced medical advertising."[72] If anything, his marketing legacy has grown even more profound after his death. If you turn on the television, night or day, you will be able to see a multitude of commercials offering a wide variety of prescription drugs. In fact, the United States and New Zealand are the only developed countries to allow direct-to-consumer advertising of prescription drugs.[73]

Arthur Sackler and his brothers would all go on to become medical doctors specializing in psychiatry. Arthur attended New York University,

"THERE WERE MANY people involved in the effort to increase opioid prescribing who really believed what they were saying. Even the executives at the drug companies convinced themselves that people were suffering needlessly and that opioids could be prescribed more aggressively. We didn't have to worry about getting patients addicted. Most professionals fell for this campaign and joined the bandwagon. There's certainly evidence that Purdue and other companies involved in the manufacturing of opioids knew that patients were having a very hard time getting off the pills. Their response was to withhold the information. Purdue instructed their sales reps to further exaggerate the effectiveness of OxyContin for chronic pain, even though there was absolutely no scientific proof to back up their bogus claims." **—Dr. Peter Whybrow, director, UCLA Semel Institute**

where he obtained both his undergraduate and medical degrees. His medical career was short but prestigious. His 1987 obituary in the *Los Angeles Times* stated, "He became a specialist in biological psychiatry and published, with collaborators, more than 140 research papers, many dealing with the body's impact on mental illness. He was the first to use ultrasound for diagnosis and identified histamine as a hormone while urging its use as an effective alternative to electric shock treatments for the mentally ill." His fortune, which grew to be enormous, was made not as a doctor but as an investor and an advertising executive. The obituary added, "Sackler later made his fortune in medical advertising, medical trade publications and the manufacture of over-the-counter drugs."[74] His dual role as a medical marketer and part owner of a pharmaceutical manufacturer proved to be a rather dubious combination, resulting in allegations of conflict of interest.

To pay for his medical school expenses, Arthur got a job at the William Douglas McAdams advertising agency, which specialized in the medical industry. He was extremely successful at his work. According to his MAHF entry, he helped Pfizer become a major player in prescription drugs for his promotion of their antibiotic, Tobramycin.[75] He would eventually purchase William Douglas and earn his reputation as the marketing innovator that landed him in the Medical Advertising Hall of Fame. In 1960, Arthur began publishing the *Medical Tribune*, a medical industry trade publication that would eventually have a million readers in 20 countries.[76]

Arthur's marketing techniques were extremely effective, but as Frances Allen, former chair of psychiatry at Duke University School of Medicine, told journalist Patrick Radden Keefe, "Most of the questionable practices that propelled the pharmaceutical industry into the scourge it is today can be attributed to Arthur Sackler."[77] Sackler understood that the most effective way to promote a drug was not by appealing to the customer but by appealing to the physician. In his campaign for Pfizer's Terramycin, Sackler had fake postcards from faraway countries sent to doctors' offices detailing how the antibiotic had treated various diseases. The postcards were signed "Sincerely, Pfizer," and doctors were targeted based on their prescribing habits.[78]

Working on another campaign for Pfizer, this time for the drug Sigmamycin, one of Arthur's advertisements featured a number of doctors' business cards with the words, "More and more physicians find Sigmamycin the antibiotic therapy of choice." An investigative reporter for the *Saturday Review* tried to contact the doctors whose names appeared on the cards, but none of them were real.[79]

A NEW MARKETING STRATEGY: LIBRIUM AND VALIUM

Sackler made much of his initial fortune marketing the tranquilizers Librium and Valium, whose campaigns promoted the use of the drugs even for those with "no demonstrable pathology."[80] One Librium ad featured a distressed-looking college freshman and suggested the drug should be used to treat the anxiety of young students. Valium's manufacturer, Roche, had conducted no studies regarding the drug's addictiveness. Years later, Win Gerson, a former Sackler colleague, told journalist Sam Quinones, "It kind of made junkies of people, but that drug worked."[81] Valium became America's first hundred-million-dollar— and then billion-dollar—drug. Sackler's page on the Medical Advertising Hall of Fame website states, "His experience in [psychiatry] enabled him to position different indications for Roche's Librium and Valium— to distinguish for the physician the complexities of anxiety and psychic tension,"[82] meaning he convinced doctors to expand the list of symptoms they would have normally prescribed tranquilizers for. "The patient would walk in," Gerson told Quinones, "[and say] 'I'm nervous all day long, doctor.' Or, 'My son's in the army.' People were walking around nervous, worried, and this drug absolutely calmed them." Years later, long after Arthur Sackler's death, an internal memo circulated at Purdue concerning the launch of OxyContin would state, "We do *not* want to niche OxyContin for just cancer pain."[83] Expanding the use of opioids would be a cornerstone of Purdue's marketing campaign. It was extremely successful, but this is what led to doctors massively overprescribing a dangerous drug.

Companies have long sought to expand their markets to the widest base possible, and it can't be said definitively that Purdue was explicitly

"HOW COULD DOCTORS have fallen for this? In fact, Purdue's messaging was very compelling. The health-care community was hearing from pain specialists who were eminent in the field. Many people became doctors because they really wanted to help patients. They were hearing that they can be much more compassionate. Purdue's argument sounded reasonable: You're confusing physical dependence and addiction. If you thought harder about it, it stopped making sense. If you started to prescribe, you would see very quickly that patients were, in fact, getting addicted." —**Dr. Andrew Kolodny, director of Opioid Policy Research, The Heller School for Social Policy and Management at Brandeis University, founder of Physicians for Responsible Opioid Prescribing (PROP)**

following Arthur Sackler's methods. Sackler was also correct that physical pain is connected to mental stress and seemed to earnestly believe that tranquilizers like Librium and Valium would help. But the drugs weren't thoroughly tested, and in seeking to cure one problem, another was created. The similarity between the promotion of Valium and Oxy-Contin is striking, and it raises questions about the marketing of powerful, habit-forming drugs. If Coca-Cola wants to reach a new market, that's one thing, but if a pharmaceutical company wants to find a new market for their prescription drugs, particularly potentially addictive ones, that's another issue entirely.

THE SACKLER EMPIRE

Arthur's aggressive tactics in medical advertising took on a new dimension in 1952, when together with his brothers, Raymond and Mortimer, Arthur bought Greenwich Village–based medical manufacturer Purdue Frederick. At the time, Purdue Frederick produced laxatives and earwax remover, as well as other over-the-counter drugs. The brothers split ownership of the company evenly into thirds. The other two Sacklers, Raymond and Mortimer, would run the day-to-day as joint CEOs, while Arthur remained at William Douglas McAdams Agency. However, Arthur's position as both part owner of a pharmaceutical manufacturer and medical advertising agency began to raise eyebrows.

In 1962, Arthur was brought before a Senate committee to answer questions about the growing pharmaceutical industry, which had recently come under scrutiny for high drug prices and monopolistic practices.[84] A memo prepared by the staff of Tennessee senator Estes Kefauver, who chaired the subcommittee, read:

> The Sackler empire is a completely integrated operation in that it can devise a new drug in its drug development enterprise, have the drug clinically tested and secure favorable reports on the drug from various hospitals with which they

have connections, conceive the advertising approach and prepare the actual advertising copy with which to promote the
drug, have the clinical articles as well as the advertising copy
published in their own medical journals, [and] prepare and
plant articles in newspapers and magazines.[85]

In 1959, chief of antibiotics at the Food and Drug Administration, Henry Welch, was forced to resign when it was discovered that he
had been paid by Pfizer to endorse certain drugs. Welch had said that
a "third era of antibiotic therapy had arrived," a phrase that Pfizer had
written in their promotion of Sigmamycin, a campaign managed by a
Sackler-owned company.[86]

OXYCONTIN: THE 12-HOUR
DOSING SCHEME

Arthur Sackler died in 1987, years before OxyContin was developed or released. Today his descendants have been waging a vigorous
media campaign to distance themselves—and Arthur—from OxyContin's rather dubious record. Although Arthur Sackler himself was not
involved with OxyContin, the methods he pioneered as a medical
advertiser would be employed by Purdue Pharma in their promotion

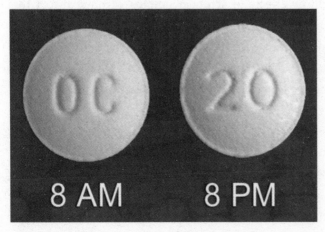

OxyContin 20mgs

GRAPHIC BY WALESKA
SANTIAGO, MEDIA
POLICY CENTER

Purdue Marketing Campaign for OxyContin, 2004
PURDUE PHARMA (STATNEWS.COM)

of OxyContin. In the early 1990s, the patent on Purdue's best-selling drug, MS Contin, was coming to an end. MS Contin, like OxyContin, was a long-acting opioid painkiller, typically reserved for cancer pain (the "contin" short for "continuous") and was used to provide pain relief over several hours. The basic logic behind drugs like OxyContin is that instead of giving a patient a direct, heavy dose of opioids, as with a morphine drip, the slow release of a small dose of opioids can theoretically provide the pain-killing effects of stronger opioids without any of the euphoria and less potential for addiction.

MS Contin had been an extremely successful drug for Purdue. An internal memo from 1995 preparing for the launch of OxyContin said, "In our focus groups, we learned that MS Contin was the 'gold standard' for cancer pain."[87]

But with the loss of that drug's patent, other companies would soon move in on Purdue's territory. A 1990 memo from Purdue noted, "Other pharmaceutical firms are thought to also be developing other controlled-release opioid analgesics . . . MS Contin may eventually face such serious generic competition that other controlled-release opioids must

Purdue Savings Coupon

PURDUE PHARMA (STATNEWS.COM)

be considered." The memo went on to say that because Purdue wanted to move into the no–cancer pain market with their opioids, "it would be unwise to 'put all our eggs in the MS Contin basket,'" in the face of upcoming generic competition.[88]

What they came up with turned out to be OxyContin, which would seek to prolong MS Contin's effective period to a full 12 hours. Much of Purdue's marketing plan for OxyContin emphasized the importance of 12-hour dosing, known in medical shorthand as q12h. Most pain killers last about six to eight hours, which means patients have to remember to take the pill several times a day. With OxyContin's 12-hour dosing, patients would be freed from what one Purdue press release described as "anxious clock-watching."[89] Purdue released OxyContin in 1996, and from that year to 2000, Purdue increased its number of sales representatives from 318 to 671 and brought the number of doctors on its physician call list up to approximately 94,000.[90]

"Very seductive," said Dr. Tauben from the University of Washington, thinking back on Purdue's promotion campaign. "Dashing men in GQ-looking outfits to meet with the women physicians, and women

"THE EVIDENCE SUGGESTS that Purdue, at the time it launched OxyContin in 1996, opened new territory in terms of the aggressive promotion of narcotics. They did things that had never been seen before. They took a drug that only sold $48 million, OxyContin, in its first year, and within four years, by the year 2000, it was selling close to a billion dollars a year. How did they do this? They did this with very aggressive marketing and promotion. They doubled the staff of sales reps. They recruited 5,000 doctors, nurses, and nurse practitioners to 40 different conventions, expositions, around the country, and with lucrative payments, they trained them to become additional sales cheerleaders for the OxyContin product. These are what is termed in the industry a K-O-L, or a Key Opinion Leader." —Joel Hay, professor of Pharmaceutical and Health Economics, USC

who were wearing skirts you wear to cocktail parties and heels that were three inches tall to come in and talk to you about their wonderful drug." As well as targeting physicians, Purdue provided coupons for patients as part of a starter program that would offer a 7- to 30-day supply. "Once you get [patients] started on these, they're going to be a continuing customer for life," Dr. Tauben said. By the time the program ended in 2001, approximately 34,000 coupons had been redeemed nationwide.[91] "By any means necessary, they're pushing this product directly to the customers and directly to the clinicians. And there weren't any brakes on that activity, other than the conscience of the clinicians," said Dr. Tauben.

Purdue and other pharmaceutical companies spent a great deal of money to convince doctors to prescribe their drugs, not just through purely educational means. From 1996 to 2001, Purdue hosted training seminars at resorts in Sunbelt states like California, Arizona, and Florida, with all expenses paid for doctors, pharmacists, and nurses.[92] Health professionals generally spend about three to four hours a day

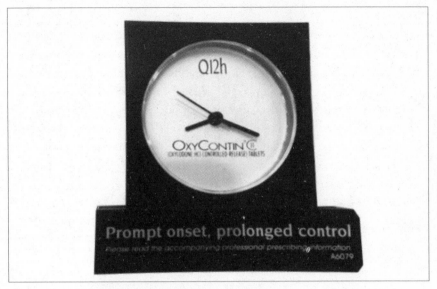

Purdue Pharma Marketing Campaign for OxyContin, 2003

PURDUE PHARMA (STATNEWS.COM)

in educational seminars at these types of conferences, while the rest of the time is free for leisure activity. Doctors insist that such enticements have no effect on their prescribing habits, but studies show otherwise. A 1992 study subtitled "There's No Such Thing as a Free Lunch" revealed that doctors who attend such seminars do tend to prescribe that drug more often following the symposium. "The physicians in this study did not feel that the largesse of an expense-paid trip to a resort to attend a seminar concerning a drug would influence their prescribing of that drug. Nevertheless, a significant and substantial increase in the prescribing of that drug occurred subsequent to the inducement," the study said.[93]

To be fair, it could be argued that attending such conferences gives doctors more familiarity with a particular drug and thus a greater willingness to prescribe it. The authors of the study went on to say that since they conducted these studies several months after a doctor attended such seminars, new evidence may have come out about the drug's efficacy or that its reputation had grown in the medical community. But pharma companies don't just offer trips to luxury resorts, sales

> **"IT ALL COMES** down to money. The drug companies that make opioids want to make a profit. Doctors know that opioids exist. They know that these medicines are out there. So why is it that drug companies employ large sales forces to go around the country, to take these doctors out to lunch, to present to them, and so on, if doctors already know these products exist? Why do you need a sales force to go and sell this kind of product to them in the first place? The answer is obvious. There are guidelines for what the sales rep can and can't say, but you're not sitting in on that lunch. I'm not sitting in on that lunch. There's no recording or transcript of it. Who knows what is said off the record, especially if a big bonus is involved?" **—David Crow, senior correspondent for** *Financial Times*

representatives fill doctors' offices with gifts like hats or stuffed animals. In the case of OxyContin, some doctors were gifted a clock with the q12 dosing schedule printed on the face. Doctors may claim to be uninfluenced by such marketing techniques, but as the study's authors pointed out, "It is unlikely that companies would spend large sums of money on marketing efforts if they were not felt to be effective." Like with the beautiful women in a beer ad, it's said these tactics are transparent and have little effect, and yet the practices persist.

Pharma companies like Purdue lavish gifts on perspective clients, but they also offer substantial rewards to their sales people who are able to bring in the most cash. A June 1996 letter to Purdue sales reps was headlined: "It's Bonus Time in the Neighborhood!"[94] and went on to say, "He who sells the 40 mg will win the battle."[95] OxyContin was originally sold in 10 to 40 mg tablets, with the larger pills being more expensive. Sales representatives were encouraged to get doctors to prescribe the most lucrative pill, not based on any medical evidence, but simply because it was the most profitable for Purdue.

DEFENDING THE SACKLER LEGACY

Today the Sackler name can be found on museums, universities, and art galleries around the globe. Arthur Sackler, in addition to being interested in medicine, was also fascinated by history and art and became a voracious art collector and philanthropist. Arthur Sackler's name can be found at Tel Aviv's Sackler School of Medicine, the Sackler Institute of Graduate Biomedical Science at New York University, the Arthur M. Sackler Sciences Center at Clark University, the Sackler School of Graduate Biomedical Sciences, and the Arthur M. Sackler Center for Health Communications at Tufts University. He founded galleries at the Metropolitan Museum of Art in New York City, at Princeton and Harvard, and in 1993, his widow, Jillian, opened the Arthur M. Sackler Museum of Art and Archaeology at Peking University in Beijing.[96]

As the controversy over opioids grew and fingers began to be pointed at Purdue and then at Arthur Sackler himself, his family has mounted a rather vigorous campaign against what they view as unfair media bias. Arthur, his family points out, died many years before OxyContin was released, and Purdue's profits from OxyContin are controlled completely by the families of Arthur's brothers, Raymond and Mortimer. On the Sackler family website, Arthur's biography was amended by a letter from his widow, Jillian, dated February 16, 2018. "Much of what's been written in recent months about my late husband, Dr. Arthur M. Sackler, is utterly false," she wrote. "None of the charitable donations made by Arthur prior to his death, nor that I made on his behalf after his death, were funded by the production, distribution, or sale of OxyContin or other revenue from Purdue Pharma. Period." She listed Arthur's many contributions, both philanthropic and intellectual, and took pains to state that Arthur's money was independent of his brothers'. Last, she claimed, "The media is accusing Arthur of pioneering deceptive marketing techniques. This is another lie. He had complete integrity."[97]

But are these two things mutually exclusive? Can one have pioneered deceptive marketing techniques and still be a man of integrity? Perpetrators of great crimes often believe themselves to be doing the right thing. Humans have an amazing capacity for rationalization and acting in the moment is very different from judging actions several years later. But as the crisis grew and the overdose death count spiraled out of control, the country demanded action. Backed into a corner, industry representatives took pains to define the crisis as one of abuse, of people improperly using these drugs to get high. Few of us bought their pathetic explanation.

Harriet Ryan is a journalist for the *Los Angeles Times* and worked on a major investigation of Purdue and the opioid crisis. She tried to interview the Sacklers for her piece but was declined. "Many of them are philanthropists. They've made a lot of money, billions from this drug, but they're not your typical sort of *Vanity Fair* rich people. Yachts, dating models, things like that. They're intellectual people. They care about science. They're dedicated to a lot of really worthy causes, cancer research, arts, Doctors Without Borders and that sort of thing," she said.

"I have been told by people that know them, that know the company and work there, that inside the company when the drug came out, they received so many letters from people who had been suffering for years with no relief who finally felt through OxyContin they were getting to be alive again in a way they hadn't for years. That they considered it a miracle drug. That was just this great feeling inside Purdue for years, that they felt like they were really helping people.

"Then to some degree the tide turned and [OxyContin] started to be called hillbilly heroin and was denigrated as a drug. But people inside the company still clung to that, that sense that they had helped people who were in really bad straits."

■ ■ ■

HUBRIS AND RATIONALIZATION are not traits exclusive to the pharmaceutical industry. But as evidence mounts against Purdue, and the country is undeniably ravaged by the opioid addiction crisis, it becomes increasingly egregious that Purdue has only accepted a modicum of blame for its practices. In fact, the company is getting ready to release a new drug that treats opioid overdose, an all-too-common occurrence in America today.[98] We shall see in the next chapter how Purdue became aware of its misrepresentations very early on but continued in its denial and rationalization, all while reaping immense profits.

CHAPTER 5

Purdue Pharma

WHILE RAYMOND AND Mortimer were busy managing the day-to-day business at Purdue, Arthur was busy researching what was to make the three of them fabulously wealthy. He told his brothers that pain was the "next big thing." That their futures were in the development and marketing of time-release opioid medicines. What was remarkable was his plan was directed at chronic pain sufferers and their primary care doctors. Arthur's passion and vision became Raymond and Mortimer's mantra fueling the exponential growth of Purdue.

In the beginning the Purdue Frederick Company continued to produce over-the-counter drugs, adding arthritis medicines and disinfectants to its repertoire.[99] As the company grew, it acquired other smaller companies, built new manufacturing plants, and moved its headquarters from New York to Connecticut, eventually changing its name to Purdue Pharma in 1991.[100] In 1966, the Sacklers purchased Napp Pharmaceuticals in the United Kingdom. It was through Napp that Purdue acquired the sustained-release technology, which lays at the heart of MS Contin and OxyContin. In 1972, Napp developed what it called the "Continus" system for sustained release of drugs, first for the asthma drug Uniphyl and later for morphine.[101]

Sustained-release systems for drugs, generally special coatings, started to be developed in the 1950s,[102] and allowed for drugs to be administered over a long period of time rather than immediate release upon dissolution in a liquid. Purdue developed their own (via Napp) in the 1970s,[103] and by the 1980s were ready to apply it to morphine.

Raymond and Mortimer Sackler
NEW YORK TIMES

Until that point, morphine had been used intravenously with a relatively short, but powerful, effect.

OPIOIDS AND PALLIATIVE CARE

Two things occurred in the 1970s that together created a perfect breeding ground for the opioid crisis: One of them was the development of this sustained-release technology and its application to opioids; the other was the rethinking of pain medicine discussed in chapter 3. Where it once was thought that long-term chronic pain patients could not be helped, it soon became accepted that not only could people with chronic pain be treated, but it was also the doctor's duty to do so.

Part of this rethinking in pain medicine was pioneered by an English doctor named Cicely Saunders. Saunders, who would eventually be honored with damehood for her innovations, was the first to establish a hospice care facility for people at the end of their lives. She played a central role in the development of what came to be known as palliative care. In 1967, she founded St Christopher's Hospice in London, which was the first center of its kind. Saunders saw that people at the end of their lives were experiencing immense pain, and she felt a desire to help ease that pain. She pioneered the idea of "total pain,"[104] which saw pain as having emotional and spiritual components in addition to the *physical*. Saunders had seen the relief that morphine had brought to dying people and expanded the use of opioids for palliative care, a practice that remains to this day.[105] It was Saunders' St. Christopher's that asked Napp Pharmaceuticals to apply their sustained-release system to morphine. The result was MTS Continus, followed by MS Contin.

At the same time that Saunders was pioneering palliative care, former army doctor John Bonica was pioneering pain care in the United States. Bonica was an army doctor during World War II, and in 1947, he left the service and began working at Tacoma General Hospital. Bonica saw pain all around him—in the veterans he treated, in his wife during childbirth, and in himself, as the years he spent as a professional wrestler to pay for his schooling caught up with him. Bonica dedicated himself to pain relief and became chairman of the University of Washington's Department of Anesthesia, where he founded the nation's first multidisciplinary pain clinic.[106] Bonica understood, as Saunders did— and even as Arthur Sackler did—that pain is much more than just physical and that in order to treat it, it must be approached from several fronts.

But while the movement that pain could and should be treated was new, the knowledge that opioids brought relief to those in pain had existed for some time. MS Contin enjoyed wonderful success in its use for cancer patients and palliative care, and doctors began asking themselves if they could bring the same relief to sufferers of chronic pain.

MS Contin became Purdue's best-selling drug for cancer pain. But cancer pain can be extreme, so powerful drugs like opioids are accepted in order to ease that pain. In palliative care there is less concern about addiction because patients are dying. In both of those cases, opioids are administered under the close scrutiny of medical professionals. In the treatment of chronic pain, patients would be responsible for administering their own doses using their own judgment.

THE FALLACY OF THE 12-HOUR DOSING SCHEDULE

Purdue conducted its initial human tests of OxyContin on a group of women in Puerto Rico in 1989. According to Purdue's record of the study, roughly half the women in the test required more medication before the 12-hour mark and a third complained about experiencing pain in the first eight hours. Despite this, when Purdue submitted a patent application two years later, it stated that OxyContin provided 12-hour relief in "approximately 90 percent" of patients.[107] Through the application process, Purdue continued OxyContin tests, and in study after study, it was shown that OxyContin did not last for the full 12 hours, as it claimed.[108]

This was a problem for Purdue. The 12-hour dosing schedule was its competitive edge in a market full of pain pills. If OxyContin lasted for only six or eight hours, it was no better than many of the other

"**THERE WERE MANY** people involved in the effort to increase opioid prescribing who really believed what they were saying. Even the executives at the drug companies convinced themselves that people are suffering needlessly and that opioids could be prescribed more aggressively and that we didn't have to worry about getting patients addicted. Most professionals fell for this campaign and joined the bandwagon. There's certainly evidence that Purdue and other companies involved in the manufacturing of opioids knew that patients were having a very hard time getting off the pills. Their response was to withhold the information. Purdue instructed their sales reps to further exaggerate the effectiveness of OxyContin for chronic pain even though there was absolutely no scientific proof to back up their bogus claims." —**Dr. Andrew Kolodny, director of Opioid Policy Research, The Heller School for Social Policy and Management at Brandeis University, founder of Physicians for Responsible Opioid Prescribing (PROP)**

I am concerned that some physicians are using OxyContin on a q8h schedule rather than a q12h schedule. Where this is occurring you need to train the representative on how to deal with it, convincing the physician that there is no need to do this, and that 100% of the patients in the studies had pain relief on a q12h dosing regimen. Another factor may be the dosing card that only goes to 120mg per dose conversion. To deal with this, it is important that the representative discusses with the physician that there is not upward limit, asking if there are any reservations in using a dose of 240mg-320mg of OxyContin. As you pointed out, most patients will have adequate pain control with doses that do not exceed these levels.

Sackler Brothers Memo to Head of Marketing
GRAPHIC TAKEN FROM PURDUE INTERNAL MEMO

painkillers on the market. Purdue's marketing campaign focused on the q12h dosing schedule. It portrayed patients using competing drugs as trapped in anxious cycles of clock-watching in four- to six-hour intervals and waking up in the night in order to take another dose. If OxyContin couldn't provide a longer dosing schedule, doctors might prescribe another painkiller.

Doctors did notice that OxyContin wasn't lasting for 12 hours, so they began prescribing it on q8h or even q6h schedules. It was imperative to Purdue that this behavior be stopped. In a 1996 memo concerning OxyContin sales, it was stated how sales representatives should work hard to convince doctors that such dosing was not needed. The memo said explicitly that "there is no need to do this [dose less than q12h], and that *100 percent of the patients* [our emphasis] in the studies had pain relief on a q12h dosing regimen."[109] If patients were not experiencing a full 12 hours of relief, the remedy was not more frequent dosing but stronger dosage. "There is no upward limit," the memo said. "Most patients will have adequate pain control with dosages that do not exceed these limits."

When OxyContin was first released, the largest pill was 40 mg, but Purdue would eventually release a 120 mg pill. The problem with raising the dosage is that a higher dose increases the risk of dependency and addiction. Opioid dependency causes strong withdrawal symptoms, the most common of which is pain. The higher the dosage, the stronger the

NYSCEF DOC. NO. 12   RECEIVED NYSCEF: 10/06/2017

Exhibit A

Relationships between Corporations and Physicians, uses of Front Groups
and Selective Deceptive Marketing Materials and Resources

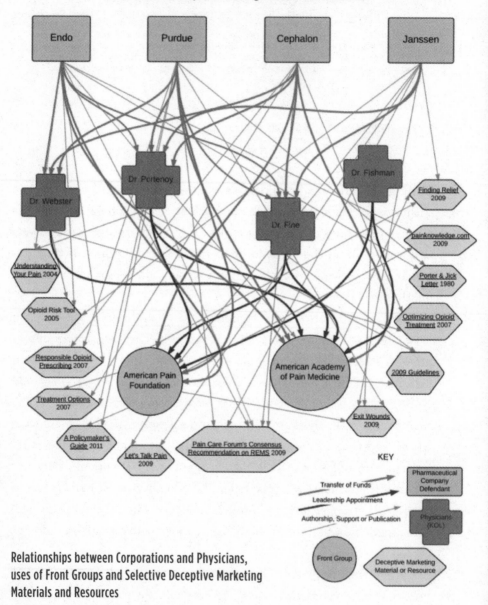

Relationships between Corporations and Physicians, uses of Front Groups and Selective Deceptive Marketing Materials and Resources

GRAPHIC FROM LAWSUIT AGAINST PURDUE PHARMA
AND OTHER PHARMACEUTICAL COMPANIES
BY BROOME COUNTY, NEW YORK,
HTTP://NYLAWYER.NYLJ.COM/ADGIFS/
DECISIONS17/020617BROOME.PDF

"THE START OF the opioid epidemic can be tied back initially to the introduction of OxyContin. At the time OxyContin was marketed, it was a very high dosage formulation that was meant to be used as instructed in a sustained-release way so that you would use it twice a day and it would deliver the drug slowly over time.

"But two important things were missed when OxyContin was first introduced. [One] was the idea that everyone would take it as intended, which means that you would only take it twice a day, and you would swallow it whole as instructed. But, in fact, it was really an easy source of opioids for recreational purposes because the drug could be immediately crushed without any difficulty, and then the entire dose that was meant to be delivered over 12 hours could be delivered within a minute.

"The second is that when OxyContin first came onto the market, it was described as being less addictive, or having limited abuse potential, because it was in a sustained-release formulation. This was information that was provided by the company and the manufacturer, and many physicians believed that this was the case. At the same time, there was a lot of pressure on practicing physicians to improve the treatment of pain because pain had probably been undertreated in hospital settings and home settings for a long time." **—Sharon Walsh, PhD, University of Kentucky**

withdrawals. Patients are then caught in a cycle of taking OxyContin to treat their pain and then having the withdrawal causing pain in and of itself.

All along Purdue repeatedly claimed that fears of addiction were unfounded. In a press release for OxyContin from 1996, the company said, "The fear of addiction is largely unfounded."[110] Purdue also pushed the idea of "pseudo-addiction"—the idea that patients who were exhibiting the typical warnings signs for addiction, requesting more of a drug specifically by name for example, were not actually addicted. What they needed instead was a higher dose. The press release went on to quote a statement from Dr. Mitchell B. Max, chairman of the American Pain Society Quality of Care Committee: "There is very little risk of addiction from proper uses of these drugs for pain relief."[111] What the press release did not say was that the American Pain Society, and many other pain and patient advocacy groups, were funded by pharmaceutical companies like Purdue, Teva, and Pfizer.[112] Purdue's OxyContin press release cited guidelines from the American Pain Society and the American Academy of Pain, but these guidelines were written by Dr. J. David Haddox,[113] who at the time was a speaker for Purdue and currently works at the company.[114]

It was also the American Pain Society that pushed the idea of pain as the "fifth vital sign." The four vital signs health professionals check for are body temperature, pulse, respiration rate, and blood pressure, all of which can be objectively measured. Pain, however, is very subjective and, as we noted earlier, influenced by a variety of factors, many of which have to do with mental health. The American Pain Society began its campaign for adopting the "fifth vital sign" in the 1990s and in 2001.

As we discussed in chapter 3, the Joint Commission asked doctors to have their patients gauge their pain on a scale from 1 to 10. However, the subjectivity of such a scale does little to help diagnose or treat pain. Following the paucity of attention and care given to pain in the past, there may have been a certain amount of guilt on the part of the "House of Medicine," which led them to adopt such imperfect methods. It should be noted that pain is not something that medicine should ignore. The Joint Commission cited an editorial in *Annals of Internal Medicine* in 1990 by Dr. Haddox (a paid Purdue speaker), which called for a different approach to pain. His editorial called for making pain "visible," involving patients in the "communication loop," and "facilitat[ing] innovation and the exchange of ideas."[115] His recommendations also called for more liberal use of opioid painkillers and stated that "therapeutic use of opiate analgesics rarely results in addiction."

PAYING FOR PROMOTION/ IGNORING THE EVIDENCE

Pharmaceutical companies spend massive amounts of money funding research and paying medical professionals to promote certain practices. It would be unfair to characterize these efforts as wholly self-interested or coercive. Much of what these companies pay for results in advancements and breakthroughs that help all of us. But there is another side to that relationship, one that is more morally ambiguous. Paid speakers are not necessarily promoting unsound ideas or practices, nor are they wholly under the thumb of their benefactors. But receiving money and support does affect people's thinking and can make people either more susceptible to certain practices or less critical of certain ideas.

In the case of opioids, Purdue and other pharmaceutical companies were able to convince medical professionals that these drugs were not as addictive as once thought, despite significant evidence to the contrary. We discussed earlier how a simple short letter to the *New England Journal of Medicine* by Porter and Jick became inflated into what some called a "landmark study." It is important to remember that this was before the internet and digitized information databases. In order for doctors to actually read a study cited by an article in a medical journal, they would have to go to a medical library and physically track it down. Doctors had trust in their peers and medical journals and believed what they were reading were extensive and properly conducted studies and not simply observations.

Do these untested articles constitute a full endorsement of the safety of opioids? Russell Portenoy did promote the use of opioids and was paid by Purdue to speak about opioid therapy. As Dr. Tauben pointed out, he has been widely criticized for recklessly promoting an unsafe drug. But it's important to look at this in the context of its time and place. At the time there was some evidence to suggest that medical technology had advanced enough that we could rethink our understanding of opioids and use them safely.

In a recorded interview produced by Physicians for Responsible Opioid Prescription, Portenoy said, "I gave innumerable lectures in the late 1980s and '90s about addiction that weren't true . . . Clearly, if I had an inkling of what I know now, then, I wouldn't have spoken in the way that I spoke. It was clearly the wrong thing to do."[116] It's important to remember that Portenoy and Foley had conducted the study themselves and seen with their own eyes patients receiving opioid treatment and responding positively without becoming addicted.

But in that same interview Portenoy said, "I gave so many lectures to primary care audiences in which the Porter and Jick article was just one piece of data that I would then cite. And I would cite six or seven, maybe ten different avenues of thought, or avenues of evidence, none of which represented real evidence. And yet what I was trying to do was to create a narrative so that the primary care audience would look at this information in total, and feel more comfortable about opioids, in a way they hadn't before. In essence, this was education to destigmatize, and

"**CDC DROPPED THE BALL** when OxyContin was released by Purdue. The FDA also dropped the ball. When you talk about the importance of regulation and proper vetting of a drug, there is a tremendous conflict of interest because the drug companies pay for the testing that ultimately gives them approval. That means there is a problem with proper regulation. The FDA's mandate is quite narrow. They are asked to assess whether the drug is safe, and this isn't safe in the sense of will it cause addiction or not. This is safe in the sense of are there dangerous side effects, could the drug end up making you sick, end up giving you a heart attack, things like this. These are called adverse events. It's not about will this drug make you addicted. And then they're asked to assess whether or not this drug is effective. Does it reduce pain? Yes or no? They're not asked this third question of if you prescribe it in very large numbers to people who have chronic long-term pain, will there be an opioid crisis?"
—**David Crow,** *Financial Times*

because the primary goal was to destigmatize, we often left evidence behind."[117] The effort was to destigmatize because it was a sincerely held belief at the time that opioids were in fact safe.

We saw in chapter 4 how doctors can be influenced by gifts and paid getaways to Sunbelt resorts, even without being conscious of it. It's reasonable to think that the same thing occurs when companies fund research and pay for speaking engagements. Are these doctors cynically ignoring scientific evidence because they are being paid to do so, or is there a trust in the system that people are unlikely to question?

According to David Crow of the *Financial Times*, "Greed fits in because drugs are big business and there is a lot of money swirling around the whole medical establishment, especially for doctors who maybe see themselves as underpaid. There are huge gains to be made by running clinical trials, by acting as an advisor to the pharmaceutical industry, and so there's this dangerous feedback loop. What you would really want are doctors to be on the frontline of protecting patients from drugs that could conceivably be dangerous for them, but instead quite often they work in tandem with the industry itself." While the bias of pharmaceutical companies' beneficiaries remains open to question, the role and actions of the companies themselves is less ambiguous. In its own tests and studies, Purdue saw that OxyContin was not lasting for the full 12 hours they had claimed. Even before it became national news, Purdue were getting reports of patients becoming addicted and even committing criminal acts in order to obtain more OxyContin.[118]

According to their 2016 Guidelines, the CDC's definition of an "addiction" is "the loss of control over use of any substance. It is a compulsive requirement to use that substance independent of its appropriateness, any time of day, all day, every circumstance requires an exposure to that substance. Then continuing use of that substance despite evident adverse consequences. The three Cs still applies: adverse consequences, compulsive use, and loss of control."[119]

PURDUE, GIULIANI, AND THE JUSTICE DEPARTMENT FINDINGS

Barry Meier is a journalist for the *New York Times* who has been follow-ing OxyContin since the late 1990s. In 2003, he authored *Pain Killer: An Empire of Deceit and the Origin of America's Opioid Epidemic*, one of the first books about the crisis. In 2007, when three Purdue execu-tives pleaded guilty to "misbranding" OxyContin and paid a combined $635 million, the Justice Department team that prepared the law-suit were forced to seal the report, which detailed the charges against Purdue. According to Meier, the team working for federal prosecutor John Brownlee was forced to seal the report by top officials at the Jus-tice Department in the George W. Bush administration. Those officials declined to follow the team's recommendations to indict Purdue and instead charged the three officials with misdemeanor crimes. The result-ing charges ended in fines and community service for the three Purdue officials. But in 2018, someone from Brownlee's team provided Meier with a copy of the 120-page report, which details Purdue's knowledge of how OxyContin was being abused and how patients were becoming addicted.[120]

When Purdue first released OxyContin, it included an insert with information about the drug, including warnings about misuse, as is cus-tomary for all drugs. The insert warned against taking the pill other than as directed and specifically warned against crushing the pill, as this would release all of the drug instantly rather than over several hours as it was meant to. Unfortunately, this warning served as a guide to poten-tial drug abusers, explicitly telling them that if the drug was crushed and snorted, or injected, then its effects would be extremely powerful.

Abuse of the drug became widespread, and according to the Jus-tice Department's report obtained by Meier, Purdue was aware of this as early as 1996. "Company officials had received reports that the pills were being crushed and snorted; stolen from pharmacies; and that some doctors were being charged with selling prescriptions," Meier wrote in the *New York Times* in May 2018.[121] The report also shows that emails were sent to certain members of the Sackler family who were involved with the company.

Because of these reports, the family of Arthur Sackler has stated emphatically that they have received no money from OxyContin sales and are in no way involved with the company's dealings. Raymond and Mortimer Sackler bought out Arthur's shares after his death.

When the Food and Drug Administration approved OxyContin in 1995, it allowed Purdue to make the claim that the sustained-release system used for the drug made it less appealing to drug abusers because it failed to quickly produce any kind of euphoria. The FDA made this decision not based on any trials. In fact, the FDA conducts no trials of its own and relies on manufacturers own data for the approval process. Purdue provided no evidence for this but made the claim simply on the theory that drug abusers favored other fast-acting painkillers.[122]

According to Dr. Art Van Zee, in his paper "The Promotion and Marketing of OxyContin: Commercial Triumph, Public Health Tragedy," the FDA is responsible for reviewing promotional materials for prescription drugs. However, FDA approval is not needed before those materials are used. Furthermore, Van Zee wrote that the FDA has a limited amount of staff responsible for approving promotional material. "In 2002," he wrote, "39 FDA staff members were responsible for reviewing roughly 34,000 pieces of promotional material."[123] The FDA official who oversaw OxyContin's approval process was a Dr. Curtis Wright, who two years later had left the FDA and was working for Purdue.[124]

The FDA had allowed Purdue to claim that OxyContin's long-acting formula made the drug less appealing to drug abusers. Purdue went even further and trained its sales force to tell health-care providers that "OxyContin did not cause a 'buzz,' caused less euphoria, had less addiction potential, and had less abuse potential." Sales people were also trained to say that "OxyContin was less likely to be diverted than immediate-release opioids and could be used to 'weed out' addicts and drug seekers."[125]

In 2007, Purdue company president, Michael Friedman; its former medical adviser, Dr. Paul Goldenheim; and its top lawyer, Howard Udell, pleaded guilty to "misbranding" OxyContin and misleading "regulators, doctors, and patients about the drug's risk of addiction and its potential to be abused."[126] Friedman was fined $19 million, Udell $8 million, and Dr. Goldenheim $7.5 million, while the company paid $600 million in fines.[127] The profits from OxyContin, however, are estimated to be roughly $2 billion a year, and in a statement following the charges, Purdue stated that the three men "neither engaged in nor tolerated the misconduct at issue in this investigation. To the contrary, they took steps to prevent any misstatements in the marketing or promotion of OxyContin and to correct any such misstatements of which they became aware."[128]

When the Justice Department team under John Brownlee initially pursued charges against the company, they had wanted jail time for its top executives. But Purdue had an ace up its sleeve: former New York mayor Rudy Giuliani. Purdue had hired Giuliani in 2002, around the time that lawyers in the federal prosecutors' office had started to subpoena Purdue's records, and officials at the Drug Enforcement Agency had begun to look at the marketing of OxyContin. Giuliani was still flush from his tenure as mayor of New York City. He had won national praise for his leadership in the wake of the September 11 World Trade Center attack and had been named *Time* magazine's Man of the Year. He had started a private consulting firm, Giuliani Partners, and was hired by Purdue to help manage the growing concern over OxyContin.

Giuliani was more than a legal consultant; he was a PR rep. He started an organization called Rx Action Alliance, made up of drug companies, law enforcement, and doctors, which said its purpose was to tackle the abuse of prescription drugs.[129] He helped Purdue tamp down an investigation by the DEA in 2004 and was personally brought back to handle Mr. Brownlee's investigation. In 2007, Barry Meier wrote in the *Times*, "[Giuliani's] selection was not by chance, company representatives said. They figured Mr. Brownlee, a younger federal prosecutor,

"AS JOURNALISTS, I think we always need to do two things. One is to go and find the people who are being affected by this crisis and talk to them and never stop talking to them. Never stop telling their story. Especially in business journalism, there can sometimes be a tendency to just write about the numbers and not write about the actual people that are affected. Second, you have to keep holding the drug makers to account. Depomed isn't a household name today; Endo isn't; Purdue is becoming one. But if you write about them enough, they will become household names. As a result, they will become more accountable. Big Pharma is supposed to be regulated by the FDA, but unfortunately, through the PDUFA [Prescription Drug User Fee Act] laws, Big Pharma is actually paying the FDA very large sums of money to review their drug applications. So we get a problem that economists refer to as regulatory capture. If the people who are actually paying for your services are the ones you're supposed to regulate, you may not be as tough on them as if you didn't have it run that way. The problem is no one wants to raise taxes to increase the size of the FDA to take care of these problems. The result is 72,000 deaths a year from inappropriate opioid overdose. [This number refers to the number of all drug overdose deaths in America, the majority of which are from opioids.]

"There has to be very strong public education, public warning, and public understanding that these drugs, while they do play some purpose in the medical environment, particularly with very serious acute pain relief, they are not the kinds of things that could be used for chronic pain, and they certainly don't belong as recreational drugs.

"The cost to society of the prescription opioid addiction problem is, just in medical care costs, around $100 billion a year. If you add in the lost productivity due to all the people that are dying and permanently disabled, it's many times greater than that. This is, in fact, a very expensive man-made public health crisis." **—David Crow,** *Financial Times*

would look up to Mr. Giuliani, who became a legend as a United States attorney in New York." Giuliani tried to convince Brownlee to back down, which he eventually did, agreeing that the executives would not have to serve jail time.

COURTESY OF PROFESSOR MATT STEFL, MARKETING,
LOYOLA MARYMOUNT UNIVERSITY, LOS ANGELES, CALIFORNIA

This concession was made only after Giuliani appealed directly to Brownlee's bosses at the Justice Department. In a 2018 interview for the *New York Times*'s *The Daily* podcast, Meier said, "There was an eleventh hour meeting between top political appointees in the Justice Department." The attorney general at the time was Alberto Gonzales, but Meier didn't say if he personally attended the meeting. Following that meeting, Brownlee and his team were told to pursue lesser, misdemeanor charges. "The message from the Justice Department was, 'you're going to have to plea bargain' . . . because we're not going to support a felony charge."[130] Many people involved in the case have no doubts that Mr. Giuliani's celebrity played a role in influencing the case.[131] Because a plea bargain was struck, the evidence compiled by Brownlee and his team was sealed.

"Someone who was upset" about the report being buried "provided me with a copy," Meier said. Mr. Meier, who had been following Purdue since the late 1990s, reported, "I was both stunned, and heart-sickened." The report had copies of the emails between Purdue's executives and members of the Sackler family, detailing instances of abuse and how they were aware that internet forums for drug abusers were praising OxyContin for its powerful effects. The Justice Department had had these emails for several years but failed to act. "Had they told the truth," Meier said, "the foundation of OxyContin's success would've crumbled."[132]

■ ■ ■

PURDUE REFORMULATED OXYCONTIN in 2010 to make it harder to abuse. The new formulation when crushed didn't turn into powder so it couldn't be snorted, and when water was added to it, a gummy substance was produced preventing injection via hypodermic needle. But the damage had been done. In the face of billions of dollars in annual sales, $634 million seems like a paltry sum. What's more, the lack of convictions for Purdue's executives sends the message that criminality can be wiped away by money and influence.

Throughout OxyContin's entire history, even as the company pleaded guilty, Purdue has maintained that it has done nothing wrong and has displayed the utmost integrity. According to the National Institute on Drug Abuse, an average of more than 130 people die every day from opioid overdose.

CHAPTER 6

The Disease of Addiction

IF THERE IS any silver lining to the opioid crisis, it's that society now better understands that addiction is a mental illness rather than a moral failing. As the opioid crisis grew, emergency rooms across the country began to fill with overdose victims and prisons began to burst at the seams with nonviolent drug offenders. The country was forced to reevaluate how it dealt with drug users. What's more, the people showing up in hospitals and courtrooms were now disproportionately white and often middle class. These were people with whom America's white, male, and upper-class politicians could sympathize. People who looked like them and their children. A "tough on crime" approach now seemed callous and short-sighted.

It must be noted, however, that medical professionals have argued for decades that addiction is a mental disease, best treated by therapy and personal growth. (A book entitled *Drug Addicts Are Human Beings: The Amazing Story of Our Billion-Dollar Drug Racket* was published as early as 1938.)[133] But in the United States, drug use was often associated with people of color. Because of the long history of discrimination in this country, calls for a more compassionate approach to drug treatment were brushed aside for a more "tough on crime" approach. (We noted in chapter 2 how former Nixon aide John Ehrlichman later admitted that the association between drugs and black people was exaggerated by the government in order to "disrupt" those communities.) This led in part to the United States becoming the most incarcerated country in the world.[134]

We will not deal with those issues directly in this book, but it should be stated emphatically that America's racism—and associating people of color with criminality and drug use—allowed the crisis to flourish. America's "War on Drugs" is the subject of a great many books that are worth reading in their own right. Michelle Alexander's *The New Jim Crow* is an excellent examination of America's justice system and how its punishments follow offenders for the rest of their lives. *Chasing the Scream* by Johann Hari looks at several countries that have had massive success in curbing drug addiction by abandoning the US-led criminalization approach and instead choosing treatment-based programs. Matt Taibbi's *The Divide* examines how the American justice systems favors the rich and criminalizes poverty, often by using draconian drug laws to incarcerate poor people. Yet it wasn't until the crisis hit suburban white communities that politicians started to see that throwing people in prison wasn't a good way to treat drug addicts.

It should also be noted, with no small amount of irony, that Dr. Kolodny, the founder of Physicians for Responsible Opioid Prescribing (PROP), believes that racial stereotyping has protected black and Latino communities from the opioid crisis. "Something that we do know

"THIS EPIDEMIC IS hitting mainstream America; it's hitting the families of policemen and lawyers and judges and politicians. Political leaders are not playing politics with this issue to get votes so much as seeing firsthand what opioid addiction is doing to their constituents and to their own families. In over 90 percent of cases, their addiction developed through prescription opioids given to them by their primary-care doctors. When you're personally affected by the drug epidemic, it's easier to recognize that addiction is a disease rather than a moral failing."
—Dr. Kelly Clark, Louisville, Kentucky

is that doctors prescribe narcotics more cautiously to their non-white patients," Dr. Kolodny told NPR in 2017. "It would seem that if the patient is black, the doctor is more concerned about the patient becoming addicted, or maybe they're more concerned about the patient selling their pills, or maybe they are less concerned about pain in that population. But the black patient is less likely to be prescribed narcotics, and therefore less likely to wind up becoming addicted to the medication." Because the current epidemic is predominately white and began with seemingly legitimate medical prescriptions, according to Dr. Kolodny, "What we're seeing now is a very different response now that we've got an addiction epidemic that's disproportionately white." He continued, "What we're hearing from policymakers, even conservative Republican politicians when they talk about the opioid crisis, many begin by saying, 'We can't arrest our way out of this. We have to see that people who are addicted can access effective treatment.' We didn't hear that during the crack cocaine epidemic."

THE DIFFERENCE BETWEEN ADDICTION AND DEPENDENCY

What is addiction? Most people think of addiction as being unable to control some habit or the use of a substance. While that is certainly part of what characterizes addiction, there is a distinction in medicine between addiction and dependency. Dependency is when a person's body is physically dependent on a certain substance, alcohol for example. But there are instances where a person can be dependent on a substance but not necessarily addicted in the medical sense. Addiction changes the person's mind in such a way that makes his or her behavior irrational and compulsive.

Dr. Chris Evans, a professor at UCLA specializing in neuropharmacology, explained, "If [addicts] take the drug for a little while, their brain will change. Synapsis will change, transmitters will change. Their brain will change. They will become adapted to the drugs, so the drug has really become a normal state for them." That's dependency. Addiction is when "the drug becomes so important to their psyche that they can't do without it. Then they become obsessed with getting the drug, they have cravings and they can't control these cravings, and they'll need to get the drug. So it becomes a sort of stimulus response. 'I'm feeling the drug's gone, I need the drug, I need it to feel normal.'"

People dependent on certain drugs often realize what's happening to them and take steps to control their cravings or seek help. Addicts, on the other hand, often generally cannot control themselves, which is what leads to damaging behavior. "If you don't have access to the drugs, you have the cravings," Dr. Evans said. "You have the strong motivation to get this drug to feel normal. So that can be a very strong drive, and this is why lot of addicts get in trouble." This is where things like criminality often become a problem. Stealing to support a habit or turning to illicit drugs like heroin when prescription drugs are no longer available. This difference between the dependent and the addicted often goes unrecognized by many people unfamiliar with the distinction. In some way it has perpetuated the misunderstanding of addiction as a moral failing.

While addiction has become better understood in the medical community and society at large, the disease itself is still rather enigmatic.

"**WITH RESPECT TO** addiction, there are a lot of misunderstandings and fallacies about drugs and how they work. About addiction being a biological versus a behavioral, versus a moral disorder. The CDC's definition of an addiction is what the standard definition implies. It is the loss of control over use of any substance. It is a compulsive requirement to use that substance independent of its appropriateness . Any time of day, all day, every circumstance requires an exposure to that substance. Then continuing use of that substance despite evident adverse consequences. The three Cs still apply: *adverse consequences, compulsive use, and loss of control.*" —**Dr. Sharon Walsh, PhD, University of Kentucky**

Medical professionals aren't quite sure what makes a person prone to addiction in the first place. It is now believed that a certain amount of the population is genetically predisposed to addiction, but the numbers vary. Experts estimate that anywhere from 10 to 20 percent of the population suffers from addiction and that risks for the disease range from genetics to environment.[135] Many people who were prescribed opioids did not become addicted and took themselves off of the drugs because they didn't like its effects. But for those people whose addiction was triggered by prescription pills, the damage was devastating.

OPIOIDS AND INCREASED ILLEGAL ACTIVITY

When OxyContin first came to national attention, it was through stories of seemingly normal people turned into addicts. Newspapers reported stories of everyday people robbing pharmacies, not for money but for OxyContin. By 2001, newspapers across the country had reported hundreds of break-ins in search of OxyContin and strings of armed robberies of pharmacies.[136] At the same time the number of people reportedly switching to heroin because they could no longer obtain prescription opioids started to rise. Purdue was aware of these incidents as early as 1996, as indicated by the emails obtained by John Brownlee and his team in the investigation leading to the 2007 plea deal. However, Purdue continued to insist upon OxyContin's safety. Mexican drug cartels noticed the rise in the demand for heroin and responded by setting up franchise-like cells throughout the country.[137] One paper tracked a 96 percent rise in reports of opioid- and painkiller-related incidents across 28 metro areas in the US from 1997–2002.[138]

There had been opioid epidemics in America before. Civil War veterans had become addicted to morphine because of their wounds, and laudanum, a mixture of opium and alcohol, was marketed to women for a variety of uses like anxiety and "female problems."[139] Heroin was invented by the Bayer company in Germany in 1895 as a cough suppressant, but a series of legislative acts in the early twentieth century banned the use of opiates except in highly controlled medical settings. Heroin remained present in American society, but law enforcement focused on black communities in the inner city. A report on heroin in Chicago from 1971 notes that records show only 17 percent of heroin addicts in the 1930s were black, but in later years when police were cracking down, the black-white arrest ratio for heroin was 7:1.[140]

According to the *Washington Post*, the difference between today's opioid epidemic and those of the past is the availability of illegal drugs to replace legal ones. The *Post* reported in October 2017 that prescription levels for 2015 were three times what they were in 1999. "Dependent Americans who can no longer get the drugs from pharmacies are turning to illegal markets in greater numbers than ever before," the *Post* wrote.[141]

THE STRUGGLE TO MANAGE THE ADDICTION CRISIS

Despite increased knowledge of addiction and the crisis in general, communities are still struggling to find ways to cope. As a mental health disease, addiction is extremely difficult to manage and requires an

"IT IS WRONG that law enforcement is insensitive to what happens with the user or the addict. I live in this community. I see the overdoses. I go and make presentations. I talk to community members. I get to talk to the parents who have lost family members from overdoses of heroin or divertive prescription pills. It's a tragedy. I've had people in my own immediate circles that have had drug-abuse problems. It's not just a law-enforcement issue. That's an important component of it and you need that, but law enforcement needs to try to impact the supply, but for us to be successful, we [also] need to reduce the demand." —**Tom Gorman, DEA special agent for Kentucky and Ohio**

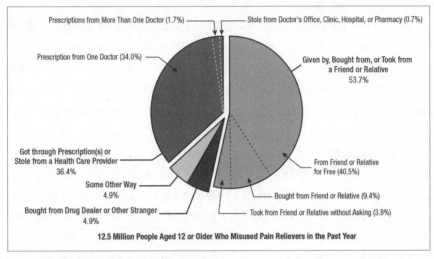

Prescriptions from More Than One Doctor (1.7%) ——

Stole from Doctor's Office, Clinic, Hospital, or Pharmacy (0.7%)

Prescription from One Doctor (34.0%) ——

Given by, Bought from, or Took from a Friend or Relative
53.7%

Got through Prescription(s) or Stole from a Health Care Provider
36.4%

From Friend or Relative for Free (40.5%)

Some Other Way
4.9%

Bought from Friend or Relative (9.4%)

Bought from Drug Dealer or Other Stranger
4.9%

Took from Friend or Relative without Asking (3.8%)

12.5 Million People Aged 12 or Older Who Misused Pain Relievers in the Past Year

Legal and Illegal Distribution Sources of Opioids in 2017

IMAGE COURTESY OF SUBSTANCE ABUSE AND MENTAL HEALTH SERVICES ADMINISTRATION (SAMHSA)

enormous amount of commitment on the part of the addicts and their social circles. Our current institutions, health care, schools, and criminal justice departments are not entirely prepared to deal with the full scope of the crisis.

Dr. Kelly Clark is an addiction physician and psychiatrist in Louisville, Kentucky, where some of the communities hardest hit by the crisis are located. "In order for us to get the right answers to this problem, we have to ask the right questions," Clark said. She went on to explain that addiction should be thought of like diabetes, a lifelong condition that a person doesn't "recover" from but learns to manage and live with. "How long do people need to stay on medicine if they've got diabetes?" she asked. "What proportion of people remain absolutely adherent to their treatment plan to treat their diabetes? We would never ask this." But oftentimes addicts are expected to complete a month-long treatment program and reenter society. "You don't go away and come back fixed in 28 days from your diabetes," she said. "You don't go away and come back fixed from your addictive disease. And by the way, do you know where the 28 days came from? That's what the State of Minnesota used to pay for. Twenty-eight days of rehab." Dr. Clark was referring to what is known as the "Minnesota Model," which is the amount of time that used to be given to alcoholics in state hospitals there. Insurance companies then adopted that as the standard amount of time for covering drug-treatment programs.[142] Despite the increased awareness of addiction as a mental disease and the necessity of therapeutic treatment, there is still a misunderstanding of how treatment works and a stigma attached to those who fail. "A medicine in and of itself does not manage addictive disease. It takes all of those pieces [medicine and therapy] to manage the addictive disease," Dr. Clark said. "But we would never, ever say, well, if you can't diet and exercise your way out of needing insulin, you're a failure." However, in a society that emphasizes and often exaggerates individual autonomy and achievement, failure to overcome an addiction, even when it's widely acknowledged as a mental health disease, is often seen as a personal failure. Furthermore, our health care is often dictated not by doctors but by insurance companies who look at numbers in the short term. Several doctors we spoke to for this project mentioned the movement of health insurance companies into "managed care" in the early 1990s. Managed care is a system where only certain doctors and services are covered. Insurance companies started refusing to cover treatments not seen as strictly medical, like physical and talk therapy, and instead preferred prescription medication.

It would be unfair to place all of the blame with institutions like health insurance companies. We, too, with our culture of instant gratification, have trouble accepting that significant lifestyle changes are the best means of overcoming addiction. "It's a clash between current

"THE NECESSITY TO meet thresholds of pain relief became oversimplified into a pain score. Doctors began to chase a pain score, which is very difficult to quantify and substantiate, particularly in chronic pain." —Dr. David Tauben, University of Washington

culture and the normal biology of the brain, which is very much reward driven," said Dr. Peter Whybrow, a psychiatrist and director of the Semel Institute for Neuroscience and Human Behavior at UCLA. "But, unfortunately, we have created a culture now where we apply directly to the patient. When that person is in pain, and doctors are prescribing opioids, then that opens all sorts of gates at all sorts of levels for addiction, which is extraordinarily dramatic." Many of the root causes of this crisis, Dr. Whybrow argued, come from our brain's emphasis on reward. "Unfortunately, human beings," he said, "we grew up in scarcity. We are actually very addicted to reward. We seek that all the time. We are fascinated by novelty. We are socially competitive. All these fundamental survival techniques, which we've had ever since the brain first began many millions of years ago, are now being reinforced by the culture we've built. Because the culture feeds on continued expansion, and continued expansion is driven by consumerism. It used to be that when we first invented the modern market society, that we didn't have very much, and so it was a very good idea to produce more goods because everybody benefited. Now we're in a situation where we have to produce goods to sustain the market society. It's flipped itself."

Addiction therapy is often concerned with limiting reward, limiting consumption. Not just of a substance but of certain behaviors and mentalities. It focuses on long-term goals and lifestyle changes, which can take a long time to produce results. Changing one's diet can yield numerous health benefits, but it's difficult for people to do because eating unhealthy food is so stimulating. Add that to a society that bombards us with advertisements scientifically designed to urge us to make certain consumer choices and you've got a culture that seems to be actively working against a healthy lifestyle. Because so many of the solutions are based on personal choice, it becomes easy to write off those who fail as lacking the constitution needed to succeed. They are thus unworthy of assistance, particularly if that assistance requires sacrifice (such as taxes to pay for social programs) on the part of those who aren't troubled by such problems.

THE FINANCIAL BURDEN OF TREATMENT

The financial cost of treatment cannot be overlooked, and who is to pay for it is a question that lingers over the fight to end the opioid crisis. "We have over 2.2 million Americans as a conservative estimate from the federal government who are addicted to opioids," Dr. Clark said. "That's 40,000 beds just for people with opioid addiction per state." Paid for by whom? "Treatment needs to be appropriate to that person. That means the right treatment by the right kind of provider with the right modality and the right place at the right frequency at the right time. Individualized care. There is no one-size-fits-all. There's no one course of antibiotics that fixes your infection here. This is a chronic disease." Who decides all that? Who pays for it? Our health-care system is not equipped to deal with a crisis on such a scale.

As director of Kentucky's Office of Drug Control Policy, Van Ingram has to be just as involved with treatment, prevention, and education as he is with the law enforcement community. According to Ingram, "It's

"WHO'S PAYING FOR the cost of the epidemic? We're all paying for the cost of the epidemic. Every taxpayer is paying the cost, every family who's struggling with someone who has an addiction is paying the cost. The costs that are incurred through the criminal justice system as a result of drug addiction are significant, and the costs to the health-care system are significant. Particularly when you don't effectively treat the addiction. Effective treatment for the addiction is one of the greatest cost savers over the long-term life of an individual. It offsets the care for so many other medical problems if you treat the addiction correctly. I think that's also part of why we need to really emphasize the medication-assisted treatment approaches (MAT), because they really bring a level of stability for many people, which keeps them out of prison, keeps them out of using health care for all of the medical problems that come with opioid addiction." —Dr. Sam Ball, Yale School of Medicine

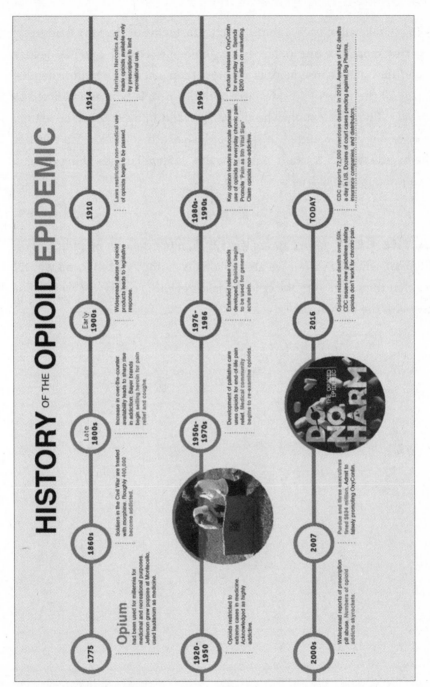

History of the Opioid Epidemic

WALESKA SANTIAGO, MEDIA POLICY CENTER

going to take all of us in a coordinated effort. One of the keys is addressing this more like the public health epidemic than a criminal justice
issue. The health consequences are more than just drug overdose deaths.
I hear all the time of suicides attributed to people who are addicted to
opioids. There are people who die in falls and in automobile accidents.
They're not even counted in the overdose death statistics. It's just not
the overdoses. It's a whole public health epidemic that's going on as a
result of our opioid drug use."

■ ■ ■

IN THE NEXT few chapters we will examine the cost of addiction on
all of us, whether or not we are personally connected to it, and we will
see that the solution to the opioid crisis lays with society as a whole, not
just with the individual.

Physicians for Responsible Opioid Prescribing (PROP)

IN THIS CHAPTER we profile several physicians and health-care professionals who heeded the call of the Hippocratic oath to practice their profession without knowingly harming their patients. Dr. Kolodny's story is a profile in courage.[143] He was not alone in signaling this abuse, but in many ways he was the first to spread the message that there was something terribly dangerous about making opioids readily available for the asking. He blew the whistle on some of the most powerful members of Big Pharma. Unfortunately, it took until 2016 for government regulators to follow suit. Dr. Kolodny agreed to be one of our key advisors during the making the documentary and the subsequent writing of the book. We were able to catch up with him for several long-form video interviews in between his very busy schedule of teaching, lecturing, giving key testimony in several important legal trials forcing Big Pharma and their allies to come to the table, and several appearances before the Senate Homeland Security and Governmental Affairs Committee.[144] Most of this chapter is taken from several longform interviews we conducted with Dr. Kolodny held between 2016 and 2018.

"My first week on the job I was told that 960 people died of a drug overdose. Let me say that again. My first week on the job I was told that 960 people died of a drug overdose in New York City last year." In 2004, Dr. Andrew Kolodny was working in the New York City health department. The head of the department, Dr. Thomas Frieden, had pioneered the city's campaign against tobacco and in the future would spearhead the effort to ban large, sugary sodas. At the time he decided that the department would use a new metric when grading the city's health: drug overdose deaths.

The health department had recently been merged with the city's mental health agency to help improve the overall health of New York City. Cities often use statistics like infant mortality and rates of disease to grade a city's health. Dr. Frieden wanted to add drug deaths to the report filed with the mayor's office. Dr. Kolodny was charged with bringing that number down.

"That would seem like an impossible task," he said. "But there were things that we could do as we studied the issue. We did things that were innovative at the time. We gave out naloxone or Narcan, an overdose antidote, through syringe exchange programs so that heroin users could be taught how to rescue their peers." Dr. Kolodny realized that lowering drug deaths is best achieved not by stopping an overdose when it occurs but by treating people suffering from addiction so that they're not using in the first place. An overdose can often result in death. But if an addict survives, it can also signal a new beginning seeking professional treatment and a commitment to lifelong sobriety.

ALARMING STATISTICS

Dr. Kolodny began to notice a difference between the patients he was treating in the New York City health department and those he began seeing when he started a private practice in Manhattan. "We were focused on overdose deaths in the South Bronx, Central Brooklyn, and East Harlem. The neighborhoods with the highest rate of drug overdose death are the neighborhoods that were hit hard with heroin in the 1970s, and crack cocaine in the late '80s, early '90s. That's where we were focused," he said of his time at the New York City health department. Those were the areas traditionally associated with drug abuse, where communities have long struggled with successive waves of drug epidemics. When Dr. Kolodny started his own private practice treating people for opioid addiction, he used the drug buprenorphine, also called Suboxone. His office was in Manhattan, and he expected to see the same types of patients he had seen while working for the city. But instead of the older addicts from the inner city, the people coming to Dr. Kolodny's office were also from the city's suburbs, from Staten Island and Long Island, from Westchester County.

"They're mostly young, with some older individuals. They're white. Their opioid addiction developed through prescription opioids. That's a sign that something's going on here," Dr. Kolodny said. So he started to look at the numbers. Using medical databases on the internet, he looked at various statistics from across the country, information that wasn't readily available just a few years earlier. "I'm looking at these reports, and I'm sure that somebody made a mistake and put a decimal point in the wrong place," he said. There was no mistake. Overdose deaths had skyrocketed, and there had been a massive increase in the number of emergency room visits for "nonmedical" use of painkillers.

Then in 2006, Dr. Len Paulozzi, a medical director for the CDC,[145] published a graph that showed the rates of overdose deaths in America alongside the sales of prescription painkillers. The graph revealed almost parallel 45-degree lines.

"When his paper came out, for me it was a point at which I felt 'aha,'" Dr. Kolodny said. "It's clear what's causing this epidemic. It's the medical community." Dr. Kolodny realized that it was doctors who had inadvertently caused the problem by too easily prescribing opioid painkillers and that the solution was more cautious prescribing. He thought that with the information now widely available to the medical community, surely the rates of prescription would come down.

BIG PHARMA AND THE GOVERNMENT VERSUS PUBLIC HEALTH

"Within the field of public health, there is an understanding that there's sometimes a tension between corporate interests and the public's health," Dr. Kolodny said. The pharmaceutical industry wasn't about to let their drugs take all the blame for a growing public health crisis and see their markets shrink as a result. The industry blamed the problem on drug abusers—people who were not taking the drug as prescribed. The pharma industry for years maintained that when taken properly, addiction rates in patients taking opioid painkillers were less than 1 percent. Furthermore, they framed the issue in terms of two competing public health crises: drug abuse and chronic pain. If the government cracked down on prescription painkillers because of a small number of drug addicts, the companies argued, then the chronic pain crisis would inevitably get worse. But to Dr. Kolodny, this was a flawed argument.

"The idea that all of the harms were limited to the so-called drug abusers wasn't true at all," he said. "In fact, overdose deaths are highest in patients receiving legitimate prescriptions for chronic pain. Hundreds of thousands of pain patients over the past decade who have become addicted to prescription opioids have died of overdoses." But the government was willing to accept the pharmaceutical industry's version of events. It's true that many people do suffer, and suffer greatly, from legitimate pain issues that can be difficult to treat. If we look at the history of how drug addicts have been portrayed and treated in the United States, it's not difficult to see why the government easily accepted them as villains, unlawfully corrupting a legitimate practice. "This focus on stopping the nonmedical use [abuse] while preserving the aggressive prescribing for everyone else, or the focus on stopping nonmedical use while completely ignoring the fact that clinicians were overprescribing, that [was] really what was fueling the crisis, not teen-agers going into grandma's medicine chest," Dr. Kolodny said. All of the efforts were focused on stopping the teenager from going into grand-ma's medicine chest as if we didn't have to worry about grandma's over-use of opioids.

"There was a fear of saying anything or doing anything that might result in doctors prescribing more cautiously, because the thinking was that if doctors started to reduce their prescribing, that would be bad for all of these pain patients who were helped," Dr. Kolodny said. The government's response to the crisis reflected that thinking. At the beginning, the response was focused on curtailing drug abuse, not over-prescription. Eventually this resulted in Purdue reformulating OxyCon-tin in 2010 in an effort to make it more abuse deterrent, as we discussed in chapter 5. The original OxyContin pill could be easily crushed into a powder, which could then be snorted or mixed with water and injected. The new pill broke into small pieces and became thick and gunky when mixed with a liquid. While this did reduce a certain amount of abuse, some studies have argued that this led many addicts to switch to heroin, causing a rise in deaths from that drug.[146] "Despite some reductions in nonmedical use," Dr. Kolodny said, "the epidemic continued to get worse. It was the wrong way to focus."

While many government agencies like the Office of National Drug Control Policy and Substance Abuse and Mental Health Services Admin-istration (SAMHSA) focused on reducing abuse only, the CDC focused on rates of prescription. Starting in 2006, the CDC had said that the roots of the crisis lay in the high levels of prescriptions for opioid pain-killers. In 2016, the agency released new guidelines concerning those prescriptions. It took some years before both government agencies and the medical community were able to get behind the effort to reduce pre-scriptions.

Purdue had spent hundreds of millions of dollars on a brilliant mar-keting campaign that involved not only flashy magazine ads but also the funding of flawed studies, which claimed to show that addiction rates were actually very low. Vast amounts of money were spent to make it appear as if the pharmaceutical industry's narrative of safe opioids was based in sound science. They were able to convince many prominent doctors in the field of pain medicine that the conventional wisdom about opioids had been misguided. "You're hearing from pain specialists who are eminent in the field," Dr. Kolodny said. "Many people become doctors because they really want to help patients. You're hearing that you can be much more compassionate. The argument sounded reasonable: You're confusing physical dependence and addiction. It seemed to make sense."

It's not always easy to convince people they've made a terrible mistake, particularly when that means taking responsibility for pain and suffering. It's understandable how many in the medical community were unwilling to believe that fault, at least some of it, lay with them. There was also the public's trust in the medical establishment to do no harm.

An enormous amount of effort had been put into creating the appearance of legitimacy for opioid painkillers. Now doctors were being told that the very prestigious institutions of the "House of Medicine" had been duped. There were other incentives within the medical community that prevented limiting opioid prescriptions. "You have healthcare systems and administrators encouraging aggressive prescribing

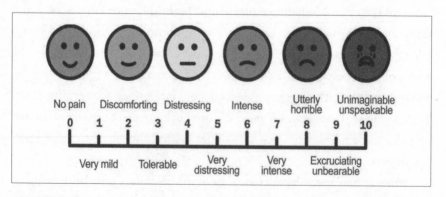

The Pain Chart

COURTESY OF PROHEALTH.COM

because of patient satisfaction scores, and the hospital needs to get good ratings," Dr. Kolodny said. "The Joint Commission, which accredits hospitals, requires that patients be constantly screened about pain. You're showing people the frowny faces and the smiley faces. There's still a lot that needs to be rolled back." Doctors could in fact be sanctioned for not prescribing opioids on the grounds that they were refusing to provide adequate medical care for their patients.

THE FORMATION OF PROP

Dr. Kolodny started trying to get the message out that prescriptions of opioid painkillers were what was driving the crisis and began trying to get other doctors to be more cautious in their own practices. Eventually those efforts led to the formation of an advocacy group called PROP, or Physicians for Responsible Opioid Prescribing. Founded in 2010, PROP has been active in lobbying both the government and other doctors about the harmful overprescribing of opioids. When the CDC released its new guidelines in 2016, it used some of PROP's own language in the statement. But the group's message wasn't always warmly received. The narrative of opioids doing more good than harm, that bringing relief to millions of pain suffers outweighed a few drug abusers, was a powerful message to overcome. "At first we were seen as on the margin, and our message was seen early on as something that was extreme," Dr. Kolodny said. "Now, five, six years later, every top medical journal is putting out articles and editorials with our messages.

"It felt lonely early on," Dr. Kolodny said, looking back. "In fact, when PROP [first] formed, there were docs from different specialties ranging from public health to pain management. When we found each other and started working together, even before we formed an organization, it was almost as if we were a support group." When they first started organizing, however, they were met with a certain amount of hostility. Industry-funded groups still paint them as unfairly taking relief away from people suffering from chronic pain. Because of industry-funded disinformation campaigns, they were seen as anti-science.[147] But eventually PROP gained more supporters, and large sections of the medical community came to accept their message. It was a relief, Dr. Kolodny said, "to find colleagues and to be able to talk to them and realize we're not crazy. It felt lonely early on. It doesn't anymore. When the CDC, one of the most respected public health agencies in the world, is putting out your message, it no longer feels lonely. When you have thousands of people marching in Washington every year, trying to raise awareness about the problem, it no longer feels lonely. It did for a while. It felt like the world had turned upside down and nobody else seemed to see it."

COUNTER-DETAILING BIG PHARMA'S MESSAGE

"PROP is a nonprofit organization with doctors from different specialties from pain, addiction, primary care, public health, and emergency medicine," explained Dr. Kolodny. "What brought us all together was a recognition that the opioid crisis—that the record high rates of overdose deaths in addiction—that it was really fueled by the medical community's overprescribing painkillers. There are really two areas where we focus on: education and advocacy. Our education materials that we put out could be described as counter-detailing."

Detailing is what drug companies do as part of their marketing campaigns. It consists of their efforts to make their products sound wonderful and flawless and to "tell the doctor why it's better than any previously existing medicine," Dr. Kolodny said. "What we do is counter-detailing education that explicitly corrects some of the misinformation that can lead to overprescribing. That communicates to prescribers that opioids are in fact highly addictive and that they don't work well when prescribed or taken on a long-term basis."

PROP was formed as doctors who had noticed on their own the problems stemming from opioid prescriptions started to encounter one another. Dr. Gary Franklin has been the medical director of the Washington state workers' compensation system for more than 30 years.[148] Washington State had been dealing with opioid addiction since the 1990s, as the pharmaceutical industry had convinced several states to adopt guidelines promoting the use of opioid painkillers. Injured workers in these states, including Washington, were prescribed opioids for injuries sustained on the job. "We all came to this problem in slightly different ways, but because of our experience, came with equal passion," Dr. Franklin said of PROP's beginning.[149] "My experience was that I was at the table in 1999, when the falsehoods from the so-called pain champions and leaders started to infuse the false teaching that addiction is rare. That there's no ceiling on the dose of opioids. That the way to treat tolerance is to keep increasing the dose, almost as an axiom," he said.

INTRACTABLE PAIN ACTS (A.K.A. PRO-OPIOID GUIDELINES)

The promotion of opioids by pharmaceutical companies and their surrogates in the medical community led to the adoption of pro-opioid guidelines in more than 20 states. State medical boards and state legislatures were convinced that opioids were safe and that they were the best treatment for those in pain. They were further convinced that any prohibitions on opioid prescription, even those limiting the amount, should be removed. "They were smart," Dr. Franklin said. "They knew that most health-care delivery is regulated at the state level. It's not regulated

"HAD THEY NOT encountered opioids either in a prescription from a physician or on the black market, because they were diverted from the legitimate medical supply chain, if they hadn't come across these drugs, they would still just be living regular lives. They would've never tried drugs. They would've never been interested in, in abusing." —Harriet Ryan, investigative reporter for the *Los Angeles Times*

by the federal government. I think the original intent was to give safe haven to doctors to be able to write prescriptions of opioids. The problem is, with that kind of language, for example in our state, one of the sentences was, 'No doctor shall be sanctioned for any amount of opioid written.' Are you kidding me? That was the language they used.

"Even if a guy's out there handing out bags of opioids in a pain clinic, and the medical board wanted to do something about it. [If] he lawyered up, with that language, there's no way they could do anything about that. This is why in most parts of the country it has been very difficult under existing laws to prevent this from happening at the medical board level. Because of this model language that passed in more than 20 states. These were called 'intractable pain acts,' and still, I think there's only one or two states, including Washington, that have repealed those acts."

Those laws were passed in Washington State in 1999, and within just a few years, the doses of prescription opioids injured workers were receiving were "going through the roof," according to Dr. Franklin.

Then the number of deaths from drug overdose began to rise, and people in the state government started to take notice. "In 2001, our

> **"THESE WERE ALL** injured workers. These were not street people, or people with lots of comorbidities, or people that had long histories of opioid use, or any kind of abuse. These were working people who came into their system and whose doctors, because of these teachings and the state law and all, put them on chronic opioids for things like nonspecific low back pain. That's how things got started. It all started because of these false teachings, because of the model laws that were lobbied on by surrogates of drug companies, like the Pain & Policy Studies Group at the University of Wisconsin, and the Federation of State Medical Boards, which were funded by drug companies to do model state policies. By the time the tsunami of terrible, tragic deaths hit us, it was really unclear as to what we should do." —**Dr. Gary Franklin, medical director for Washington State Department of Labor and Industries**

brilliant pharmacy manager, Jaymie Mai, at our Department of Labor and Industries started to get requests for death benefits or pension benefits from some of our injured workers," Dr. Franklin said. "The death benefits were based on death certificates that said, 'Unintentional overdose, or opioids, or toxicity of opioids, prescribed opioids.' Here it was just a couple years after the 1999 changes in the laws. After all the acolytes were out there saying, 'That's the new standard of care.' All of a sudden, we start to see people dying. These are injured workers who came into our system with a low backache and were dead three years later from an unintentional overdose of a drug given to them by their doctor."[150]

HIGH-DOSE OPIOIDS AND INCREASED PAIN

In Boston in 2003, PROP co-founder Dr. Jane Ballantyne[151] was working at Massachusetts General Hospital and authored a paper following observations of opioid-prescribed patients there. "Patients who were treated with very high doses of opiates were actually floundering," she said. "Not only were they doing badly medically and socially, but they also were not getting good pain relief. In fact, it occurred to us that their pain might be even worse than it might have been had they not been treated with opiates."

Scientists in the lab at Mass General had been testing opioid painkillers on animals, and what they were seeing there matched what Dr. Ballantyne and her colleagues were seeing in humans. "Something happens when you take opiates long term, particularly at high dose, that actually alters pain. That maybe [opiates are] even making pain worse. But certainly it's not making pain better," she said. "We now know that there are shared mechanisms that when opiates are given chronically for a long time, and continuously, there are adaptations in the nervous system that cause three things. One is opioid tolerance. One is opioid hyperalgesia [increased sensitivity to pain]. A further thing that happens is that pain can actually worsen, or you get sensitization for pain itself. The mechanisms, they aren't completely shared, but they certainly overlap."

Elsewhere in Washington State, Dr. Michael Von Korff[152] was researching the opioid issue at the Group Health Research Institute in Seattle. "I'd done a study that showed that chronic pain patients using opioids long term had an increased risk of overdose, particularly those on higher dose regimens," he said. "When I talked about this at a meeting here in Seattle, an anesthesiologist approached me and said that her son had died of an overdose. She wondered if I would get involved with a group of parents and other people that were trying to do something about it." Dr. Von Korff started participating in phone calls and meetings with other doctors, trying to get something done about the growing opioid crisis. It was on one of these phone calls that he first spoke with Andrew Kolodny.

"Andrew has a deep interest in public policy and a deep understanding of how regulation works. I come from an academic background—I'm a researcher—so I know a little bit about policy, but I don't have the same depth of understating that Andrew had," Dr. Von Korff said. "Andrew had worked in government and he was really interested in how you could influence public policy. It was his idea to propose a change to the opioid label. We filed a petition with many opinion leaders in public health and medicine who signed that document and filed that with the FDA."

Jane Ballantyne moved to Seattle in 2010 to join the UW Medical School faculty. Shortly afterwards, she was asked by Dr. Kolodny to join the newly formed group of physicians from around the country that would become Physicians for Responsible Opioid Prescribing. "Dr, Kolodny asked me to join PROP because I had written an influential paper about the problems associated with the long-term effects of prescribing high dose opiates for the treatment of chronic pain and the fact that their continuous use may be making pain worse rather than better for patients." She said, "I would be a good person to join PROP because of my perspective of what opiates do in terms of making pain actually worse when used in high dosages."

■ ■ ■

As evidence of the crisis became more and more apparent, and doctors began communicating with one another about addressing the crisis, it became clear that some sort of advocacy group needed to be formed. "All four of the original members came at it from different experiences and with different expertise," Dr. Gary Franklin said. "It's almost like the Four Horsemen of reversing the opioid epidemic. You know we're on our steeds and we're trying to get ahead of this thing and to reverse something that should have been reversed by the leaders that started the problem 10 years ago."[153]

Dr. Kolodny remains a driving force behind PROP. "Andrew had a lot of experience working with changing federal policy and understood all the nuances of, say, filing a petition to change FDA policy. None of us had that experience," Dr. Franklin said. Other doctors have joined the cause and serve on PROP's executive board. The group is mainly made up of doctors and others in the medical profession, but there are specialists from other fields as well. Dr. Kolodny regularly makes the rounds at universities, government hearings, and various news programs. He and other doctors from PROP have written op-eds for the *New York*

"I DO THINK this is one of the worst public health disasters in US history. What makes it so awful, in a way, is that it originates from the very source in our society that people look to for help. That is, doctors. I think there's something particularly painful and poignant about that. Not only for the millions of people who have suffered but also for physicians, for people who went into this profession in order to help others and find themselves at the epicenter of this horrible disaster. [Doctors] find themselves as the cause of harm. And that's very, very sad for patients and very, very sad for doctors." —Dr. Anna Lembke, Stanford University School of Medicine

Opioid Overdose Deaths versus Deaths from Automobile Accidents

COURTESY OF PROFESSOR MATT STEFL, MARKETING,
LOYOLA MARYMOUNT UNIVERSITY, LOS ANGELES, CALIFORNIA

Times and other prominent newspapers here and abroad. In addition to the message that overprescribing was driving the crisis, Dr. Kolodny is emphatic that the crisis is one of addiction and not abuse.

"You'll hear people talk about a prescription drug abuse crisis or a heroin abuse crisis. You hear the term *abuse* used a lot," Dr. Kolodny said. "In fact, industry loves to frame the problem as an abuse problem. I was at an FDA meeting, and I spoke right after the representative for Purdue Pharma. We each were given five minutes to testify. In the testimony from Purdue Pharma you only heard the term *abuse* used over and over again. You never heard the word *addiction* even once. What we're dealing with is an addiction epidemic and to call it a drug abuse problem, it doesn't just miss the point, it's misleading. If we were to only focus on curtailing the overprescribing and do nothing about the fact that these people have this condition, then overdose deaths are going to remain very high until that generation dies off. Heroin will keep flooding in to meet the demand for it, so we also need a response to make sure that people who become addicted receive effective treatment for their addiction so they don't die of an overdose.

"From 1996 to 2018, more than 400,000 Americans have died from an opioid overdose," Dr. Kolodny said. "That's more than the number of Americans killed during the 20 years fighting in Vietnam, more than the number killed in Iraq, Afghanistan. More than all of those conflicts combined."

It's clear that we need to first understand how addiction works on the body before we can provide long-lasting and effective solutions to combatting the epidemic.

CHAPTER 8

Understanding Addiction

ACCORDING TO A 2016 report from the surgeon general's office, one in seven people will develop a substance abuse disorder at some time in their lives.[154] Substance abuse disorders, commonly referred to as addiction, have a neurological basis that is still only partially understood. Its roots remain something of a mystery. Addiction and its accompanying disorder, dependency, are often conflated by the public. They are separate and unique conditions. As we discussed in chapter 6, dependency is when a person physically needs a substance, whereas addiction is far more destructive. Addiction takes over and changes how a person thinks and acts.

According to Dr. Chris Evans,[155] a research scientist at UCLA's Semel Institute for Neuroscience and Human Behavior, "Addiction occurs when the drug becomes so important to [a person's] psyche that they can't do without it. They have cravings they can't control," he said. "It results in permanent changes on the molecular level within the brain. Individuals become obsessed with getting the drug. It becomes a sort of stimulus response. 'I'm feeling the drugs gone, I need the drug, I need it to feel normal.'"[156] This leads many addicts into criminal behavior, or to ignore important responsibilities in order to get their hands on their drug of choice. With dependency, a person can realize what is happening to them and be able to take steps to deal with their disfunction.

Until very recently, addiction was thought to be a moral failing, something that happens as the result of a person's poor choices. It was not considered a health issue. Today, as medical science has advanced, addiction has come to be understood as a disease of the brain. Many doctors now compare addicts to individuals afflicted with cancer or diabetes, needing medical treatment rather than punishment. There is more work to be done in destigmatizing addiction, but significant progress has been made in public understanding of addiction as a disease. It is true that a person's poor choices can lead them to substance abuse disorder. But in the opioid epidemic, many people became addicts simply because they followed their doctor's orders.

OPIOIDS IN RURAL AMERICA

According to Van Ingram, executive director of the Kentucky Office of Drug Control Policy,[157] going back to 2,000, "the DEA recognized ten areas of the country by zip code as having the highest prescribing of opioid painkillers. Five of them were in Kentucky."

Official numbers range widely as to how many people became addicted to opioids through prescription medication, but they are as

"RURAL STATES ACROSS America are considered the 'ground zero' of the opioid epidemic. Kentucky was hit hard because there were many individuals working in coal mines or at other physically arduous jobs who suffered from legitimate pain. [They were] living paycheck to paycheck and often without adequate health insurance. [They] couldn't get appropriate health care and instead turned to opiates for relief. Many medical practices essentially became 'pill mills' where no questions were asked before writing—or rewriting—prescriptions as long as payment was made on the spot." —Katherine Eban, investigative journalist, Fortune Magazine. www.donoharmseries.org. Do No Harm documentary interview with Van Ingram. 2017.

high as 80 percent.[158] However, there is no doubt that the overprescribing of opioid painkillers has fueled an epidemic that has spiraled out of control. Opioid pain pills became sought-after on the black market. When pills were no longer available, or became too expensive, many users switched to heroin. Much of the heroin is now sold with fentanyl. It is far more potent—and undetectable. Heroin mixed with fentanyl has caused an even greater spike in overdose deaths. As a result of wider distribution from Mexico and China, heroin prices dropped, and the drug made its way into communities far from the urban centers traditionally associated with chronic drug use. Rural and suburban Americans have now become addicted in record numbers, and entire communities have been devastated.

Dr. Sharon Walsh[159] is a professor of Behavioral Science, Psychiatry, and Pharmaceutical Sciences at the University of Kentucky and director of the Center on Drug and Alcohol Research. Dr. Walsh researches opioid abuse and works on improving access to medication-assisted treatments (MAT) for individuals suffering from substance abuse disorders. "When I first came to Kentucky and began studying people here with opioid addiction, they were all using prescription opioids," Dr. Walsh said. "I could tell you exactly when they came in which drugs they would tell me they were using because I knew what was available on the street. But no one ever reported using heroin. If they did mention that they had used heroin, I could almost bet that it was because they had been visiting someplace else. That they had been to Chicago or they had been to Cleveland, because there really was no heroin in Kentucky, historically.

"Now we have a prescription opioid epidemic. We have a huge population of people who are addicted. From their prospective [they] need to continue using just to feel normal. We have very inexpensive transportable heroin being introduced throughout the countryside. I don't think that there are any regions that don't have heroin availability now in the US," Dr. Walsh said. "For years the number of people on methadone treatment was stagnant, but with the opioid epidemic, that number has exploded."

At the same time Karyn Hascal, president of the Healing Place,[160] Louisville's nonprofit treatment facility estimates that less than 10 percent of the people in need of treatment are actually able to receive it. "When someone is seeking treatment and they're really ready for treatment, because they are in a desperate condition, that's when they finally call and say, 'I really need help.' Often, what they're being told is, 'Okay, we'll put your name on the waiting list and we'll let you know when we have a free spot.' That is really a situation that we must change. We need to be able to have treatment on demand, because what we are seeing is that people are dying from their drug addiction while they're sitting on the waiting list. If they could get into treatment, that would be a life that we could save."

WHAT MAKES OPIOIDS SO DANGEROUS

One of the reasons that the opioid epidemic is different from other addiction crises is that one dose of an opioid can lead to overdose and often death. Medically, opioids cause sedation, and when that occurs,

"**THE CDC HAS** been doing excellent work regarding the opioid crisis. The Food and Drug Administration, in my opinion, has been making decisions that have just made things worse. In fact, if you could go back in time, had they told Purdue Pharma at the beginning of the epidemic when they were introducing OxyContin, 'You can promote OxyContin in hospices, to palliative-care doctors, for patients with end-of-life care, but we're not going to let you market this drug to the primary care doctors and the family doctors, and the dentists.' Had they done that, I don't believe we would have an epidemic today." —**Dr. Andrew Kolodny, director of Opioid Policy Research, The Heller School for Social Policy and Management at Brandeis University, founder of Physicians for Responsible Opioid Prescribing (PROP)**

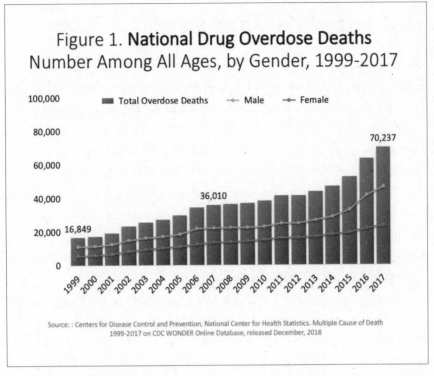

National Drug Overdose Deaths

COURTESY OF CDC WONDER

the brain is less able to regulate the body's functions, in particular the ability to monitor breathing. The most common cause of death from opioid overdose is when the brain fails to realize that breathing has slowed or even stopped and the person suffocates. Another significant driver of deaths is that a person's tolerance can change over a short period of time. "We know that when someone goes into, for example, a detoxification center or they're put in jail," Dr. Walsh said, "they no longer have access to opioids. Their tolerance level is reduced because they're not using any longer. What happens when they're released is that they don't recognize this dangerous change in their tolerance level. If they relapse and go back and use the same amount of drug that they used before, that dose becomes fatal and they die."

THE ADDICT'S JOURNEY

To understand addiction, we have to understand the journey of the addict. Their stories are varied, but there are common threads throughout each that help us better understand and appreciate the scope of the crisis. The revolution in thinking on addiction was achieved partially through breakthroughs in medical science that shed new light on the disease but also through greater empathy and understanding of the victims' dilemma. The treatment of addiction is a daunting task because addiction seldom exists by itself. There are often other medical and psychological conditions that complicate a patient's treatment, such as home environments. Treating addiction is not just about treating one condition but many issues in combination.

Dr. Michelle Lofwall[161] is a practicing psychiatrist certified in addiction medicine, working at the University of Kentucky's Center on Drug and Alcohol Research. Kentucky, along with many other Appalachian states, was hard hit by the crisis. Some observers believe that

"THE BIGGEST PROBLEM we now have is heroin laced with fentanyl. It is one of the most potent opioids on the marketplace. It is being illegally synthesized and imported, then mixed into heroin on the street. People are not aware of that. Someone can use it one time and die. They're not going into that first-time use thinking, 'I'm going to use this drug because I'm going to die from this.' It's a big risk they're taking, because when you're using something that's being sold on the street, you have no idea what's actually in it.

"We are in the midst of an opioid epidemic that is unlike any that we've seen before in the United States. It continues to spread, and we are experiencing really high rates of morbidity and mortality associated with this epidemic. It's related both to the use of prescription opioids, and the spreading of fentanyl-laced heroin throughout the country." —Dr. Sharon Walsh, University of Kentucky

pharma companies specifically targeted these communities because of the intense manual labor that takes place there. "Most of my patients come in with a chief complaint that they're addicted to an opioid," she said. "This is most frequently heroin, but if you were to ask me the same question 10 years ago, it would've always been prescription opioids." But opioid addiction is not the only problem Dr. Lofwall's patients struggle with. "We really individualize treatment within each patient. Patients will frequently have other comorbidities, including psychiatric affective disorders, major depression, and acute anxiety disorders. They'll have other medical illnesses that they may not even know they have. Everyone who comes through our doors will be screened for hepatitis C, HIV, and will be given a full physical exam."

The first step for every addict is getting clean from their drug of choice. Once that happens, the real work of confronting the psychological and emotional issues that lead people to addictive behaviors begins. That is a project that lasts for the rest of the addict's life.

Treatment is not only for the addict themselves. Families have a huge impact on an addict's recovery, both in positive and negative ways. For that reason, most recovery programs try and to involve the addict's family. As Dr. Lofwall explained, "Other family members will have therapy. They may have spouses that are also addicted. We'll work to get them into treatment. Frequently, family members that aren't addicted are supportive of the patient being in treatment. We'll try and involve them in the treatment as well."

CHAPTER 9

The Survivors

Broken, but Unbowed

A DOCTOR'S CALLING: SAVING HIS TEENAGE PATIENTS

Dr. Fred Holmes is a pediatrician in Vermont who started his first practice in 1972. As the opioid epidemic grew, it spread not only to areas once untouched by chronic drug abuse but to younger populations as well. Dr. Holmes left his regular pediatric practice and began focusing specifically on young addicts after the number of young people dying from overdoses rose in Vermont. "In the world of pediatrics, children don't often die," he said. "Maybe from trauma, maybe from a serious malignancy. But asthma and seizure disorders and serious infections, we're usually fairly good at [treating those]. In the world of opiates, good kids were dying, and a lot have died since I started doing this work."

If overcoming addiction is difficult for an adult, for teenagers the struggle can be so much harder. "That combination of physical variables is not something that a teenager is well attuned to," Dr. Holmes explained. "The other part of addiction is the behavior. It totally encompasses your life. It affects the way that you make day-to-day decisions. It affects your relationships with other people. It affects your relationship with yourself. This combination of both the physical manifestations and addictive behavior are a double curse for a youngster who walks into this situation at age 13 or 14 and thinks they can just walk out at age 19 because they don't want to do it anymore. Essentially their whole adolescent developmental period has been colored and distorted by dependency on opiates."[162]

Teenagers who become addicted often remain stuck in those years. Their emotional development is taken over by their addiction, and when they finally come out of it years later, they haven't always learned the skills necessary for leading a productive adult life. For many young people who become addicted in their teens, when they eventually get clean in their early twenties, they have the maturity and the life skills of a teenager. They are then tasked with rebuilding their life into something they've never really experienced, clean or addicted.

"On one hand there [are] the physical aspects of dependency on opiates and being tapered off," Dr. Holmes said. "On the other hand, there are resources to help them rebuild their lives, to find housing, to find food, to find transportation, to complete their education. The difficulty is that [addictive lifestyle] behaviors, through no fault of their own, have become so ingrained in their lives that it's not just 'take this prescription and see you in 10 days, you'll be all better.' It is a major life-altering experience. Unfortunately, many of the kids that I took care of came from families that were not endowed with a lot of strength and resources. In many there was a lack of mutual affection [or] members

"I THINK THE BEST WAY to manage this epidemic is to stop new cases from feeding into it. That's what we did with Ebola. We knew that the virus was going to affect the people that it already infected. But by limiting new cases you really control the epidemic. I think that's where all of our prescribing initiatives need to be. We need to prevent patients who have never had these drugs from being started on them. Then you won't face weaning somebody with addiction and all the failures and challenges of treating addiction." **—Dr. Jeanmarie Perrone, emergency room physician, University of Pennsylvania**

with stable jobs and healthy expectations."

Rebuilding one's life—or in the case of young people, building one's life—after addiction is the real work of overcoming one's disease. Getting clean from a drug is often the easy part. There are medications that can help an addict get off of a drug and help them physically recover. (Of course, detoxing from opioids is an extremely painful process, the fear of which causes many addicts to refuse doing so and prolongs their addiction.) It is the mental and spiritual process of reworking one's mind so that drugs are not used as a problem solver. That process can take a lifetime.

A FATHER AND HIS DAUGHTER

Haley is a college student from San Francisco who has been struggling with addiction since the age of 12. Her story is a familiar one. Addicts often describe a sense of detachment from their peers, a feeling of isolation, and of "not fitting in." Drugs appear to be the antidote to this problem, making them feel better in social situations and helping them find community among drug users. "It was right before my 12th birthday," she said.[163] "It was actually before I ever touched weed or alcohol or anything. I was just handed pills. I didn't know, I was so young, scared to ask questions. So I just started taking pills and drinking and just doing anything that anyone wanted me to do." Before long, she had moved on to heroin. She remembers the first time she used it intravenously. "Despite the illness I felt like for the first time there was this warmth. This thing just came over me and I knew that my life was going to drastically change since then, and it did." Haley's description of a warm feeling, a sense of belonging is one told by many heroin addicts. Looking back, Haley described how she felt when she was younger and why she felt attracted to drugs in the first place. "I always felt really scared of a lot of things," she said. "I wouldn't necessarily call it anxiety or feeling insecure or something, because I just think that's just part of being a kid. But I remember never wanting to be around people and I had a

Do No Harm Documentary
MEDIA POLICY CENTER

really tough time with my parents. A divorce and all this stuff. Younger siblings who were difficult, and I was just always alone when I was a kid. It was hard. I started doing drugs really young, so I think I missed a prime time in my life where I'm supposed to make connections and feel uncomfortable and take risks and all that stuff. I never had that opportunity. I wanted to be alone. I wanted to just sit and take the easy way out and not connect with anyone."

This is a refrain told by many addicts: the feeling of isolation and then drugs providing an antidote. Instead of learning to naturally deal with situations and emotions that are necessary for navigating an adult life, the addict is able to cut himself or herself off and experience a fabricated sense of wellness. Indeed, that is much of the allure of drugs and why substance abuse is often rampant in blighted communities. That instant gratification is also why it is so difficult for addicts to remain clean once they've kicked a drug. The addict uses drugs as their coping mechanism, but once sober, they must truly learn the skills necessary to cope with life's ups and downs.

Haley was sent to a 90-day rehabilitation facility, but she ran away and started using again. She fell into the same patterns of lying and detaching herself from people. In rehab, she was evasive and didn't fully give herself to the program. She returned home, but at the insistence of her mother was sent to a therapeutic boarding school.

"Boarding school is where stuff got really real," she said. "I was forced to work with this therapist who was like, 'I'm not going to be nice to you, I'm not going to enable you; when you're ready to work, then it's going to be a relationship, but until then, you just need to get your stuff together and be honest and then I'm willing to listen.' I needed that because I was really stuck. I didn't want to uncover layers. I didn't really want to feel."

This unwillingness to be honest, with others as well as one's self, is perhaps the greatest challenge in overcoming addiction. Even those who don't suffer from addiction can be reluctant to confront their emotional issues. "I was there for two years. I felt like an onion, like they were just peeling back layers. I was really sad, and I had to acknowledge that. Then I was really angry. It was like all of these emotions and all of this stuff

"**FOR THE NEXT** three days, I stayed in the house, downstairs. Literally, in front of the front door. Not allowing her to leave. There was screaming and yelling and fighting, and [she] was fighting with [her mother], fighting with me, physically restraining her. This went on for two or three days."

And I said, 'You know what? This is it. This is it. You have to go. You have to go somewhere. We can't help you.' She [was] yelling and yelling, and then finally, like a split second of lucidity, she looked me in the eyes, and she said, 'Well, if you're going do this, you better do it right fucking now.' And to me that was like, boom! Saturday morning we were on a flight to a rehab facility in Tucson, Arizona." —**Scott, Hayley's Father**

that I'd never really had the opportunity to feel. That was crazy," Haley said.

It took two years of hard work before Haley was ready to fully re-enter society. Haley was fortunate enough to come from a family that had the resources to provide such intense treatment. She was young enough that she had no one depending on her for their survival. But many addicts are not so fortunate. They have people who depend on them and responsibilities that need their attention. They don't have the money for prolonged stays at comfortable treatment centers.

MOMS IN RECOVERY: PREGNANT AND ADDICTED

Dr. Daisy Goodman, RN, PhD,[164] is the nurse-midwife for the Women's Health Coordinator at Dartmouth-Hitchcock Medical Center's Moms in Recovery Program. Located in rural New Hampshire, it is the country's leading treatment program that deals with pregnant women addicted to opioids and their infants. "Babies aren't born addicted; babies are born dependent physiologically on opioids. They don't struggle with the brain chemistry changes of addiction that adults do. I know that neo-natal abstinence is a transitory condition, and if well treated the babies have very good outcomes, so it's really about providing the services [for] recovery support for the moms that allow them to be good parents. When I see a baby who has a prolonged hospitalization because they needed additional treatment, I think, 'I'm glad the baby will be okay.'" Dr. Goodman added, "I'm worried about the mother because I know the extreme guilt that they go through. That mom needs extra services and extra support from us."

According to Dr. Alison Holmes,[165] lead physician at the Moms in Recovery Program, "If you have a problem with opioid dependence and you are a pregnant woman, you're actually not supposed to stop taking your medication abruptly. Because it is withdrawal during preg-nancy that's dangerous to the baby before they are born. We like the mothers to get into a treatment program." Dr. Holmes continued, "The good news is that the condition is treatable and that hospitals, according to the report, are responding with programs that wean newborns off the drugs and help their recovery with cuddling programs and efforts to increase skin-to-skin contact. Our approach to these babies when they have withdrawal symptoms is very family centered. We have them stay with their parents, and the parents, by parenting, help them with their withdrawal systems much more than a neonatal intensive care unit and medications can do. We also very firmly believe that providing care and comfort helps the parents in their own road to recovery." Diana Salzinger is a mom in the program: "This is the only time I've ever successfully stayed clean and sober since I started using opiates. It's the only time."[166]

Dr. Goodman concluded, "We absolutely can do more, and we have to do more. It is very important that we don't lose our support for treatment. We need more federal money in this area. We need a full continuum of support services from outpatient practices like ours all the way through residential treatment for moms. Our hospitals need the support to take care of patients adequately. Substance abuse is a chronic disease process. Like any other disease, it is extremely expensive if you go downstream and then have to pick up the pieces. If we can prevent harm further upstream, with prevention and treatment at earlier stages

"**AS A JOURNALIST** back in 2012, I did some stories on babies who were born dependent on opioids. Those were some of the saddest stories I've ever reported. Especially as a mom, going into neonatal intensive care unit, where half the babies born dependent on drugs, was just a horrible thing to see. I mean, they shake; they cry and scream. It's just a terrible thing. And it just really brought home to me in a, in a visceral way that this epidemic affects people who should never be touched by this."
—Laura Unger, *Louisville Courier*

of the disease, much better outcomes at a much lower cost can be the result. It is essential that we have as many services as possible to offer to our families."[167]

SAFEGUARDING CHILDREN FROM OPIOID POISONING

Dr. Julie Gaither is an epidemiologist and fellow with Yale School of Medicine.[168] She studies opioid injuries in vulnerable populations, specifically children. Her research revealed that hospitalizations for prescription opioid poisonings have almost doubled in the entire pediatric population, and she also found in very young children, those one to four years of age, that hospitalizations actually doubled in a span of 16 years.

Dr. Gaither said, "It takes one or two pills for a child to overdose and possibly die from these medications. It's important for physicians when they prescribe opioids to an adult to ask, 'Is there a child in your home?'" If the answer is affirmative Dr. Gaither follows up with, '[I] tell them to get a lock box they cannot open. Opioids need to be kept out of the hands of little kids.'

"**THE MAIN ISSUE** that we see in the newborn nursery is that the newborns, just like anyone who is dependent on an opioid medication, can go through a pretty significant withdrawal syndrome. If you have a problem with opioid dependence and you are a pregnant woman, you're actually not supposed to stop taking your medication abruptly. Because it is withdrawal during pregnancy that's dangerous to the baby before they are born. We like the mothers to get into a treatment program. They can help them with their problems of addiction, but also maintain them on a safe steady dose of opioids to keep withdrawal under control." —**Dr. Alison Holmes, Dartmouth-Hitchcock Medical Center's Moms in Recovery Program**

"The most vulnerable among us are suffering from these medications. No family should have to go through having a child taken to the ER unresponsive, lifeless, and sometimes [these cases are] fatal. The child often ends up in the ICU, and that's a burden that I hope for no one, for no family to endure.[169]

"Nearly 10,000 children and adolescents have died from opioid poisonings in the United States since the epidemic began 20 years ago. That's 500 kids a year, on average, who are dying from an entirely preventable cause. And for every child who dies, another four are poisoned severely enough to require hospitalization.

"Sadly, I expect these grim statistics to only grow worse in the coming years. As a society, we've paid little attention to how children and adolescents—a group that makes up one-quarter of the US population—have been harmed by prescription and illicit opioids. Virtually every measure enacted to contain this epidemic targets adults, even though Americans across the lifespan, from neonates to the elderly, are affected."[170]

ADDICT OR LOYAL CUSTOMER?

Shayna Akin is a recovering addict who has battled addiction since she was a teenager. She has been in and out of the Beit T'Shuvah[171] treatment center in Culver City, California, both as a patient and now, for 18 months, an employee.

"I tried to get into every rehab probably in California," she said. "I had no insurance, I had no money, and nowhere would take me. Nowhere. But Beit T'Shuvah did." Shayna became addicted as a teenager after being prescribed opioid painkillers for a sports injury. "Now I work here. I get to help women and men that go through the struggles that I went through. I've had a lot of trauma since I've been here. My aunt committed suicide. I've been to six funerals. I've watched my friends die all around me or they're in prison. But I've learned that I don't need the

PAIN RESCUE TEAM HELPS SERIOUSLY ILL KIDS COPE IN TERRIBLE TIMES

The Benioff Children's Hospital at the University of California, San Francisco is a place where the sickest children go for leading-edge treatments. It employs alternate techniques including traditional Chinese medicine as part of the hospital's integrative pediatric pain and palliative care program. Their emergency response team for pain combines traditional pharmaceutical pain care with other techniques to ease the suffering of the sick children who populate the rooms there.

The interdisciplinary team includes primary care physicians, anesthesiologists and nurses. There is also a clinical psychologist, a massage therapist and someone who practices hypnosis — as well as an acupuncturist who treats patients with both acupuncture and acupressure.

Robyn Adcock is a University of California, San Francisco pain relief specialist, "We see cases in the hospital that are end of life or very chronic serious illness, or extreme pain cases — where their primary team maybe wants more support and managing the pain piece," Adcock says.

"Studies estimate that 20% of children worldwide have chronic pain. That could range from frequent stomachaches to debilitating pain from cancer. And the majority of those children will grow into adults who also are in chronic pain," says Christine Chambers, the Canada research chair in children's pain at the Centre for Pediatric Pain Research at Dalhousie University in Nova Scotia.

"So, at a time when addiction to opioid painkillers is a crisis, finding alternative ways to manage pain and provide comfort is crucial, she says. Because not all pain can be taken away." Chambers says research shows most children, even in hospitals, don't get adequate pain care. And sometimes doctors just can't eliminate the pain.

"Every clinician who works with a child in pain hopes that we will be able to take away all the pain," Chambers says. "That isn't always possible."

So this interdisciplinary approach, Chambers says, helps kids manage their pain, ease it and live with it. Research backs up many of the techniques, she continues, including physical therapy, hypnosis and even distraction.

"There's a super strong evidence base in favor of distraction," Chambers says. That's where art and music therapy come in, because these can take kids' minds off their pain.

Unfortunately, Chambers says, this type of pain care is rare, especially for children. The team in San Francisco is one of only a handful across the U.S.

Stephen Wilson is the chief medical officer at UCSF Benioff who founded the IP3 team a decade ago, "The team still relies on traditional painkillers, including opioids, to help the children. But, he says, acupuncture may be more effective against nausea than a medication. And a massage therapist can ease muscle aches; a psychologist can help with the existential fear; and art or music therapy can distract children from their pain. Together these interventions can make the experience of illness less awful."

Reported by Alison Kodjak, NPR

drugs. I just need to feel my life. To be uncomfortable. To not medicate myself when I don't like the way I feel. To learn how to live life."

Like many addicts, Shayna spent years using drugs as a coping mechanism for past trauma. Instead of confronting her troubles, she blocked them out. Instead of learning how to be a productive member of society, she learned how to game the system to get drugs. "I went to the doctor and I told them I was depressed, and I was sad, and I couldn't leave the house. I had so much anxiety. They prescribed me Xanax. I was using [opioid painkillers] and Xanax together. It was probably a couple weeks later that I got into heroin. I kept that relationship with the doctors. I was a full-blown heroin addict [shooting intravenously], and I would go into the doctor and I would wear full sleeves and look all innocent. I'd look up on Google beforehand the different symptoms to different things. I'd go in there and I'd tell them that I had those symptoms, and they'd prescribe me whatever I needed.

"I would take Xanax; I'd sell the Xanax to support my heroin habit. I got to really learn the system of pills. I would go doctor shopping. I would have illegal doctors that I knew of. I would have friends of mine—well, 'friends' of mine, all using buddies—go in and we would pay [the doctors] and they would prescribe us whatever we wanted, Oxy-Contin, then we'd sell that and go back in and get more of it. The progression of that was really, really astonishing. I was living on the streets for 10 years, basically, shooting heroin. These doctors were playing into my addiction."

Many doctors, pharmacies, and drug manufacturers were aware of people like Shayna, and the massive amounts of drugs being prescribed and distributed. Yet they looked the other way because of the amount of money that was made. On a spreadsheet, Shayna was not an addict but a loyal customer. As of this writing, not only drug manufacturers like Purdue are being sued for their role in the epidemic but also wholesale distributors such as McKesson, and even national retail pharmacy chains like CVS and Walgreens. Plaintiffs argue that the vast numbers of drugs going out could not have gone unnoticed and that these companies allowed it to continue because of their huge profits.

DOCTORS AND ADDICTION

Doctors themselves are not immune to addiction. Dr. Joseph DeSanto is an addiction and internal medicine specialist in Newport Beach, California. "How did I get addicted? Well, how much time do we have?"[172] he said. "Unfortunately, intelligence has nothing to do with it. A lot of things have been shown to lead someone to addiction. First, you have to have a genetic component to it. You have to have a genetic vulnerability that makes you susceptible to addiction. Then given the right set of circumstances . . ." Dr. DeSanto first became addicted in the 1990s after a back injury. As a doctor he had easy access to medication and no one to scrutinize his actions. "Vicodin was actually available as samples," he said. "You can walk into a sample closet as a private-practice physician and you could just grab a couple Vicodin and then hand them to your patient. They were able to try it, and if it worked you [could] write them a full prescription. It was marketed to us back then as not being as addictive as we thought. [I] grabbed a couple off the shelf when I hurt my back and my life changed after that."

People who do not have a genetic predisposition to addiction tend not to like the effects of powerful drugs. "Most people who take Percocet or Vicodin, or a narcotic drug like that, have a typically not nice reaction. They get sick, want to roll over, and go to sleep," Dr. DeSanto said. "The real, true opiate addict takes [the drug] and feels energized. It removes all their anxiety. It makes them a little looser, a little bit more comfortable. It actually gives them energy to do the things that they want to do, an addition to feeling good. So, why wouldn't you want to repeat that over and over again?"

But these effects wear off. Once the effects of the drug have disappeared, withdrawal sets in, and that's where the trouble begins. "I think I knew I was out of control when I attempted to stop on a number of occasions and was able to do it," Dr. DeSanto said. "Then I reinjured

"I'VE INTERVIEWED A lot of these people, and you can kind of sense that something is not right with them. It's terrifying because it could be you. It could be your child. It could be your parent. Some people are always going to be drug seekers. There is a segment of our population that had they not encountered opioids, either in a prescription from a physician or on the black market, if they hadn't come across these drugs, they would still just be living regular lives. They would have never tried drugs. They would have never been interested in abusing.

"I find opioid addiction just terrifying. I have a six-year-old, and I started talking to her about staying away from drugs and staying away from pills. It's crazy when she's only in the first grade, but I never want her, or anyone I love, to go through such a horrific experience." —**Harriet Ryan, Los Angeles Times**

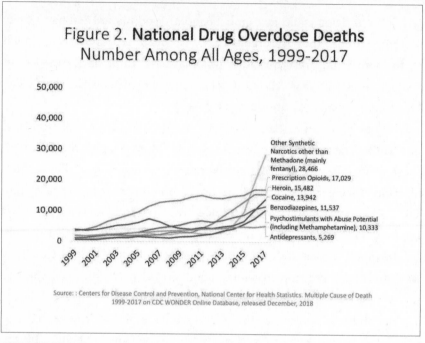

Figure 2. **National Drug Overdose Deaths**
Number Among All Ages, 1999-2017

Source: : Centers for Disease Control and Prevention, National Center for Health Statistics. Multiple Cause of Death 1999-2017 on CDC WONDER Online Database, released December, 2018

CDC WONDER, 2018

myself and had to take more medication and realized that the cycle was starting over again. For a lot of people with pill and narcotic addictions, it tends to go like that. Then towards the end, you just can't stop and it just keeps rolling until an inevitable end. Which, for a lot of people, is death."

The number of deaths from overdose is what makes this drug epidemic different from the past. Opioids are much more powerful than drugs like cocaine and methamphetamine. The chances for overdose and subsequent death are significantly higher than with other drugs. Fortunately, new overdose relief drugs like Narcan have saved many lives, but the number of deaths from opioid overdose are still staggering.

THE LONG ROAD TO RECOVERY

Recovery is a long and painful process. Addicts will often choose circumstances that most people, those without a mental illness, would find unacceptable. Shayna Akin spent 10 years living on the street, homeless and addicted to drugs. "It's sad because my story started off when I was 14 years old having shoulder surgery to legitimately treat the pain I had," she said. "I came from a great family in an upscale community. I think that was kind of the jumping off part of it. I shot heroin for 10 years."

Twelve-step meetings are full of people exchanging stories the general public has trouble understanding. Why would this young woman from a comfortable background choose to live on the street for 10 years shooting heroin? How could a licensed doctor abuse these drugs he knew were so damaging? Addiction is such a pervasive mental illness that it makes perfectly rational and intelligent people act insane. "When you're in the deepest, darkest part of your addiction, there's nothing that can stop you," Dr. DeSanto said. "There's no human power that can get in the way of you. It becomes almost like a survival instinct. What you think may happen to you gets pushed so far into the background. This is what I try to explain to people that are not addicts. That the consequences become so distant and quiet. Whereas a normal person would take that as a warning sign, an addict does not have that going on in the brain.

"You just have to have the right genetics. You have to have the right environment. You put those two in combination and then a prescription and it's really hard to stop," Dr. DeSanto said. "I don't know if anybody here has dealt with an opiate addiction, but it's something that takes over your life completely. You really don't have a choice once it starts, at least I didn't. I can't speak for anybody else, but I know I didn't."

When an addict finally reaches recovery, it's usually because they're at the edge of dying. Many of them have lost everything but their own life. An addict's rock bottom is far lower than what most people would even dream of experiencing.

When addicts do recover, their lives are forever changed and they often consider their "sober date," the first day they stopped using drugs, like a second birthday. Twelve-step meetings frequently celebrate these

Dr. DeSanto's interview, Media Policy Center, 2017, from *Do No Harm* documentary
DR. DESANTO

days with cakes and candles just like any other birthday. Many addicts talk about feeling reborn and finding new hope within the recovery community. There is a sense of commitment to other addicts and an acknowledgement that one cannot become sober on one's own.

"People ask me all the time if I would go back and change the time when I first took my first prescription. I'm not sure," Dr. DeSanto said. "I don't think I'd be sitting here talking to you. I don't think I'd be helping the amount of people that I'm helping now. Having done what I went through, you learn a different language, and being sober for five years, you really pay attention to what's going on in the world."[173]

Many addicts go on to work in recovery or otherwise make some kind of lifelong commitment to the recovery community. People can go for years, decades even, being sober and suddenly relapse and the process starts all over again. Recovery is a painful process, and that in itself keeps many addicts from seeking the help they need in the first place. "It's like you built up a beautiful life for yourself and you don't want to show up to it," Dr. DeSanto said. "You keep avoiding it and putting it off until tomorrow and putting it off until tomorrow. Then you start to develop this fear of things that you really shouldn't be fearful of. Addiction perpetuates fear, in some people anger. [In] most people remorse and guilt. Talk about having to deal with something! Try remorse and guilt. The guilt of what I had done, [and then to try] to come back into society.

"Being sober is being stable and reliable and being present, for better or for worse. When you're newly sober, trying to manage your emotions is the hardest part. When you're taking your family through that, it kind of looks a little crazy on the outside. You have to be patient with somebody who's getting sober in the beginning. Then we get better at navigating through that. It's made me a better parent. My kids can finally look at dad and know he's not going to be falling asleep at three in the afternoon. He's going to be going to functions; he's going to be present; he's going to care."

Finding hope and purpose outside chasing a high is an integral part of the recovery process. Sadly, for many people who are addicted to opioids, it's not enough. The body is forever changed once it's become dependent on opioids. Many doctors now insist that medication-assisted treatment is a necessary part of maintaining sobriety. In the next chapter we will cover the debate between MAT and abstinence only, but the evidence for the success of MAT is undeniable.

"For me Subutex is something that is not a solution, but it is a tool and it helps keep me alive every day," Shayna said, referring to a brand of buprenorphine pill. "This isn't something that I do and that's the cure. I use it along with 12-step meetings, my program, AA, HA, NA [Alcoholics Anonymous, Heroin Anonymous, Narcotics Anonymous], whatever it takes. I have a sponsor. I do my steps along with medication-assisted therapy. I don't think it's the answer for everyone and I wouldn't recommend it for everyone. I'm not a doctor, but in my experience, I couldn't get sober to save my life. I was so close to dying this last time. I had abscesses all over my body; I kept OD'ing; I really am super lucky to be here today.

"Medication-assisted therapy has helped me. I don't crave drugs anymore," Shayna said. "That, along with the 12-step work, the

Shayna Akin in recovery, from *Do No Harm* documentary
WALESKA SANTIAGO

obsession to use has absolutely been lifted. I used to be able to close my eyes, and I'd picture the word *heroin* in my head. I'd obsess and obsess and obsess over it until I had to do it. These days I don't have those feelings. I don't have that impulse to go get loaded or this is too much I

"WHAT CAN WE do about this? In this country we consume 99 percent of the world's hydrocodone combination products. We use over 80 percent of the world's oxycodone products. One hundred twenty-nine people in this country die every day from an opioid overdose. We use far too many of these drugs in this country. Until we get these numbers to go down, I'm not sure what else we can do to slow this epidemic.

"Thirty-four percent of all the deaths in Kentucky had fentanyl in the bloodstream. Fentanyl is 30 to 50 percent more powerful than heroin. We have people out there who think they're taking heroin, the same heroin they bought last month or last week, and it turns out to be a completely different drug. One that is far deadlier because it is laced with street fentanyl." **—Van Ingram, executive director of the Kentucky Office of Drug Control Policy**

can't deal with this. I know that whatever I'm feeling is going to pass, and that's the beauty of the medication-assisted therapy for me. It gives me room where I'm not going to just go make a mistake. It blocks the opiates so that I don't crave them. And even if I did have a thought about them, I would have [a] longer time in between making that bad decision."

CHAPTER 10

Talk Therapy

DR. RICHARD RIES is an addiction specialist and psychiatrist at Harborview Medical Center in Seattle.[174] He regularly sees patients in recovery and has met with some of the same patients for years. The following is an edited transcript of a meeting he had with three patients who agreed to have their session recorded. One aspect of a 12-step recovery program is being wholly honest and forthcoming with your addiction and the things you've done as part of it. Many addicts live lives that those who haven't suffered from addiction, what the 12-step lingo refers to as "normies," have trouble understanding. Twelve-step meetings are meant to be nonjudgmental environments where addicts can come to terms with their past and focus on their future in a setting with people who have shared their experiences. Hopefully this transcript will help to shed light on how addiction distorts a person's thinking and leads to an incredibly unstable life, and how difficult it can be to finally get—and stay—clean.

2018 THERAPY SESSION WITH DR. RICHARD RIES

Dr. Ries: It's been about a year for you right now, but I think you know each other pretty well. If we were to add up the amount of time you've been clean over the last five years, it's been like 98 percent of the time.

Glen: It's only when I went off the Suboxone. [that he wasn't clean]

Dr. Ries: Why'd you stop?

Glen: You know, if I could explain the insanity of addiction, I probably wouldn't be here.

Dr. Ries: But do you remember what was going through your head?

Glen: No. What was going through my head is I had run out of Suboxone. The prescription had run out and I was going through withdrawal. I had to take care of the withdrawal and nothing else mattered.

Dr. Ries: How about you, Aubrey? How did you get to three years?

Aubrey: I've been trying to get clean and stay clean off of one chemical or another since I was 15.

Dr. Ries: And you're how old now?

Aubrey: Thirty-three. So, when I'm clean, I'm newly clean. Then when I'm not, I'm not. There's, like, no break. There has to be, like, this huge catastrophe that happens for me to get clean again.

Dr. Ries: You have to hit bottom.

Aubrey: Yeah. Like I have to hit bottom, and normally my bottom is harder than the bottom that was before.

Dr. Ries: What's different about now? You've got three years. That's a lot of time.

Aubrey: I just got so, like, burned. Like I was just so done. With using, the life, what my addiction had stolen from me, my kids, everything. I just couldn't live like that anymore. And part of that story is Harborview and Suboxone and these recovery groups. And my church. So that's my number one go-to that has supported me through all the ups and downs of the last three years, which I had never had before. Like spirituality was always the piece that was missing every time I tried to get clean. But this time it's been my foundation.

Dr. Ries: Great. Janet, how did you get to where you are?

Janet: Over the last, let's see here, 16 years, I've had about 14 surgeries. One due to an accident, so I ended up getting dependent on all those pills, medications, opiates. So I came here three and a half, four years ago? Somewhere in that time frame. And started on Suboxone, and I've been fine ever since.

Dr. Ries: Has it been easy?

Janet: No.

Dr. Ries: What do you think have been your biggest struggles?

Janet: Family.

Dr. Ries: The opiate part of things, for you, has been fairly easy?

Janet: Yeah.

Dr. Ries: So, the just getting off opiates and being on Suboxone and stabilizing, that part of your recovery's been pretty easy.

Janet: Yep.

Dr. Ries: But you've had other challenges.

Janet: Yep, that was the start. That was the foundation, and there's been a lot of ups and downs with my family. My kids, you know, that's been tough.

Dr. Ries: You got into opiates through the surgery?

Janet: Yep.

Dr. Ries: [to Aubrey] How did you get into opiates?

Aubrey: Heroin.

Dr. Ries: And how did you get into that?

Aubrey: I started when I was 13, on cocaine. I grew up in a very abusive and dysfunctional family.

Dr. Ries: Streets?

Aubrey: Yeah.

Dr. Ries: Tough life?

Aubrey: Yeah.

Dr. Ries: Abuse?

Aubrey: Yeah.

Dr. Ries: And got into heroin at a very young age. Smoking, shooting . . . what?

Aubrey: I went from smoking crack to shooting heroin by the time I was 17.

Dr. Ries: Was it supporting other dysfunctional habits?

Aubrey: Yeah.

Dr. Ries: How about you, Ashley? How did you get into things?

Ashley: Where to begin? I grew up in a household that was, on the outside, pretty normal. Nobody in my family had any addiction issues. I was a little rebellious. I experimented with drinking and marijuana and cigarettes and then, towards the end of high school, I started experimenting with opiates.

Dr. Ries: How old are you now?

Ashley: I am 30. And been to a number of inpatient and outpatient treatment [facilities] over the last seven years.

Dr. Ries: Seven years and about how many treatments? Five treatments? Ten?

Ashley: Probably about eight.

Dr. Ries: Eight treatments.

Ashley: Pretty constantly in some sort of treatment for the last seven years. I came in here this last year, so it's been crack and IV heroin use that brought me in here. And I have about four months clean with the Suboxone right now. I come to Harborview three days a week for intensive outpatient with another group of women, and I love it. I actually want to be here.

Dr. Ries: So, we're not bending your arms?

Ashley: No, and I remember, it makes me laugh, the first time I came and saw you, and I wanted to stop using, and you suggested Suboxone. And you said, "Let's do it right now, today!" And I just, I was in shock that it was available right then and right now. I couldn't handle it. I ran out of your office. I said—

Dr. Ries: You did run out of my office!

Ashley: But I said, "I'll be back later!"

Dr. Ries: That's not a figure of speech. You ran out of my office.

Ashley: Yeah, because I just couldn't believe. I couldn't wrap my head around it that I could be helped right now, right this minute, that I would never use again after this moment. So I had to go back out for my final hurrah. Which lasted probably another week or so.

Dr. Ries: Wasn't even that long.

Ashley: Yeah.

Dr. Ries: And then you were back in my office.

Ashley: Yep.

Dr. Ries: And then what happened?

Ashley: Then I started the Suboxone and started going to my women's outpatient group. And haven't stuck needle in my arm since.

Dr. Ries: Couple of other issues that I think are interesting: There's a lot of sort of conflict in the news and in the papers and this and that about 12-step issues and medication-assisted treatment. Specifically, buprenorphine. Can you be on buprenorphine and can you work recovery? Can you be on buprenorphine and have some sort of spirituality?

Aubrey: Absolutely.

Dr. Ries: Can you work buprenorphine and work the steps?

Glen: Absolutely, because you have clarity of thought. I have that clarity of thought. I can focus on the aspects of recovery. I can focus on the steps. I can be mindful of what I am doing.

Ashley: I just find it so frustrating, personally. A lot of the 12-step groups are open to using medications. Some are very close-minded about all sorts of things, and I just choose not to attend those meetings. But I'm also on antidepressants, antianxiety medication, OCD. It's basically the same for me. I had no idea that Suboxone could help eliminate my cravings. Like is that even possible? Yeah. It's a miracle. It did. It really helped that.

Glen: If you can do it without medication, hey, that's a blessing. If you need the medication, well then, it's a blessing too. Anything that can keep an addict or an alcoholic clean for any measure of time is a miracle as far as I'm concerned, and like I've said before about Suboxone, I've told you before . . . When I first took Suboxone, it was the first time in years that I told someone I actually feel alive. It was the first time I felt 100 percent again in a very long time. And it's funny, just crossing the street here, and I was telling my friend, "Wow, I feel really alive!"

Ashley: It lets me be my authentic self. It doesn't change me.

Glen: The drugs were the wall. I think once you recover, you recover spiritually, mentally, and physically. Your real self is finally coming through when you have a degree of clean time. All the stuff that I was suppressing, whether it be depression or anger or disappointment or pain, whatever, finally I can actually handle life on life's terms. Today. I don't need the crutch.

Dr. Ries: What words of wisdom, experience, strength, and hope, whatever, would you offer to the general public? People who don't have opiate addiction are going to watch or read this and try to understand opiate addiction. What are some words you would offer to help them try to understand what it was like for you when you were on the tipping point, when you were struggling to break free? When you were trying to get better but couldn't?

Janet: It's not a choice. It's a physical problem that takes over your emotions and mental everything.

Dr. Ries: I put it in the way of, when you're in opiate withdrawal, the opiates are steering the ship; you're not. Glen, did that happen to you, trying to stop but getting back to using? You just told us when you ran out of Suboxone and started using. What was that like? What were you telling yourself?

Glen: I knew that when I went off and I went on a binge, I knew that it wasn't going to last. I knew that any day now, there was going be, "I can't keep doing this." When I run out of money, or for whatever reason. Plus, I knew that everything I had built up, I was about to lose again, so I didn't want to do that again. I didn't want to do that anymore because I had the tendency to sabotage myself. But this time, it's much different this time.

Dr. Ries: What's it like for you, when you've had some clean time, you've got some insight, and you sort of feel like you've kind of got a handle on your addiction, and then now you're using again?

Ashley: It's very demoralizing. It's just . . . it is a cycle. And you feel completely helpless to stop it. I do usually have to wait until everything falls apart. So far I haven't been able to put myself back on my feet and not lose everything.

Dr. Ries: If you use, you just, phew.

Ashley: Yes. Until I can't anymore, until—

Aubrey: I'm the same way.

Ashley: Until I have no money, no more places to steal from, no more people to use, you know. No more place to live. And I'm on that very edge. And that's when I come back and ask for help. And it's very frustrating. I wish I was further along in my life, but I can't say that. This is my journey. It was meant for me to be where I am now, so I can teach other people. I don't regret that I've lived through what I have. I mean, it's been very, very difficult and very painful.

Ashley: For people that are struggling, I would just say, get help now, and—

Dr. Ries: Don't run from it.

Ashley: Right. Because you're gonna lose. And when you start recovery, just give yourself a chance. And give yourself a chance, and just keep giving it a chance. Because when you use, you stop growing.

Dr. Ries: Right.

Ashley: And there is a side of you, within, that you're not in touch with anymore. And as you recover, those things are going to start coming to the surface. You can find out things that you didn't know about yourself, and that's one of the beautiful things about recovery. It's not just that you're going to get your mental awareness back, and your emotions, good or bad, but you're going to find out things you didn't know, and likes and dislikes that you didn't know. Kind of a whole new world is going [to] open up.

Glen: Right, yeah. You find out you're not such a bad person after all.

Ashley: I mean, it's not going be all lilies and roses or anything, but it's possible, and I just can't say enough good things about it. Just hang in there. Keep giving yourself a chance. A lot of people have been great, and especially here. Everybody here is very knowledgeable and understanding and looks at me and speaks to me like a person.

Janet: Yep.

Ashley: Like a real human being. This is recovery from life. Everybody needs this.

Janet: Mm-hmm [affirmative].

Ashley: Everybody can benefit from what we're doing here because life isn't easy. We're set up to fail. Just getting a little helping hand, understanding, empathy.

Dr. Ries: Empathy?

Aubrey: I had a doctor here that had no empathy, and I ended up going other places, other than coming here. So, if you have empathy, try to just listen. Don't think about what the person is saying and try to judge what they mean. Just listen.

Glen: You still have . . . your basic needs have to still be met. You lose your shelter, your place to maintain yourself. You lose all your property. The hardest thing is, you have to have . . . your basic needs have to be met before you can focus on staying clean, I think. It's hard to live under the bridge and stay clean and stay off the drugs.

Dr. Ries: Yeah.

Glen: You have to meet someone's basic needs first before they can get to work.

Ashley: Oh gosh, for me the hardest thing about recovery right now is repairing relationships and taking care of myself, being selfish now and watching out for me, what's best for me. Instead of taking care of everybody else.

Janet: I would say the hardest part is being sick and facing your family because you're so degraded, and they catch on to that, and they feel degraded for you, and it's just like a really tough, extremely tough spot. But as you get into recovery, that exchange sort of gets a lot better. They're proud of you; you're proud of yourself. You feel better. Withdrawals aren't there; the cravings aren't there. The pain is much better. So you get the respect back from your family. And you learn how to take care of yourself.

Dr. Ries: You're sort of saying the hardest part is in that cusp from being sick, just starting to be well, dealing with trying to get respect back.

Ashley: Yeah.

Dr. Ries: That you've lost.

Janet: Yes.

Aubrey: In my journey, I've been at the very bottom of rock bottom. It's my life. Just slowly climbing out of that hole is the hardest thing. Repairing the damage, dealing with financial issues, dealing with legal issues. All while trying to get your basic necessity needs met as well. So, it's just life. Just trying to slowly get out of the hole.

Dr. Ries: Yes.

Aubrey: I chose to see you because you listen, and you exude caring and understanding humility. . . . You don't degrade us. You don't look down upon us. You just listen and do what you can to support us on our journey upward. And because of that, it has made all the difference in the world to me.

Let's Face It
COURTESY OF PROFESSOR MATT STEFL, MARKETING,
LOYOLA MARYMOUNT UNIVERSITY, LOS ANGELES, CALIFORNIA

■ ■ ■

In the next chapter we're going to look at the ways in which the crisis has been addressed as well as some of the possible solutions. Dr. Holmes, a pediatrician in Vermont, has been working with young addicts for nearly 10 years. For him, the solution is not just with the addict themselves. "I think that ultimately, the solution is going to lie in societal changes. The ways in which we address the needs of our children when they're very young. The way we offer the support that they need when they're in school and struggling. Particularly in the teenage years. [We need to] let them know that we love them, that they're our kids. That we assume in a societal manner a parenting role for them.

"Unless they feel that somebody loves them, they're not going to be able to love themselves enough to do the hard work that's needed," he said. "If a youngster holds up South Main Grocery and it's his first offense, he gets one response. His third episode for the same offense, he'll go to jail, which is not in any way in his best interest. If we can only take some of the money that's being wasted on corrections and law enforcement and devote it to the care of young families with their first child so that their parenting skills and the strength of the family improves, we'll be way better ahead with more appropriate expenditure of our resources. If every pediatrician were to address opiate addiction in the developmental stage as they meet with their kids regularly. [If they] knew enough about it, knew enough to screen for it, and understand the treatment algorithms and programs and resources within their community. What a difference! You wouldn't see what we're seeing now."[175]

Policy makers are finally beginning to understand this. It's cheaper and far more effective to treat an addict through empathy and support than through punishment and incarceration. We discussed in earlier chapters, but it bears repeating, that this change in public opinion on drug treatment occurred only after white America was affected. Unfortunately, as the CDC reports, the epidemic is spreading to all communities as cheap opioids have become more available.

CHAPTER 11

Medically Assisted Treatment (MAT) or Abstinence?

AS THE UNDERSTANDING of addiction has grown, so has the number people working to keep people off opiates for good. But within this group there is sometimes a conflict. There are different views on how an addict should approach recovery. While these two camps are not necessarily mutually exclusive, they sometimes find themselves at odds with one another.

Medication-assisted treatment, or MAT, is the process of weaning addicts off of powerful opioid drugs like heroin or fentanyl by providing them with less potent ones in a controlled setting. Historically, the most common drug for this has been methadone, and methadone clinics began to appear across the country in the late 1970s and 1980s. More recently, the drug buprenorphine has replaced methadone as the preferred drug for MAT. Buprenorphine is commonly sold under the brand names Suboxone or Subutex. It is sometimes combined with the drug naloxone, which is the principle drug in Narcan, the nasal spray now commonly used as a rescue drug for opioid overdose.

Advocates of MAT argue that because opioids' effects on the brain are so powerful, an addict can never truly beat their own addiction. Instead, a small dose of an opioid drug, like methadone or

"THE SYMPTOMS THAT you experience when you come off, if you've been on opioids for a while, can be months of insomnia, leg kicks in the middle of the night, depression, and fatigue. Even a patient who took their medicine exactly as prescribed and then comes off can have months of feeling lousy, especially when they know in the back of their mind, all they would have to do to feel better again is to put one pill in their mouth to overcome their cravings." —Dr. Andrew Kolodny, director of Opioid Policy Research, The Heller School for Social Policy and Management at Brandeis University, founder of Physicians for Responsible Opioid Prescribing (PROP)

buprenorphine, should be administered on a regular basis in order to satisfy the body's craving for opioids. Opponents of MAT argue that addicts trying to recover are simply exchanging one addictive drug for another and that they are failing to address the deep-seated social and emotional issues that lay at the heart of addiction. Patients are often required to maintain low-dose opioids over several years, if not the rest of their lives, leading critics to argue that MAT does not actually free recovering addicts from addiction. MAT may be a preferable alternative to overdose, but it will not allow the addict to break from addiction in a way that an abstinence-based program of spiritual recovery can.

Yet the advocates of MAT argue that the method is based in sound science and has been proven time and again. France had a massive heroin problem in the 1980s and 1990s. When they changed the laws regulating buprenorphine, making it so that any doctor could prescribe the drug, heroin overdoses dropped 79 percent in four years.[176]

THE ORIGINS OF MAT

Medication-assisted treatment has been tested for decades in laboratories around the world and was first pioneered in New York City following World War II. Dr. Mary Jean Kreek[177] is professor and head of the

Screen shot of Dr. Kreek from *Do No Harm* documentary

CREDIT TK

Laboratory on the Biology of Addictive Diseases at Rockefeller University. We had the opportunity to spend an afternoon with this trail-blazing research pioneer at her laboratory at Rockefeller University.

What follows is part of the conversation we had about how she and her team developed methadone treatment as the first medically assisted treatment for opioid addiction in the late 1960s.

As a medical student at Columbia, Kreek was hired by Dr. Vincent Dole at what was then called the Rockefeller Institute for Medical Research. Dr. Dole was starting a new line of work on addiction treatment, a field that at the time had few doctors and scientists working in it. Dr. Dole also hired a psychiatrist named Marie Nyswander who had written a book entitled *The Drug Addict as a Patient*.[178] Together they spent six months performing research and collaborating with social workers and occupational therapists. At the end, they came up with a novel approach to addiction treatment.

"Heroin addiction had become the scourge of New York City and New York State," Dr. Kreek said.[179] "Dole had served with the late Louis Thomas on the Board of the Health Research Council of the City of New

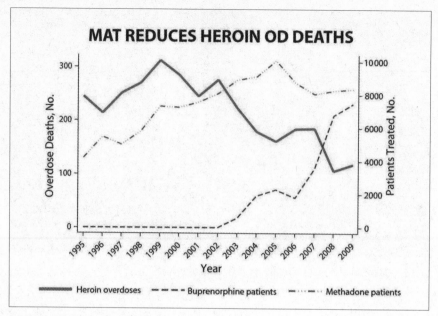

MAT Reduces Heroin Overdose Deaths

NATIONAL INSTITUTE OF DRUG ABUSE

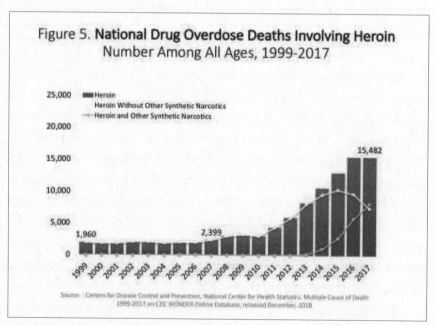

National Drug Overdoes Deaths Involving Heroin

NATIONAL INSTITUTE OF DRUG ABUSE

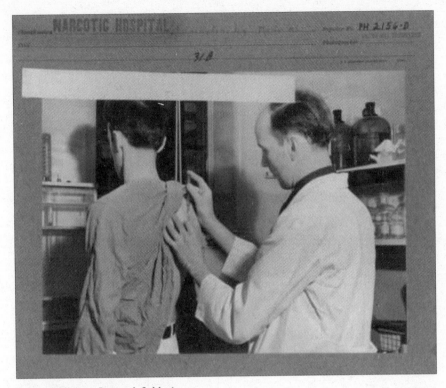

Heroin Addicts as Research Subjects
NARCOTICS HOSPITAL ARCHIVES, LEXINGTON, KENTUCKY

York. They had recognized that no doctors and no scientists were work-ing in this area."

The problem was—and still is—that addictive diseases are not part of the medical school or nursing school curriculum. In fact, I had been taught, both at med school and in my house training, if a . . . excuse the word . . . junkie . . . or addict comes through the door, send them to the local city hospital." Dole saw that addicts were not being taken care of and that there was scant literature on the subject. He did find a few articles concerning heroin addiction from the Public Health Hospital in Lexington, Kentucky.

"They were looking for a nonaddictive pain medication," Dr. Kreek said. "But they used to bring in heroin addicts as research subjects. They were people who had been sent to prison. This was in the days before it was not allowed to study prisoners. Some physicians and nurses would also show up. They had started self-administering opiates as part of their hospital work, particularly anesthesiologists and surgeons who had ready access to opiates all the time. So there were two strange populations together in Lexington. They [were looking] for a nonaddicting medicine. They weren't really thinking about treating the heroin addiction or identifying or preventing or managing it. Although there were some marvelous scientists and physicians involved in that effort." The answer would come from Dr. Kreek's and her partners' exhaustive research and drug trials at Rockefeller University in New York.

As a medical student, Dr. Kreek had done research into endocrinology, the science of glands that secrete hormones into the blood. Some hormones can physically change the brain when the body has too much or too little. Dr. Kreek wondered if the same thing was happening with drug addicts. "What is the brain doing? It's like an endocrine disorder, which I was already studying. Like an endocrine disorder but here it's a drug. [It] comes from the outside. Heroin, I had a feeling, would change your brain just like thyroid hormone . . . too much or too little changes the

"**THE STIGMA OF** the disorder plays into why prevention and treatment are not emphasized. The other piece of it is that many of us are in denial and don't want to believe that this could really be happening to young people. Oftentimes [it's] not only youth themselves, but their family might not be quite ready to accept that there's a need for treatment. In the case of opioid addiction, the idea that a son or daughter could be addicted to opioids at 16 or 17 is one of the most difficult things that any family could come to terms with. Distraught parents will spend a long period of time trying to get their child back to the way they were. Oftentimes trying to do that with treatments that are not effective. Either the person finds the right treatment by the time they're in their early twenties, or their risk of overdose and significant health problems increases dramatically." —**Dr. Samuel Ball, Yale School of Medicine**

brain. Or when you don't have enough sugar metabolism, insulin defi-
ciency: Diabetes, Type I and Type II, changes the brain and what you
think and your behaviors."

Seeing that heroin was physically changing the brain in the same
way that other conditions did, Dr. Kreek, with doctors Dole and
Nyswander, decided that the best way to treat heroin addicts was with
medication. "I could see we needed a medication," Dr. Kreek said. "The
medication probably needed to be a look-alike. In other words, like
heroin but not like heroin . . . just like we use [with] thyroid replace-
ment." She presented her findings to her colleagues at Cornell Medical
Center, where she had been working as an intern before Dr. Dole hired
her. "Everyone looked at me astonishingly, but I have to say, nobody
said you're doing the wrong thing," she said.

Dr. Kreek and her colleagues decided that a medication was needed,
but it wasn't clear what kind would be the most effective. When Dr.
Kreek suggested that the medication should be an opioid, she was met
with some resistance. Heroin addicts had been treated with morphine in
the 1920s to little effect. Instead, Dr. Kreek argued, a long-acting drug
was needed, one that provided a small dose over a long period of time.

"We went through the literature, and there was only one long-acting
medication that was an opiate," she said. "We all agreed that it would
probably be ideal to go in with an opiate, which would act at the same
part of the brain as did heroin or morphine. Marie [Nyswander] had
already done it." They interviewed hundreds of heroin addicts and found
that when they couldn't get heroin, they used morphine, and used
it more frequently than heroin. "I also learned what a couple of very
famous heroin-addicted surgeons did. They would give themselves
morphine once an hour. That was making a steady state as opposed to
the on-off [of intermittent drug use.]" Dr. Kreek started looking into
the research of opioid drugs and found what she was looking for in the
drug methadone.

THE DEVELOPMENT OF METHADONE

According to Ralf Gerlach in his book *The History of Methadone*,[180] the drug was first developed and synthesized at the I. G. Farbenkonzern laboratories in 1939.[181] Cut off from a supply of poppies for morphine production, the company was forced to produce a synthetic opioid. "When the war was over, the allied troops sent in people that were medically sophisticated to look at places like Bayer," Dr. Kreek said. "You can call it spoils of war, positive spoils of war." One of the people sent over was a young army doctor named Ray Hood. He read the company's research and saw potential in methadone.

Hood returned to the US and starting testing methadone on patients. At the same time, a Harvard professor named Henry K. Beecher (a famous anesthesiologist who pioneered, among other things, observations of the placebo effect[182]) was doing his own research on what became Bayer's studies. Independently of one another, Beecher and Hood found that methadone lasted for four to six hours. "When Beecher and Hood, independently, gave a single dose of methadone to relieve pain," Dr. Kreek said, "they would find pain relief for about the same duration of action as morphine. They were injecting it, of course, but they found an onset that was fairly rapid when they injected it, and they found it lasted for about four to six hours."

Kreek, Dole, and Nyswander began testing methadone on patients. They were men who had been convicted of drug crimes and suffered from heroin addiction. "Our patients were criminals," Dr. Kreek said. "They were people that had been in and out of jail, 14 years or more of heroin addiction. The criteria we set initially: They had to have been detoxified at least once in one of the numerous detox centers where people were really essentially going cold turkey or might be given a tapered dose." The Public Health Service Hospital in Lexington, known as Narcotic Farm, had used methadone for dose reduction in heroin addicts, but only to a very limited extent. Dr. Kreek and her colleagues decided that administering the drug orally was preferable to injections—and only once a day.

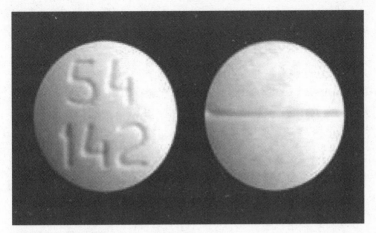

Generic Methadone
WALESKA SANTIAGO, MEDIA POLICY CENTER

"We started with low doses. Then we went slowly, slowly upward," she said, "being sure they weren't falling asleep. We found that if we did that slowly over about four weeks, we could go from a safe 20 milligrams up to what we had predicted might be a cross-tolerance-providing dose of 80 milligrams a day.

"We conducted studies that we referred to in the paper as 'narcotic blockade.' We took a group of patients who'd been stabilized into a double-blind study for four weeks. Every day I would walk in and intravenously inject heroin, or morphine, or saline, or methadone, or another very powerful narcotic used in the clinic. Each day I would watch the patients for the next two hours.

"They couldn't feel anything, except when I gave them morphine, and they'd say, 'Pins and needles! Pins and needles, that feels like morphine used to feel.' And then that would go away. When we got to the higher doses of methadone, it was even a stronger blockade, so nobody felt anything except a little pins and needles."

Dr. Kreek continued her studies by giving increasing amounts of heroin to her patients. "Scary study," she said, but it worked. "[We] found that none of our former heroin addicts, now patients (important semantics) could feel the heroin [high]. We exceeded 200 milligrams.

Two hundred milligrams, at that time, would have cost thousands of dollars on the street. Way beyond what anyone could have afforded. It was at that set of studies that we knew we had it. We had medication that didn't render people high, but they also didn't go into withdrawal or [get] sick. Drug craving went steadily downward. I would have patients say, 'Doctor, I'm not dreaming about drugs anymore.' 'Doctor, I dropped out of high school in the tenth grade. I kind of would like to go back.' 'I have not seen my parents for years.' 'I'm beginning to feel like I might have normal sexual function again.' And I was to study each one of those things as time went on."[183]

Methadone treatment would become widespread in the United States and Europe, but it's not without its problems. Methadone is still a powerful drug and can be abused. It causes a certain amount of euphoria and has been criticized as simply replacing one drug with another. But when administered carefully in a controlled environment, it can provide a stable treatment that keeps people from injecting heroin and risking the possibility of overdose. In recent years, buprenorphine has come to replace methadone in most medication-assisted treatment programs. Buprenorphine can provide the addict with a sufficient dose of opioids necessary for them to stave off craving, but without many of the messy side effects of methadone. Addicts are able to function

"I GOT OUT of jail. My apartment was completely wrecked from the police, and I looked at myself in the mirror. I had two choices: to put one foot in front of the other, or I was going die. This time it's taken a lot more work. I went to a treatment center after I had relapsed. They talked to me about medication-assisted therapy and prescribed me Subutex. Subutex is a brand name of buprenorphine [generic]. This is a tool that is helping me to stay alive every single day. I have a sponsor. I do my [12] steps along with medication-assisted therapy. I've been sober for 10 months now. I really am super lucky to be here today. I really didn't think I was going make it." —Shayna Akin, in recovery

as they normally would. Whereas methadone makes a patient groggy, buprenorphine allows them to function normally.[184]

CAN MEDICATION-ASSISTED TREATMENT (MAT) HELP PREVENT RELAPSE?

Dr. Richard Ries has worked with addicts for nearly 40 years. "You can focus on just the chemical part of addiction. Like is the person still using or not?" he said. "Or when we talk about addiction recovery, we [need to] talk about a spectrum of not only getting away from using drugs, but from improving some of the things in your life that have fallen apart during drug use. Those would be relationships. Those would be general function. Those would be things like jobs, health, doing better with people, being more straight forward, honest, dependable. All of those kinds of things."[185]

Dr. Ries, like most doctors who work in addiction medicine, is an advocate of medication-assisted treatment, or MAT. Medication-assisted treatment is when an addict takes a supplementary medical opioid to stave off the addict's now natural inclination for those drugs. Traditionally this has been methadone, which is taken daily and administered at clinics around the country. While methadone has its benefits, it is still a powerful drug and comes with its own issues. "Methadone fully blocks the opiate receptor, occupies it, is moderately psychoactive, moderately sedative," Dr. Ries said. "It's federally regulated and requires people to do some pretty serious life changes to be involved with it. Methadone treatment requires people to go to certified methadone centers, stand in lines. It's very paternalistic and very regimented. A lot of people with opiate addiction need that kind of regimentation because they've been out of control for years. That's an element of treatment that's absolutely required."

But the sedation that comes with methadone leaves many people unable to fully function after dosing. This is of course a preferable alternative to using a stronger drug and risking overdose, but methadone treatment presents its own set of issues. Fortunately, medical science has provided newer, better drugs that allow people to function much better day to day. Buprenorphine is now widely used in MAT as a preferable alternative to methadone.

MAT doesn't solve addiction on its own, and addicts are still recommended to attend some kind of emotional or spiritual recovery program. The most common of these are the 12-step programs first pioneered by Alcoholics Anonymous. "Half the [12-step] meetings you go to," Dr. Ries said, "you're going to hear somebody saying, 'You know, I'm struggling with my addiction, but I'm getting a lot better. I tried getting sober on my own without medications five times and I ended up half dead or dead

"**THE MOST DIFFICULT** part of withdrawal is that, I don't know how to put it, it's like your body needs it. But you're also dependent on taking a pill at a certain time of the day, or how many you take, and that pill's not there. Not anymore. So that was the hardest part to get over, what I call the dependency on that drug.

"Now I can actually stay awake at work. I'm not exhibiting what looked like drunken behavior. I had a woman that lives in my building say to me, 'You know, you really scared me a couple years ago when I was trying to drive behind you. You were driving like you were drunk.' That was because of the opiates. I don't drink.

"I felt pretty miserable for a few days. Nauseous, hot, cold, restless legs, not being able to sleep. You might throw up; you might get diarrhea. There's a whole array of stuff. It's not as bad as people think it is, because within about three days, you're beginning to feel better. You still have a lot to withdraw from. But I just found that once I got to that point of accepting [the medications they] gave me, and why [they] gave it to me, things began to open up. [I was] more alert, better at work, better with my dog, my cat. I just had more energy." —**Linda Gianotti, recovering elder addict, Hanover, New Hampshire, http://donoharmseries.org. Do No Harm documentary interview with Linda Gianotti**

twice. Was lucky enough to be saved. Now I'm on buprenorphine and I'm coming to meetings and I've got a sponsor and I'm getting better.' That's a win, win."[186]

"The chances of somebody getting sober using just abstinence, even if they go to tons of meetings, even if they do lots of talking, even if they go to residential care, even if they do all of that, they've got about a 5 percent chance of not relapsing within the next three months," Dr. Ries said.

"You've got a 90 to 95 percent chance of relapse within a few months of abstinence-oriented treatment. And that research, some of the best research around that was done by the Clinical Trials Network and published by a friend of mine, Roger Weiss, at Harvard. They looked at just pill-taking people mostly. They're younger, mostly not with long-term opiate addiction. They gave them buprenorphine either in a quick withdrawal or in a longer withdrawal. The longer withdrawal worked better. People stayed in treatment longer. They use less. The first group stopped MAT at one month; the second group stopped at three months. Within three months, it didn't matter which group you were in. Whether you had a lot of therapy, whether you had almost no therapy. Whether you were in a quick withdrawal or less quick withdrawal, within three months 90 to 95 percent of people were back to using.

"I could make any person in the world dependent on opiates who had absolutely no pain to start out with," Dr. Ries said. "After three months, if I tapered their opiates off to half of what they were taking, within two or three days, all the joints in their bodies would ache. They'd be nauseated, they'd be throwing up, and they'd be saying, 'I'm sick. I must need opiates to make me better.' Well, that's true. They'd be in opiate withdrawal. So it became a challenge for primary care docs, as well as patients with pain, to know whether their pain was reoccurring or whether they'd become tolerant on opiates and now they were going into withdrawal, even on the same dose."

The science is pretty clear now that once a person has become opioid addicted, it follows them for the rest of their life, and their brain's genetic makeup is forever changed The idea of not using MAT to treat opioid addiction, Dr. Ries said, was like treating any other illness without medication. "The way I think about it is we wouldn't dream of treating bipolar patients or schizophrenic patients without a basis of medicine," he said. "And then we use psychosocial things on top of that medicine. We wouldn't dream of treating them just with talk therapy. I think you need to think of opiate addiction in that same way. You need to stabilize the opiate receptor and then build other treatments on top of that."[187]

SOBRIETY VERSUS RECOVERY— THE LIMITATIONS OF MAT

Still, there are many who are critical of MAT and its insistence that a person remain tied to a drug. Furthermore, much of what drives a person to addiction is not something that can be treated with medication, they argue. Taking a drug to replace another may prevent overdose, but it doesn't take care of the emotional damage that goes hand in hand with addiction.

For more than 30 years Harriet Rosetto,[188] director and founder of Beit T'Shuvah, a drug rehabilitation center located in Los Angeles, has treated addicts using an abstinence-only program based on the 12-step process laid out by Alcoholics Anonymous, overlaid with the Jewish faith.

"I think that by and large it's another drug to get off a drug. It treats the symptom, not the disease," Harriett Rossetto said. "There's a difference between sobriety and recovery. If you're just approaching the drugs, then maybe it's better than shooting up and dying. But it doesn't address the things that [Beit T'Shuvah chooses] to address, which are the feelings and the sense of void that underlie the need to escape and anesthetize yourself. That's what the recovery piece is. That's what the spiritual, emotional, existential parts of the disease are."

Rossetto acknowledges that the cognitive behavioral therapy of 12-step programs is not mutually exclusive with MAT. However, she argues that MAT is still making a person use a drug to feel a certain way. Rossetto said that MAT and spiritual recovery could only work in tandem "if you're not stoned and loaded all the time. Because there's a certain amount of feeling and even discomfort that's necessary in order to deal with the issues. How do you tolerate discomfort?

"Sobriety is just about drugs or alcohol or gambling and the other compulsive activities. Recovery is about addressing the emotional, spiritual, and existential issues of being a human being that people try to escape through using drugs. Not all people want to engage in recovery. So is medication-assisted treatment better than overdose and death? Yes. If you just want to be able to get up and not have to shoot heroin and go to a job, then to be on Suboxone is probably better than to go look for heroin and go to prison or die."

Furthermore, Rossetto sees MAT as an extension of the pharmaceutical industry exercising its power over society. "I think it's Big Pharma that's pushing that model and people are looking for simplistic solutions to what are complex issues," she said. "The whole industry of recovery has changed, and it's big business. There are big companies buying up lots of little treatment programs. And there's marijuana-assisted treatment. There's all kinds of stuff. People are making a lot of money in this business. The treatment industry has become, in many ways because of insurance billing, [full of] practices that are really unhealthy. There are programs that are giving people drugs because insurance won't pay if you come in sober. So you have to come in loaded. I mean, a lot of nasty stuff is happening. There are programs charging $60, $70, $80,000 a month. That's the [model] the pharmaceutical companies are [promoting]. The government's emphasis [is] on medical-assisted treatment."

Medication certainly has its place, according to Rossetto, but once the early work of detoxing a patient is done, the role of drugs should be finished. "I think when a person is detoxing, medication is useful," she said.

Harriet Rossetto has devoted herself to finding the most meaningful of healing outcomes. "The ultimate goal should be spiritual recovery,

"**IN 2015, WE** became the first Southern state to have a syringe exchange program. The program is a lot more than about exchanging needles. A person in the syringe exchange program is five times more likely to get into treatment. A person in the syringe exchange program can get medical services that they couldn't access otherwise. They now have a safe place that they can go and ask questions and learn about the treatment options that are available to them." —**Van Ingram, executive director of the Kentucky Office of Drug Control Policy**

the kind that makes a person not look to drugs in the first place. My point of view is not popular and not universal. But I have maintained my mission, what I set up 30 years ago. I'm the founder, and it's the way I want to work. People come here [and] get well because of connection to community and to authentic relationships. There are returns because recovery is a lifelong, crooked path. Sobriety and recovery may go together, but people relapse. If they want to continue their work of recovery, then they return. So if your only measure is length of sobriety, then you're only measuring the symptom."

THE CASE FOR MAT

On the other side of the MAT debate there are people like Dr. Andrew Saxon[189] at the Harborview veterans' hospital in Seattle. As to the controversy over medication-assisted treatment, Dr. Saxon has some rather strong words. "So if it's controversial, it's because people don't listen to science and they're ignorant," he said. "Because there's the so-called recovery community, [which] often consists of in-patient treatment programs that don't have physicians and don't provide [MAT]. They want to make money by getting people with opioid use disorder to come there for 28 days and be taken off of their opioids and get no medication. That's very unsafe. There's only controversy because people are ignorant. So I would put that in the same class as there's people who are somehow against vaccines. Vaccines are the greatest public health intervention that's ever been created, preventing the spread of these terrible infectious diseases that people used to rampantly die from. Yet getting vaccines is controversial. Well, it's not. It's scientifically proven and safe and has made life for human beings in developed countries much better. I would put this on that same order. Anyone who says there [is] some reason not to do that is ignorant and anti-science and may be out to make a profit for themselves."[190]

Dr. Saxon admits that methadone has its issues and that not everyone responds to it. But, he says, like with other medical conditions, different people respond differently, and the goal is to find the right treatment for the right person. Although not allowed in the United States, Canada has had some success with limited trials of prescription heroin. "Medication treatment with heroin is a good idea for patients who fail methadone," he said. "Methadone is a great medication and it works for many, many people. But it doesn't work for everyone, and so it would just be like treating high blood pressure. Some people respond beautifully to one medication and other people don't respond to it. So you need a different medication for those people. Heroin-assisted treatment is, I think, a very reasonable plan for the people who are not responding to methadone. The studies in Canada and in Europe have shown that those people do better. But people who fail methadone, if you randomize them to either continue on methadone or get the heroin-assisted treatment, people with the heroin-assisted treatment tend

"IT'S BUPRENORPHINE OR Suboxone, which is an opioid; it's a partial agonist opioid. It's a little different from the other opioids. It may sound crazy to use that. I've just spent this 45 minutes telling you the way in which doctors have been prescribing opioids has led to a public health catastrophe; now I'm telling you we need more opioids for people who are addicted. But I am telling you that." —Dr. Andrew Kolodny, at a presentation to a gathering of California District Attorneys in San Diego, 2014

to do better in terms of not using as much and not getting involved in criminal activities and that sort of thing.

"I just want to reemphasize that every patient that has opioid use disorder should be treated with medication," Dr. Saxon said. "Because not using medication, you get very poor results. And we have the medications to treat the people and we just need to scale up. Everyone who has that disorder should be getting treatment in this very rich country with a lot of resources. Yet the majority are not getting treatment. So we all need to work hard to make the good treatments that we have available to everyone who needs it."

CHAPTER 12

Public Health Campaigns and Legal Actions

AS AN OPIOID problem grew into an epidemic, so, too, did the response grow from small isolated efforts to confront the crisis into broad national and international ones. While significant progress has been made in several areas, no amount of money exists that will provide every person with every adequate treatment. The opioid epidemic is one made up of interwoven issues—addiction, medicine, and health care, to name but a few. There is no one single solution, no magic bullet. Responses to the opioid crisis have come from individual community activists as well as federal agencies. All are necessary; none are sufficient. Even if there were a so-called "magic bullet," there is nothing we can do that can bring back the hundreds of thousands of lives lost, the families devastated, or the lives turned upside down. However, alongside this tragic and infuriating story of negligence and greed, there exists stories of hope and resilience, led by a growing number of professional and lay people doing what they can to try to bring an end to this deadly man-made crisis.

Combating the opioid epidemic will take myriad efforts, each addressing a different aspect of the crisis. Addicts need treatment, cities need money, and families need healing. The good news is that there are solutions at hand. However, as in all things related to the opioid crisis, good news is coupled with the frustrating truth that these solutions have been in front of our faces for a long time. Tragically, it took hundreds of thousands of deaths for the country to finally pay attention. But action is now being taken, and the full scope of this pushback is not yet organized or fully realized.

EDUCATION AND ADVOCACY

Dr. Andrew Kolodny has been fighting this battle for more than a decade, and his knowledge of the public sector has kept him as a driving force behind the organization he co-founded, Physicians for Responsible Opioid Prescribing (PROP). "I want you to think about how you would bring any disease epidemic under control, whether it's Ebola or measles," Dr. Kolodny said, speaking in San Diego. "Think about it for a moment. How do you bring disease epidemics to an end? There are really two things that you do: The first thing is you have to prevent new cases of the disease, meaning you contain it; the second thing is you see that people who have the disease receive effective treatment for it so the disease doesn't kill them."[191] For this reason, PROP focuses their efforts in two areas: education and advocacy.

According to Dr. Kolodny, "Advocacy has mostly been focused on the Food and Drug Administration, which is the federal agency that regulates pharmaceutical companies," he said. The FDA "is supposed to prohibit drug companies from promoting their products for conditions

"IN THE MONTH of June alone, we turned 400 men away from our detox unit. We have 24 beds in our detox unit for men and 24 for women. We are actually able to manage the female population pretty well, but we are just completely overwhelmed with the need of men seeking our services." —Karyn Hascal, The Healing Place, Louisville, Kentucky

Who Will Be Affected by Rescheduling?

the AMERICAN ACADEMY of PAIN MEDICINE

Dependency or Abuse?
AMERICAN ACADEMY OF PAIN MEDICINE

where they're not safe or effective. We've been trying to get the FDA to properly enforce existing laws that would make it illegal for the drug companies to promote opioids for common conditions." Prevention focuses on ensuring that doctors and their patients know the dangers involved with prescription opioids. It was the inaccuracies and outright lies told by the pharmaceutical industry that led to the overprescribing of opioids in the first place.

When people began to realize that something was going horribly wrong with prescription opioids, the pharmaceutical industry responded by trying to portray the problem as strictly limited to drug abusers. It wasn't that people who were taking these drugs as prescribed were becoming addicted, surrogates for the industry said, but that people were knowingly taking these pills in harmful ways.

HOW THE OPIOID LOBBY FRAMES THE PROBLEM

"It suggests that what we're dealing with is a problem of people behaving badly," Dr. Kolodny said. "Taking dangerous drugs to try and feel good, to get high from the drug. They're accidentally killing themselves in the process. The problem is these people [are] behaving badly and how do we stop them from doing that? That's not the problem. The problem is an epidemic of addiction, meaning the number of people with the condition of being addicted to opioids has skyrocketed over a short period of time. Once addicted, people need to use an opioid simply to avoid feeling awful. It is true that some people developed opioid addiction taking pills for the effect, using pills recreationally. Many more developed opioid addiction by taking the pills exactly as prescribed by a doctor."

> **"RICHARD SACKLER INDEED** went into the field to promote opioids to doctors alongside a sales rep. When he returned, Richard argued to the Vice President of Sales that a legally required warning about Purdue's opioids wasn't needed. He asserted that the warning 'implies a danger of untoward reactions and hazards that simply aren't there.' Richard insisted there should be 'less threatening' ways to describe Purdue opioids."
> —Richard Sackler Memo to VP of Sales, Massachusetts Attorney General's Brief Against Purdue Pharma

A PUBLIC HEALTH CRISIS

If the problem is one of addiction, then the solution is treatment. Many states and cities across the country have expanded their health-care systems in recent years to include drug treatment programs. Sentences for nonviolent drug offenders have been reduced, and in many places,

"HOW CAN YOU not have hope? Which is why recovery is so powerful for these people. It is because they've been hopeless for so long. We take the hopeless and helpless, and we give them help. We infuse them with hope. We do it through spirit, through mind, through body, through science. We are the place where all of it comes together. Watching the excitement of scientists, and the excitement of clergy, and the excitement of therapists, and bringing everybody together, it fills my body with electricity. As I'm talking, I'm all charged up about it." —**Harriet Rossetto, Beit T'Shuvah recovery center, Los Angeles, California**

addicts can seek help with no fear of legal punishment for drug possession or even selling drugs in some cases.

Brandon del Pozo[192] is chief of police in Burlington, Vermont. Burlington is Vermont's largest city and is in a region hard hit by the opioid crisis. Burlington, like other cities with high rates of crime related to opioids, has recognized that the issue is one of public health, not necessarily criminality. "I grew up as a teenager during the war on drugs and the crack epidemic in New York City," Chief del Pozo said. "I spent almost 20 years as a New York City police officer, and I saw that there is a role for locking up drug dealers. But that's not what solves this problem. This is first and foremost a public health crisis, and it has a law enforcement dimension. It's not a law enforcement crisis that happens to do with public health. Our focus here is really to make sure that all the police work we do serves a legitimate public health end." The so-called "war on drugs" focused on punishment. It imposed strict sentences for drug offenders and spent an enormous amount of time and money on arresting drug users. Far from solving anything, the "war on drugs" simply exploded the prison population and devastated communities.

"If it's arresting a drug dealer," del Pozo said, "it's going to be for a reason that we can demonstrate has a positive public health effect. If you're a person who's addicted to heroin, if you're somebody who, at a low level, is selling heroin to feed his or her addiction, it's not clear to me that the answer is an arrest. We want those people to get treatment, we want them to return to society as sober, productive members. That's not about a war against them—that's about making sure the police outcomes and public health outcomes are in tandem."[193]

TRAINING FOR OVERDOSE TREATMENT

So how does a city achieve public health outcomes in tandem with police outcomes? One way is by better training officers to deal with drug addicts and giving them the resources to help people suffering from overdose. "The first thing people talk about is accountability, and police are in the accountability business," Chief del Pozo said. "We do want people to be responsible for the crimes they commit when they're addicted to drugs, but they [have got to] be alive to be responsible. We believe in the widespread distribution of Narcan, or naloxone. Our officers carry it. Centers here give it out to citizens." Narcan is the brand name of naloxone,[194] a drug that blocks the body's opioid receptors and can be used to rescue people suffering from opioid overdose. Cities across the nation have begun distributing naloxone to their first responders and even to children in some cases. Narcan comes in a nasal spray, which is relatively easy to use and has saved countless lives over the past few years.

"The fire department has it, and we've already saved a lot of lives, collectively. My police department, plus the other agencies, just with people having real unfettered access to Narcan," Chief del Pozo said. "Responsibility can't be levied against a person who [has] died from an overdose. But more interestingly, what we're doing is hiring a public health coordinator. The police department [hired] an opiate policy coordinator. That person's job, in addition to [an] addiction and recovery advisor that we have working with us, is to make sure that our police responses are the appropriate public health related responses.

"We leave a lot of value on the table when we don't coordinate with probation or parole, with the people who do reentry, the people who

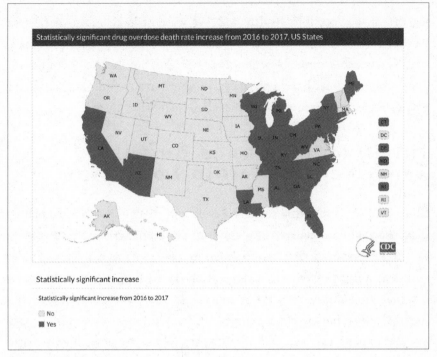

Drug Overdose Death Rates Increase from 2016-2017

CDC WONDER

provide shelter, the people who give treatment, the people who help people with mental illness. We leave a lot of value on the table when we don't work with those other groups to make sure that citizens are getting the treatment that they need to get out of this predicament. Right now there's no unified response. Everyone's in their silos doing their jobs. Their intentions are all good." Burlington's response is one that more and more cities across the country are starting to replicate or establish their own version of. This comprehensive approach has produced better results in a few years than the "war on drugs" did in decades.

"If an addict gets out of jail for a burglary," del Pozo said, "but then he goes back to the very same couch that he was sleeping on before he committed the burglary, he's going to start using heroin again, and he's going to commit burglaries again. He's going to become not only a public safety risk but a public health risk. We want to make sure that we're working with the right people. For example, if somebody gets out of jail, they've done their time. Now they may be clean, but they're unemployed. They probably don't have a place to live, they have a criminal record, and we're just going to create a vicious cycle if we let that go on."[195]

THE IMPACT OF RACE ON THE APPROACH TO OPIOID ADDICTION

Chief del Pozo's thinking reflects a welcome change in the approach to drug use that has occurred as a result of the opioid crisis. It is a change far too long delayed. One that was ignored for years as countless people suffered in needlessly long incarceration only to be released to a society that looked down on them and refused to help them back into a normal and stable life. This change was delayed for so long in large part because of America's sad history of racism. When drugs like heroin were associated with communities of color in the inner city, politicians only saw a "tough on crime" solution. But when the crisis started to affect white America, the narrative changed to one of compassionate concern. "Something that we're seeing that's different from our previous epidemics," Dr. Kolodny said, "is that policy makers are responding in a different way now that we have an epidemic affecting mainstream white America. When you had drug epidemics that were concentrated in the inner city in minority populations like heroin in the '70s and crack cocaine in the late '80s, early '90s, the response from policy-makers was a law-enforcement approach. What we got was the war-on-drugs and tough-on-crime approach.

"You're seeing a very different approach today, and not just from liberal politicians, but with conservative politicians as well. When they talk about our current opioid addiction epidemic, they all start off the same way. They all start off by saying we can't arrest our way out of this problem. You didn't hear that when it was an epidemic affecting blacks and Latinos. What I think is happening is you now have an epidemic

"WE'VE GOT TO get to a point in this country where we are willing to spend real money and sacrifice in order to make sure that for everyone that hits rock bottom, there's a bed; [that] the treatment that's available will work for them, whether it's 12-step, medically assisted, or otherwise. And that it's long enough because 30, 60, or 90 days under Medicaid or insurance isn't enough when you're facing a heroin addiction. That may take longer than six months to kick even some of the basic symptoms."
—Andrew Beshear, attorney general of Kentucky

hitting mainstream white America; it's hitting the families of policemen and lawyers and judges and politicians. They're not playing politics with this issue to get votes so much as seeing firsthand what this epidemic is doing to their constituents and to their own families. Now I think when you're personally affected by a drug epidemic, it's easier to recognize that addiction is a disease rather than a moral failing."[196]

CASEY'S LAW

Charlotte Wethington[197] lost her son, Casey, to heroin overdose. Like so many of those lost in this epidemic, Casey didn't grow up in a troubled household, in a poor neighborhood, or with few opportunities. "This is rural, beautiful, middle-class at the very least, Kentucky," Charlotte said. "I never thought that heroin would come to our house, because [when] you say the words *Morning View*, it sounds so idyllic. How could heroin, which has such a harsh, criminal, dirty connotation that goes with it, because of the stereotypical idea of what someone who's addicted to heroin looks like. How could that come to Morning View, Kentucky?"[198]

Casey got into skateboarding and other adrenaline-fueled sports. He was a risk-taker, according to his mother. "I thought of him as just being a typical little boy that was just rough and tumble and liked to try things," she said. "In the end, that was a very big detriment and an influential factor in his becoming addicted." His mother believes Casey started with pills, like many young addicts do, and when he attended the University of Cincinnati, the city environment provided him with easier access to drugs.

"I guess the first time that I really knew, it came straight out of Casey's mouth," Charlotte said. "After his first overdose, they were releasing him from the hospital because they couldn't hold him because of his age. He was choosing to leave.

"We were walking down the hall that day, he [was] in his hospital gown, because we didn't have a clue where his clothes were. He looked at me and he said, 'Mom, I have a love affair with heroin.' I had no clue what that was all about. Heroin? And then a love affair? How does that happen to have a love affair with a drug? That was when I knew for sure what was going on with Casey."

Casey Wethington died of a heroin overdose at the age of 23. His mother, distraught, determined that no other parents should have to feel the loss of a child as she and her husband had. "When Casey died, I said, 'Casey died, and an advocate was born.' That's who I'll be for the rest of my life," she said. "I know that there are so many families who have not found their voice yet. Those of us who have been active, hopefully we can be that voice until they find their own. Because it is going to take all of us to turn this around."

Charlotte traveled to the Kentucky state capitol, Frankfort, and began lobbying for better education and funding for drug-treatment programs. Because Casey was an adult, he was able to check himself out of the hospital and could only enter a treatment program voluntarily. "We had no means of intervening on his disease," Charlotte said. "While we really didn't understand the seriousness of his disease completely, we did finally realize that our son was not going to be able to seek treatment on his own. Because of his age we were not allowed to intervene on his behalf. We were told that we were trying to take his rights away from him. In fact, what we were trying to do was give him the right to live.

"As time went on, we saw Casey continuing to spiral down, the disease tak[ing] more and more control of his life. Of course, because [addiction] is a brain disease, [it took] control of his brain to the point that he was incapable of making the right decision for himself.

"We were told the best advice, if you can call it the best advice," Charlotte said, "was that Casey had to want to [get help], [had to] lose enough and hit bottom. That was the mantra that was repeated to me over and over again, regardless of who I spoke with. Whether it was the professionals in the field, whether it was a layperson, whether it was a person in a 12-step program. The message was the same. Because I was just a mom, and had no credentialing in addiction, and really was just such a novice at knowing anything about addiction at the time, I bought into that . . . I bought into that."

Eventually Casey did check himself into a detox program. And after six days he checked himself out. At the hospital, the nurses told Charlotte Wethington the same thing. The addict has to want help, and that the only way that addict will want it is by hitting rock bottom. "So he has hit bottom," Charlotte said. "Casey now resides at Spring Grove Cemetery. What's left of Casey's body is there. I know that his spirit is with us always. But that's the reason for Casey's Law, that there was something more that was needed, other than wanting to [get help], [other than] losing enough and hitting bottom."

Casey's Law is a Kentucky state law that allows for friends or relatives of a drug addict to petition for a court order to compel that person into treatment and to stay there. The law is modeled off a Florida law called the Marchman Act and has been replicated in several other states. But passing the law was no easy feat. It took several years for the Kentucky state legislature to vote it in. "[State Representative Tom Kerr] introduced the bill in 2003," Charlotte said, "and it did not pass. It did not make it out of committee, in fact. I asked him then in [the] 2004 legislative session if he would be willing to go back and introduce it again. He said he would.

214 DO NO HARM: THE OPIOID EPIDEMIC

"We went back again in 2004, and I thought, 'Well, I've got a leg up,' because I had gotten acquainted with the committee it was assigned to in 2003. I had done, I thought, considerable education. I thought, 'Well, this will be easier.' [But] it was assigned to a different committee. The committee chair again refused to call it up for a hearing. And again, it died in committee.

"But being the persistent person that I am, I went to our state capitol, Frankfort, and I just talked to people who had been supportive of Casey's Law. I asked, 'What am I doing wrong? What can I do better? Help me understand how to navigate this system.' One of the senators, Senator Katie Stine, said, 'There's a bill that has made it out of the House that's germane to yours, and I think if you could get your language amended onto that bill in the Senate it stands a chance of passing.'

"My senator, Damon Thayer, was willing to do that. He amended the bill. It made it out of the Senate unanimously and came back to the House for a final vote. My representative, Tom Kerr, allowed me to be

"OPIATE RECOVERY IS an area where our young people are leading the way. There are folks who have historically been addicted to opioids [who] haven't come out of the closet about that. I really appreciate that younger individuals are willing to talk through the stigma around opiate use and addiction and say, 'Hey, this is a problem that I have. This is a genetic predisposition, in many cases, and I'm going to not be ashamed of that. I'm going to deal with it.' I think the longer we keep it in that stigmatized area, the less likely we are to talk about it openly. The less likely people are to get the help that they need, and other individuals are going to be judgmental until they're educated about it. Our youth are doing us a huge favor. [They] are not as willing to say, 'Oh, I'm not going talk about this.' They're willing to say, 'I'm going tell you what I went through, and I want your support.'" —**Dr. Barbara Thomas, senior director of Counseling and Psychological Services at the University of San Francisco**

his page that evening. I sat with him on the floor of the house. At one point in time, he just kind of nudged me and said, 'This is like a movie,' because the sponsor of the bill had been told that unless he voted against it, that they were going to kill his bill altogether.

"He said, 'Before I do that, I want to speak to this amendment,' and it was like a movie. All these legislators started turning their lights on to speak. They told about how they had families that were coming to them and begging for help with their adult children, and [how] they had nothing to offer them. So, in that eleventh hour of that 2004 session, Casey's Law passed.

"It became effective July the 13th of 2004. And so, for 16 years now, we have had the Matthew Casey Wethington Act for Substance Abuse Intervention as a Kentucky statute."[199]

According to the Louisville *Courier-Journal*,[200] 230 petitions were filed under Casey's Law in 2017, and while success in treatment is never a given, the law and its widespread support are indicative of the great lengths cities and states are now going to in order to provide treatment for drug addicts.

THE SAFE STATIONS PROGRAM

One of the nation's most successful programs for guiding addicts to treatment started in Manchester, New Hampshire. It was there that a young man, similar to Casey Wethington, walked into a fire station looking for help. This young man, Cameron, had hit rock bottom and wanted to get help but didn't know where to turn.[201] So he walked into a local fire station, presumably due to firefighters' dual role as paramedics, and told them he had a drug problem and asked for help. The firefighters put him in contact with a treatment center, and Cameron eventually got back on his feet.

Manchester fire chief Dan Goonan heard about this and asked himself why this couldn't work for other people as well, and the Safe Stations program was born. After two years, Manchester fire stations had taken in more than 3,000 people in search of substance abuse treatment. Cities from all over the country started calling and asking how they could replicate the program. In spring of 2018, key Washington officials, including President Trump, visited Manchester to learn about the Safe Stations program.

The Safe Stations program, Casey's Law, and other community-level responses are encouraging examples of what can be done on the local level. But like all things, they need money. Many of the people going into treatment cannot afford to pay for it, and drug treatment is just one aspect of a crisis influenced by countless factors. In September of 2018, funding for the Safe Stations program became the subject of controversy in New Hampshire as the governor wanted to transfer safe interdiction sites to hospitals rather than fire stations. Chief Goonan's program is paid for largely through grants and donations. Their partner organizations, however, like treatment centers and medical facilities, receive state funding that is tied to the Safe Stations program. If the Safe Stations program is transferred to hospitals, it is unclear if those treatment centers will continue to receive that funding.[202]

FUNDING TREATMENT VIA LAWSUITS AGAINST BIG PHARMA

Securing sufficient and steady funding is a challenge for any public-health program. Central to funding the myriad programs aimed at combating the crisis are the enormous amounts of money that were made by Big Pharma and many in the health-care field. Currently there is a coalition of more than 40 state attorneys general working with more than 100 local communities on lawsuits directed at these entities. Working with a group of lawyers, led by attorney Mike Moore, they are looking at the enormous profits pharmaceutical companies have made—and continue to make—as a source of money needed to fund and operate comprehensive treatment strategies.

Moore is a former attorney general for Mississippi and now works in private practice. As attorney general of Mississippi, he successfully sued 13 tobacco companies for lying about the addictive effects of nicotine and won the largest corporate settlement in US history, $246 billion. Moore personally received none of that money, only his salary as state attorney general. After the Deepwater Horizon oil spill in the Gulf of Mexico in 2010, Moore oversaw negotiations between BP, five states, and hundreds of municipalities.[203]

"I came up close and personal with the three leaders of Purdue in 2005 when I had them down in Jackson. I sat across the table from them and they told me straight to my face that the only people that get hooked on OxyContin were criminals. People who abuse the drug and crush it up and shoot it in their arm. People aren't addicted to it. They're 'pseudo-addicted.' There's no way for them to get addicted to this drug. There's less than [a] 1 percent chance of them getting addicted and they have this crushproof technology—all this bull, you know? A year later, we produced a bunch of documents and the Feds indicted them. They all plead guilty. That's why I first got involved."[204]

In response to the mounting evidence, former Purdue CEO (and son of one of the founding brothers) Richard Sackler advised blaming the addicts. "We have to hammer on the abusers in every way possible," the lawsuit quoted Sackler as writing in an email. "They are the culprits and the problem. They are reckless criminals."[205]

Moore is involved with a series of lawsuits against not only drug manufacturers but against distributors as well. Purdue Pharma is, because of its promotion of OxyContin and the accompanying marketing campaign, a target in almost all of those suits. Other drug companies that sold their own brand of opioid painkillers are being targeted as well. "We have about 33 states that have actually filed cases now against various defendants," Moore said in an interview with the authors. "Purdue is involved in almost every one of those cases. Some of the states have outside counsel like me. Some of the states are doing it themselves with their own staff. Alabama has filed in this federal MDL [multidistrict litigation] up in Cleveland."

Mike Moore works out of a small office in Orlando, Florida, but according to him, every state in the union is either involved in or looking into litigation. "There's about 33 states who joined the effort," Moore said. "And then the other states are all still investigating. They're very much involved. Some have decided to do it through subpoenas and other things rather than through actual lawsuits. But all 50 states are focused on Purdue and other defendants and distributors."

Other defendants include companies like Rochester Drug Cooperative, InSys, the McKesson Corporation, which markets its own opioid painkiller, Oxaydo,[206] and even drug distributors like CVS pharmacies. "You got Janssen, which is Johnson & Johnson; you got Indo; you got Teva, which used to be Cephalon; you got Allergan on the manufacture side. Then you got the three primary distributors, which are Cardinal Health, AmerisourceBergen, [and McKesson]," Moore said. "In my view, the large drugstore chains played a role in this. Walgreens and CVS and Walmart, Rite Aid. Those companies bear some responsibility and need to step up to the plate. So there's lots of players, and then there's a hundred little players out there."[207]

The goal is to get these companies to pay for the damage they've done. To try and staunch the bleeding of those suffering from opioid addiction and to prevent more people from becoming addicted. Many of these companies have already acknowledged a certain amount of responsibility, but they maintain that the issue lies in drug abuse, not the inherent danger of their products. But while companies have

"I'VE HAD FRIENDS die in my arms. I've watched people go to prison for life because they couldn't not have this drug that the drug companies know is so addicting. People are dying because of it. I almost lost my life because of it." —Shayna Akin, in recovery

committed some funds, there is no amount of money in the world that can provide everything that's needed, nor can money bring back the lives lost or destroyed by addiction. Purdue has committed to paying for treatment programs,[208] and McKesson has committed $100 million toward combating the crisis. These are token amounts compared to the task at hand.

"If you put a damage file together, we need $500 billion," Moore said. "Well, they [the pharma companies] don't have $500 billion. So, the real question you have to ask yourself is: If you had to pick a number? If you had $2 or $3 billion a year for the next 10 years, could you have an impact on the problem in some fashion or form? The answer is, 'Yes, you could.' You just have to be efficacious in how you spend the money. There's a clear effort to try to figure out what that efficacious effort would be before we ever accept any resolution from these defendants. Now, they're not there yet. Nobody's offered that kind of money yet. You're just trying to figure out what's a feasible amount of money that you could actually get. Then what could you do with it?"[209]

There are countless things that can and should be done with the money. One of the reasons these suits are coming from states and not individuals in class-action lawsuits is because of programs like Safe Stations. When the opioid crisis really started to hit, state and local public health services were the ones tasked with cleaning up the mess. First responders, hospitals with public funding, state workers compensation programs, and other such government-funded bodies were stretched thin trying to keep up with the steady stream of addicts and overdoses coming through their doors. Moore and his colleagues are trying to get the pharmaceutical and other complicit companies to pay for these programs.

"There's not enough money—all the companies don't have enough money to do that," Moore said. "But we can try to recover enough money that has an impact on three areas. We can try to provide a reeducation of America. Education and prevention programs for young people in order to try to prevent this from ever occurring again.

"Then, obviously, money for treatment across the country to try to expand what we're doing already and maybe try to force insurance companies and others to cover treatment. There's three or four million opioid dependents. We're trying to make a dent in that in some fashion. That doesn't mean that all those people will seek treatment. It just means that we can try to provide a treatment in the most cost-effective way we can. The third is to have a real robust emergency response program for providing naloxone and other antagonists [opioid overdose treatment drugs] that will save lives. Keep people from overdosing, treat people that need treatment, and reeducate the country in such a way that we prevent this from ever happening again. It's like a three-legged stool. That's the goal.

"I'm an encourager. That's what I am. I encourage people to get involved in this fight and do something about it. I try to bring people together. That's my forte here. I just try to build consensus and collegiality and keep people focused on solving a problem. And that's what I continue to do."[210]

Moore won $250 billion from tobacco companies. When asked about similarities between the opioid case and tobacco, he said this: "There's similarities and then there's a difference. The tobacco companies were cash rich and they could easily raise the price of their products to pay for the gigantic settlement that we got from them. Although the settlement was $250 billion, it was paid over years and years, so it's $8, $10, $12 billion a year, over forever. This one is a little bit different. You have people dying every day from overdoses. It's not like you have people smoking cigarettes for 35, 40 years and dying of cancer. They're overdosing today. We need [an] immediate infusion of cash. The idea would be to pound these guys as hard as you can pound them. Take every last cent you could possibly get out of and put it to immediate use."

Indeed, immediate use is not fast enough. People continue to die every day from opioids. With the synthetic drug fentanyl now on the scene, the risk from overdose is even higher. In fact, according to the CDC, 2017 saw more than 72,000 overdose deaths. The is the highest figure yet, although for the first time since 1990, according to the CDC, there has been an actual drop in overdose deaths.[211]

There is not yet a timeline for the lawsuits pending against the pharmaceutical companies, and the sad reality is those companies have the resources to drag the process out for as long as they can. Moore has said that the amount of money he hopes to get from these companies may bankrupt them. Bankruptcy, frankly, is far less than they deserve. The evidence is quite clear that these companies knew as far back as the late 1990s that people were becoming dangerously addicted. The number of pills going to rural communities was in the millions. Far beyond what their populations would need even if every person in the county were taking their drugs as prescribed. The evidence is clear that these companies profited in the billions of dollars on the backs of those innocent victims.

"Whenever you see 70,000 people a year die from something that ought to be prevented, it gets your attention," Moore said. "Frankly, it's an opportunity to do some good. When people ask me what I hope to accomplish, I'm focused on trying to resolve the opioid epidemic. If you ask other lawyers what they're trying to do, they may say they're trying to make a bunch of money or they're trying to recover a bunch of money. I'm trying to just play a small role in getting people to save lives. That's why I have a sense of frustration about it because I think this could get resolved this year. But we're going to have to take people to the law. Which means take them to a trial date and see if they want to go to trial or if they want to resolve the case. When we go to trial, they're going to lose big, and these companies, some of them may not be in existence anymore. Because it will certainly drive some of them to bankruptcy."[212]

In March of 2019, the *Wall Street Journal* reported that as a result of the large numbers of lawsuits pending against them, Purdue Pharma is exploring filing for bankruptcy.[213] It is unclear how this might affect the billions of dollars in compensation at stake, but a spokesman for Purdue said that the company was intent on remaining "strong and sustainable."[214]

Mother and Child
MEDIA POLICY CENTER

A RISE IN THE DEMAND FOR TREATMENT

According to the CDC, from 1999 to 2017, more than 700,000 people have died from drug overdose. Not all of those deaths were from opioids, but in 2017 alone, 68 percent of the over 70,000-plus deaths were from some kind of opioid. The CDC estimates that an average of 130 Americans die every day from an opioid overdose. It describes three waves of opioid deaths in the past two decades. The first wave, from 1999 to 2010, was when deaths from opioid prescriptions steadily rose. The second wave began in 2010, when there was a spike in heroin overdoses. (We noted in previous chapters that some have pointed to the reformulation of OxyContin that took place in 2010 as a driver of increased heroin use.) The third began in 2013 when synthetic opioids like fentanyl arrived on the market and drove up deaths even higher.[215]

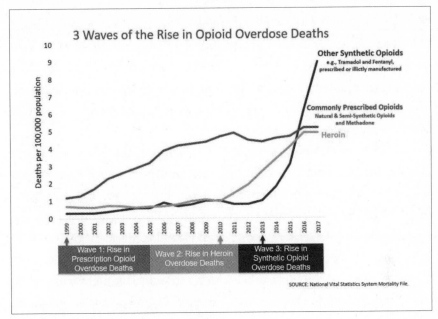

3 Waves of the Rise in Opioid Overdose Deaths

COURTESY OF THE NATIONAL VITAL STATI,STICS SYSTEM MORTALITY FILE

Alongside the deaths, countless numbers have sought treatment for their addiction. Public and private medical facilities have been flooded with people trying to get clean. Some are able to kick their habit, going on to live happy and productive lives. Others struggle in their addiction and are caught in cycles of sobriety and relapse, never fully freeing themselves from drug dependence. Those who relapse should not be considered failures. Their recidivism merely illustrates the difficulty of maintaining a healthy sobriety. Keeping clean from opioids is made all

> **"MY SON, HE** had virtually no chance of stopping just by free will. The behavior that he exhibited that started a lot of my anger, with regard to stealing from us and everything else that goes along with the chaos of addiction . . . [the drug] hijacks your brain, and all of that behavior changes who you are. The real Nicholas, his personality, was hijacked by that drug."
> **—Eric and Holly Specht, Founders of Northern Kentucky Hates Heroin**

the more difficult by the physical changes the drugs make to the brain. This is why so many medical professionals we've spoken to have insisted on medication-assisted treatment (MAT) as a cornerstone of a healthy recovery. A number of doctors have made the comparison to diabetes, arguing that no one would ever suggest weaning themselves off insulin after a few years of treatment.

Access to treatment has expanded in the past few years, but it still lags far behind what it should be. State and local budgets have been drained as communities divert funds to emergency services and treatment facilities. Yet treatment facilities are still overwhelmed with the number of patients seeking help. Karyn Hascal is president of The Healing Place, a long-term residential recovery program in Louisville, Kentucky. "We used to fill up at nine o'clock, ten o'clock at night. Now we're full at nine o'clock in the morning," she said. "Some people sleep behind the building to try to be there when a bed opens up."

When The Healing Place opened in the 1980s, most of the patients were treated for alcohol or cocaine addiction. In those days, Hascal said, if the facility had no open beds, that patient could return in 24 to 48 hours. However, "the scenario today is so much more dangerous because if a young person comes to us seeking help and we don't have any space,

"**WE HAVE ALWAYS** looked at experimentation, and that kids should be able to try things. If you smoked pot a few times, what's the big deal? But with pain pills and opioids, that's not a possibility. You can't have that weekend where you went crazy. I mean, I've talked to people who can describe in detail where they were sitting, what they were doing that first time they took a pill because it represented just a complete departure from the life that they should have had. It's not something that you can just experiment with in college. It will take over your life. I've become a complete hardliner on that. These pills are totally dangerous." —Harriet Ryan, reporter for the *Los Angeles Times,* http://www.donoharmseries.org. Do No Harm documentary interview with Harriet Ryan. 2018.

we don't have any beds, they go back to the street. The lethality level of the heroin and fentanyl is so outrageous that they may not live to come back."

The Healing Place has 740 people in residence every day, Hascal said. At the time of the interview, they were working on expanding their facilities and services. "But the reality is, if we opened a new building tomorrow that nearly doubled our capacity, we still wouldn't begin to touch the need."[216]

■ ■ ■

WHEN WE'VE SPOKEN to doctors about what can be done about the opioid epidemic, almost all of them have said that the expansion of access to MAT is an integral part of the answer. Of course, the first thing they say is "don't start using." That may seem obvious, but it's important to remember that many of these people got addicted via a doctor's prescription. "Turning off the tap" is another phrase that comes up a lot. Doctors and the general public need to be educated about the dangers of opioid medications and understand that even a doctor's orders can be dangerous.

No other American public health effort has required a coordinated and dedicated response involving health care, legal, educational, and governmental communities. Recent court cases highlighted by victories in Massachusetts, Ohio, and Oklahoma offer the hope that funds will be found to treat far more victims than was thought possible just a few years ago.

CHAPTER 13

The Beginning of the End?

THE OPIOID EPIDEMIC has been with us for decades now. It began with the introduction of OxyContin in 1996. The marketing campaign for OxyContin was built on years of misinformation and created an environment where the prescribing of powerful opioid drugs for everyday chronic pain was not only acceptable but also a doctor's obligation. People were in pain, and if doctors didn't prescribe opioids, they were denying their patients the best treatments available. Advocates for opioid use argued that these doctors were guilty of not fulfilling their responsibilities.

In the earlier parts of the twentieth century, after opioids had been banned from everyday products like cold remedies and women's health products, the drugs became reserved for only the most severe cases of cancer and acute pain. Doctors were taught to use opioids cautiously. Changes in the use of opioids began in the 1960s when Dr. Cicely Saunders developed the modern hospice movement in the United Kingdom. She sought to provide more humane care for people at the end of their lives. Rather than watch dying people agonize, Dr. Saunders began to use opioids to ease their pain. There's little concern for addiction when patients are already dying. But through that movement, the medical community began to rethink the use of opioids and their potential for other ailments.

In the 1970s, many more in the medical community started to take a second look at opioids. New technologies had created medical miracles in the past. It wasn't so far-fetched to believe that the immense power of opioids could be harnessed and used casually to treat everyday pain. New coatings for drugs were invented in the late 1970s that allowed for the slow release of drugs into the system. Opioids were certainly powerful and potentially dangerous when given in large doses, but what if they were introduced slowly, over a period of several hours? To some extent this worked. New drugs were produced that gave relief to patients suffering from cancer pain. MS Contin, which used a slow-release polymer coating, became Purdue Pharma's best-selling drug. Then Purdue and other drug manufacturers went a step further. What if those drugs could be used for everyday patients suffering from chronic pain—the aches and soreness we all feel? If left untreated, chronic pain can grow and become even more debilitating, preventing people from working or engaging in an active life. What if we could use these new technologies to make chronic pain a thing of the past? It was a question worth exploring. People in pain certainly need treatment, and experimentation is the driver of innovation. If the medical community could do it, why not try?

Fast-forward to the 1990s, where evidence initially appeared to suggest that time-release technology could make opioids safe for everyday use. As a result, Purdue's OxyContin was approved in 1995 by the FDA for general release.

But the experiment ultimately failed. The drugs were still too powerful. They didn't last as long as Purdue claimed, and they made people physically and mentally dependent on opioids. Their painkilling abilities were too often coupled with intense withdrawal symptoms, which caused pain on their own. Patients were taking the drugs more often than they should. When they complained that their drugs weren't lasting, doctors prescribed higher doses. Recent disclosures[217] revealed a cover-up by Purdue Pharma that is a significant part of lawsuits in Massachusetts, Ohio, and Oklahoma courts. Purdue's marketing campaigns were directed at primary care doctors who were told, repeatedly, by prominent institutions within the medical community that opioids were not as addictive as once believed. In the case of Purdue's new blockbuster drug OxyContin, doctors were told that the slow-release formula actually lessened the risk of addiction.[218]

Doctors told their patients that they could take the drugs more frequently if they wore off before the 12-hour mark. Purdue's patent and approval from the FDA relied on the 12-hour claim. It needed to be 12 hours in order to maintain the competitive edge over other companies that were now getting into the marketplace with their own brand of opioids. Don't prescribe more frequently, doctors were told by Purdue; prescribe in higher doses. Their literature read, "Those patients you're seeing that appear to be addicted, who are showing the classic warning signs for addiction, aren't actually addicted. They're displaying a new condition, 'pseudo-addiction,' where patients look like addicts simply because they're not getting enough of the drug." The answer wasn't to take them off the drug but to raise the dosage—and, as a result, make more money for Purdue.

Doctors complied with this. There was trust in the system. Medical journals like the *New England Journal of Medicine* and prominent doctors had all told them that opioids were safe, that denying their patients opioids was needlessly cruel. What they didn't realize at the time was that the authors of those studies in medical journals, those speakers who presented at prestigious conferences, had often received funding from drug manufacturers. Industry-funded lobbyists convinced state legislatures and medical regulatory agencies that these drugs needed to be prescribed. They convinced lawmakers that pain, a wholly subjective experience, needed to be measured alongside conventional objective indicators like pulse and blood pressure. Pain became the "fifth vital sign."

THE SPREAD OF AN EPIDEMIC

Big Pharma's plan began to unravel out of control. Patients were taking the drugs more frequently, and some were even dying. Because of their potentency, pills found their way onto the black market and abusers found ways to circumvent the time-release formula. They crushed and snorted the pills. Or mixed and crushed them with water and injected the mixture. Some doctors' offices became "pill mills," handing out prescriptions to almost anyone. A number of pharmacies filled their orders without question. Pills were being sold in incredible numbers. Numbers that, if the pills were taken as prescribed, could provide a steady dose to everyone in the state, let alone the sparsely populated rural counties where they were being sold.[219]

When pills became too expensive, or a prescription ran out, many turned to heroin. Heroin, which once was limited to metropolitan areas, found its way into the lily-white suburbs of middle America. Drug cartels responded to the increased demand for heroin and flooded the country with cheap drugs. What had once been grown far from the United States was now being grown just across the border in Mexico, where poverty and corruption allowed cartels to flourish. Cartels had grown rich satisfying America's demand for cocaine in the 1970s and '80s, and now the heroin market was making them even richer.[220]

Then a new drug appeared on the market: fentanyl. Like other opioids, this was a drug that had been used in medicine but only in extreme cases. Now it was being mixed into the heroin being sold on America's streets. Indistinguishable to the naked eye, the synthetic opioid fentanyl is even more powerful than heroin and made an already devastating drug problem much worse. Public services, already stretched thin by an unprecedented number of addicts, had to scramble to combat an ever-expanding epidemic.

THE TIDE HAS TURNED

Yet there is some good news and hope for the future. Headlines appear almost daily in newspapers across the country telling stories of addicts turning their lives around, new medications and programs to distribute

"BY 1999, THERE'S no question that Purdue knew that people were dying from their drug, OxyContin. Instead of doing something about it, they just continued to spread the lies. Just like the tobacco companies. They spread lies about the addictive nature of the product. Instead of stepping up and doing something about it, they just had lots of excuses and continued to build their company. Instead of selling a few hundred million dollars' worth of OxyContin, they ended up selling billions of dollars' worth of it. Other companies jumped in the same way. The distributors who were delivering the pills to all these little towns should have known better. You can't deliver five million pills to a town of 800 people. You've got to know there's a problem there somewhere and they didn't do anything about it. Everybody knew what was going on, but it was driven by money.

"Every time they'd get caught doing something, they just had an excuse, 'Well, we just don't have the sophistication and we didn't really know.' They're still giving excuses like that even in 2018. They knew that there was a huge problem. It became evident as the opioid deaths continued to rise and especially in the last 18 years. You've seen thousands and thousands of people [die]. Then they cut off the supply. Everybody did what they needed to do. They limited prescriptions, and they told the doctors they can't [prescribe as much] anymore. But when you cut off the supply of pills, people that are addicted are going to go do something to keep from getting sick. They go to heroin and fentanyl, and now the numbers have escalated even further. I blame the companies for that. I mean, you can't go out and set the fire and then never try to put it out. All they did was [fan] the flames. They never did anything really to try to turn it around. That's why I really think they have some huge responsibility for this." **—Mike Moore, attorney**

them to those in need, and communities coming together to prevent future addictions and deaths. At the same time, the enablers of the crisis, drug manufacturers, distributors, doctors, and pharmacies are all in the crosshairs of everyone from individual citizens to state and local governments. As of this writing, hundreds of lawsuits are in process against drug makers and distributors who, plaintiffs argue, turned a blind eye to the damage these drugs bring because their profits were enormous.

Responding to overwhelming public pressure, Purdue and other drug companies have begun funding treatment and recovery programs and have taken steps to prevent overprescribing and abuse. But those efforts hardly compare to the money spent by public health agencies trying to stem the tide of addiction. Plaintiffs in many of these cases are not looking for cash compensation necessarily; they're looking for enough funding to expand drug treatment programs and for reimbursement for the money already spent by cities and states.

Drug companies maintain their innocence. They say that the problem lies with drug abusers and corrupt medical professionals. The media and aspirational lawyers are using corporations as an easy enemy in a complex and opaque crisis, they say. Yet internal documents obtained through legal actions tell a different story.[221] They show that company executives knew about the vast numbers of pills going out, about the people becoming addicted, about the damage being done. Their initial reaction was not to limit the sale of opioids but to try and change the narrative.

Some of these suits will be decided soon, but a final settlement and the disbursement of funds may take years. A major court decision is currently brewing in Ohio,[222] and legal experts believe that this suit will serve as a bellwether for future litigation. Yet regardless of the outcome of this particular decision, the losing side will undoubtedly appeal, and cases are bound to be dragged out for as long as possible.

Even without money, many communities are finding ways to turn back the tide in their own way. Needle exchange programs across the country, long proven to reduce rates of transmittable diseases, are now hubs for overdose prevention drugs and access to treatment programs. Prevention programs are in most schools. And, importantly, addiction is now looked upon as an illness to be treated rather than a criminal offense.

RESISTANCE TO CHANGE

Education's a great way to provide foundation, but unfortunately, most people have a lot of difficulty changing," said Dr. Lewis Nelson of Rutgers New Jersey Medical School. Dr. Nelson is chair of the Department of Emergency Medicine and has watched the crisis grow to epic proportions. "Change is often manifested through regulatory change, and that's often met with a lot of resistance because once people have a set way of doing things, they don't like to change very much. It occurs when we are resistant to not using pain meds, [or] being open to trying alternative strategies to manage pain."

The changes needed to properly address the opioid epidemic will ultimately disrupt health-care institutions and their methods of getting things done. It's quite natural for people in those networks to find certain changes to be suspect. Furthermore, regulatory changes are not always well thought out. Politicians like to show that they are taking action, but the changes they implement are not necessarily proven to be effective. "It's the way laws are made," Dr. Nelson said. "Unlike medicine, where, in order to make a change, we want evidence. We want validation of any change we're going to make. In the law, they just make changes. In legislative action, they just make changes that kind of sound good but don't really carry the evidence to support their impact. So, not surprisingly, a lot of things that we put in place regulatorily have been met with unintended consequences."[223] But regulatory change is necessary to put an end to the epidemic. All the doctors we spoke to stress the need to limit the amounts of opioids that are being prescribed. Of course, this can't be achieved purely by regulation. There are changes that medical providers and everyday citizens need to make on their own.

"When you put money out there, people go after the money as they best know how to do it. So a lot of places are opening up addiction treatment centers, and they don't really have the knowledge and the credibility to do it. But there's money available, so they go after the money. When you look at who's running these addiction centers and what their outcomes look like, there's really a lot of bad medicine being practiced."[224]

CORRUPT TREATMENT CENTERS

There are no shortage of stories about so-called "treatment centers" opening up, often in Sunbelt states like Florida and California, that do little more than warehouse people trying to recover. "You've probably seen some of the pieces in and others about what went on in Florida, like in Delray Beach, where doctors or people were just opening up addiction practices. Flying patients down there, draining their insurance policy, and then just throwing them out. Now they're stuck in Florida, without any place to live, and they're still addicted. That's because there's money [to be made], so it breeds bad practices."

The *New York Times* piece Dr. Nelson is referring to, "Haven for Recovering Addicts Now Profits from Their Relapses,"[225] tells the story of how Florida became a haven for sober homes. But while many legitimate centers flourished, so, too, did scams and corruption. "The state of Florida licenses haircutters, yet we don't license any of the people involved in the supervision of young adults suffering from substance abuse, far away from home, without means," Delray Beach mayor Cary Glickstein told the *Times*. "These desperate patients and family members are getting exploited and abused."[226]

Not all treatment centers are exploitative. Many of them do great work and have helped countless people recover from addiction. Dr. Nelson talked about the tension between abstinence-only programs and medication-assisted treatment discussed in chapter 9. Dr. Nelson is very much in favor of MAT but says that the cognitive behavioral therapy aspect promoted by the 12-step system is necessary for recovery as well. "I should say [drug] recidivism isn't necessarily a real failure," Dr. Nelson said. "It's just an impediment or a stumbling block, just like people who develop hypoglycemia when they are on diabetes treatment. [That] doesn't mean that the whole world comes to an end. It means we have to try a little bit harder and better next time. We have to come up with a better approach or better understanding of what treatment is like [and] what the expectations are for success. We need to really parse out better who's going to do best with which medication and which of the subgroup will actually do okay without medication, and there are some that do. Non-medication isn't all failure. There are some people that can do it. But most people don't do very well with that. The really big solution is at the beginning. It's preventing addiction. I still think we have a long way to go with that."[227]

ACCOUNTABILITY AND REGULATION IN PAIN TREATMENT

The problem is people are still in pain, and those people need to be treated. "We don't have great non-opioid pain treatments," Dr. Nelson said. "There are some, but they're not great. So many people wind up getting opioids to treat their most severe forms of pain. The threshold to get opiates is still too low. Particularly to get opioids for more than a dose or two. If you come in and you're in really bad pain, or you are post-operative, you need to get opioids for a day. Nobody's going to argue that. The problem is, the more you give somebody opioids, the more their chance of developing long-term opioid use, meaning dependence or hyperalgesia, which means that the pain gets worse because you're on a pain medicine. Not in spite of being on a pain medication. It's because you're on a pain medication."

At the same time, non-opioid medication treatments for pain are being developed. This is where Dr. Nelson believes good regulation can play an important role. "Regulation and accountability," he said. "The same accountability standards as hospitals, for example, in terms of quality metrics. With hospitals, we're always looking at outcomes and the metrics and benchmarks. We don't do that with these other programs. You have to hit this marker, but there's nothing that you are required to really do to maintain that, and we just have really poorly regulated addiction treatment programs."

Both the FDA and the CDC put out regulations, but those are often nonbinding resolutions, according to Dr. Nelson. Those agencies need to set regulations that are able to make drug companies and medical providers accountable for their practices. "There's so many drugs on the market and they just keep putting them out there," Dr. Nelson said. "The FDA is relatively powerless to do anything about it. They are a regulatory agency for determining whether or not a drug should be on the market, not whether or not we have too many drugs on the market. They don't really have the ability to do that.[228]

"If you have an oversight team on a local level that implements best practices," he said, "particularly evidence-based best practices, maybe that's a mechanism that we could take from the large governmental level down to a local level, through these opioid stewardship programs." Dr. Nelson said he had been working on trying to put something like that together.

"We're trying to say [that] at a local level you need to have a pain management SWAT team," he said. "An addiction treatment SWAT team that can come in, target, and manage the problem just like the antibiotics stewardships did when there were resistant bacteria developing in various different clinical practices. I like that model because it's been proven to work for antibiotics, and it might be part of the answer. [With] the opioid stewardship programs, [medical providers] can regulate opioid dosage on a more local, personalized level at their own institution or practice. As for people that run their own practice, there might need to be other mechanisms. If you're a private practitioner in the community, you might need a state-based regulatory stewardship program to monitor those people. It might be a good mechanism to sort of look at things both at a 20,000-foot view and then bring it down to the weeds level."[229]

Elsewhere doctors have been coming together to produce guidelines for opioid prescription and other medical practices concerning pain. Dr. David Tauben, chief of Pain Medicine for the University of Washington, has been in medicine since before the crisis began. Washington had a significant problem with opioids because in the 1990s, drug companies had told the medical community that their drugs were safe. The state workers' compensation program began to prescribe opioids for people hurt on the job. He and other doctors in Washington developed guidelines for the state. Washington wanted rules for what the compensation would and wouldn't pay for. As part of that effort, Tauben and his colleagues were able to assemble guidelines for both the prescription of opioids and pain treatment.

"It's a Washington State combined agency," Dr. Tauben said. "It had Medicaid, the Department of Corrections, just public employees folks. They set guidelines for care of the population that they're responsible for providing the health insurance for. They were called the Agency Medical Directors' Group. They brought in, through [Gary] Franklin's leadership, probably 30 people finally after we started to get going on this. Across the state of Washington, [they brought in] clinicians and academics. These agencies had the authority just on the basis of their standard rules for what they're going to pay for and what they're not. They're saying that if you're taking care of these populations, our experts have come up with these education guidelines."

But those were simply education guidelines. Things to be taught, not necessarily practiced. They weren't mandatory. In 2010, Washington State took some of those guidelines and turned them into law, becoming the first state to take such an action. "So I joined the telemedicine program where we're able to mentor, give educational guidelines just like we did in the beginning," Dr. Tauben said. "Let's hear about the case, inform about other things. Let's see what's better, and let's help to get control of dose[s], certainly. Don't go higher on the dose, and [offer] some measured, kind, humane, and empathic strategies to reduce those who were already on the high doses.[230] Certainly [don't] let people get a high dose again."

THE NEED FOR A MORE HOLISTIC TREATMENT FOR PAIN

One of the continuing problems Dr. Tauben sees, and one that was mentioned by Dr. Nelson as well, is that pain treatment still relies too heavily on opioids. Dr. Tauben now runs the University of Washington pain clinic originally opened by John Bonica. Bonica was the first to take a holistic approach to the treatment of pain, one of the first to understand pain as a biopsychosocial condition. The best way to treat pain, Dr. David Tauben says, is not with medication but with an array of treatments to assuage the many influences that can cause pain.

"That's behavioral and physical measures," Dr. Tauben said. "Exercise is an anti-inflammatory. Now we see it in advanced research work. It produces anti-inflammatory molecules when you exercise. Sleep is an anti-inflammatory and an analgesic. We know that now. Gathering your thoughts in a meditative state is an analgesic, reducing the salience of pain. How important is pain to you as an organism right now, and later, and even in your imagination? What is the meaning of that pain? That is an analgesic effect.

"That would be great to have learned as a medical student," he said. "And we're teaching them that now. We've reset the pendulum for the medical students to be wary, and hopefully to identify when their [patients] are addicted. To know when they are not, and to recognize better the non-pharmacological [treatments]," he said. "Patient education and self-management techniques are the most effective treatment for pain when it persists and persists in a way that reduces function. There are more than opioid strategies. So at the training end, big impact."

Yet his hope comes with a warning. "[For] the folks who are in practice right now, they're just getting hammered by guidelines and rules," Tauben said. "My fear [is] this could be doing wrong for taking care of pain." Doctors are now refusing to treat pain or have anything to do with opioids. "We're seeing that all around the country," he continued. "'Chronic pain, I don't take care of chronic pain. Pain medication, we don't prescribe any pain medications.' Physicians won't even go into the prescribing of opioids whatsoever. So the pendulum can swing to the point of doing great harm and increasing suffering needlessly. It's important to see shades of gray."[231]

THE DARTMOUTH-HANOVER MEDICAL CENTER TRIALS TO REDUCE OPIOID PRESCRIBING

Dr. Richard Barth[232] is a lead surgeon at Dartmouth-Hitchcock Medical Center in Lebanon, New Hampshire, and professor of surgery at the Geisel School of Medicine at Dartmouth.

"I'm a cancer surgeon, so I take care of patients with tumors of the breast, with pancreas cancer, with liver tumors, melanoma. Those are the type of patients that I see. As a surgeon who writes opioid prescriptions, I felt it behooved us to figure out how we could have an impact on this problem."

Dr. Barth continued: "We prescribe opioids for patients who have had surgery because we want to try to help them to get over the pain from their surgery. What studies have shown is that patients that are opioid-naive, that haven't taken opioids in the past but then have surgery, are at an increased risk of becoming long-term opioid users. Unused pills often end up being abused by other people. This is called diversion and can lead to addiction and overdose."

Dr. Barth decided a quantitative-use study was warranted. "We tried to figure out how many opioid pills are prescribed for the most common operations that we do. We went back to 2015 and looked at five of the most common operations that we performed. The lumpectomies for breast cancer, lumpectomies and lymph node removals, laparoscopic cholecystectomies, removing the gallbladder, and hernia repairs, both laparoscopic and open hernia repairs. We analyzed the five most common general surgical operations we performed. It was a total of about 650 patients, and all we did was look to see how many opioids they were prescribed after they had their surgery."

They found that some patients were prescribed five pills, while others were prescribed as many as a hundred opioid pills for one of the more serious operations. There was wide variation, and, in general, the average number was about 30 pills for each patient.

Dr. Barth continued, "Then we called the patients to find out how many pills they actually took. What we found was only about a quarter of the opioid pills that were being prescribed were taken by the patients. It was clear that we were overprescribing these opioids."

Dr. Barth said, "As physicians, we have the obligation to take care of our patients pain, and these opioids are prescriptions that you can't just call in a refill[for]. Patients have to come back in and get a refill, and especially when you're in a rural environment like we are, a lot of my patients come from a couple of hours away to have surgery. It's an effort to come back and get a refill. Therefore lots of times, doctors will just say, 'Make sure you give them enough pills so that it takes care of their pain and they don't have to come back.'"

Dr. Barth and his team came up with prescription guidelines stating, "For a partial mastectomy, five pills should be enough to satisfy 80 percent of the patients. For gallbladder removal, cholecystectomy, 15 pills should do the job." They published their results in the *Annals of Surgery*. Up until then, these guidelines did not exist.

They found that patients don't really need as many opioids as were normally dispensed after an operation. Dr. Barth's paper showed it was 53 percent less than what they would have prescribed if they had kept dispensing at their old rate. In fact, for all five of the operations, the number of opioids pills that were prescribed dramatically decreased to approximately half.

Dr. Barth concluded: "We were taking care of their pain just fine because less than 1 percent of the patients ended up needing an opioid refill. We were able to dramatically cut, by more than half, the number of opioids that were prescribed and we still took care of our patient's post-op pain."

Dr. Barth also educated surgeons about alternatives to opioids. Studies have revealed that the combination of acetaminophen, which is Tylenol, and ibuprofen, which comes in multiple forms like Advil and Motrin and Aleve, is actually much more effective than opioids for taking care of acute pain.

UNETHICAL RELATIONSHIPS AND THE FAILURE OF THE FDA

One of the issues with rules is the people tasked with making them. Often the people who make the rules are the very people those rules are meant to affect. Not surprising, the rules end up having little effect or leave easily exploitable loopholes, the "revolving door" between regulatory agencies and the companies they are supposedly regulating.

According to Dr. Kolodny, there are already a number of laws on the books that would have prevented much of the opioid crisis in the first place. "If the FDA had properly enforced [those laws] when Purdue introduced OxyContin, I don't think we'd have an epidemic today.

"The law is the Food, Drug, and Cosmetic Act," Dr. Kolodny said. "It's a law that says that drug companies can only promote their products for conditions where the products are proven safe and effective, and those conditions where they can demonstrate that the drug is safe and effective. That becomes the drug indication. You let drug companies promote their drugs for that on-label indication. For conditions where a drug is not proven to be safe and effective. Where the risks are likely to outweigh any potential benefits, those conditions or uses should not go on the drug label. You don't let drug companies promote for those conditions.

"Because if [the FDA] had properly enforced that law, they would have told Purdue, 'OxyContin sounds like a drug where the risks outweigh the benefits if it's being prescribed for some moderately painful

Comparison of Opioid Prescriptions Pre versus Post Provider Education:

Operation	Mean Number of Opioid Pills Prescribed (SD)			Median Number of Opioid Pills Prescribed		
	Pre	Post	Reduction	Pre	Post	Reduction
Partial Mastectomy (PM)	19.8	5.1	.74242424 = 74%	20	5	.75 = 75%
PM with sentinel Lymph Node Biopsy (PM SLNB)	23.7	9.6	.59493671 = 59%	20	10	.5 = 50%
Laparoscopic Cholecystectomy (LC)	35.2	19.4	.44886364 = 45%	30	15	.5 = 50%
Laparoscopic Inguinal Hernia Repair (LIH)	33.8	19.3	.42899408 = 43%	30	15	.5 = 50%
Open Inguinal Hernia Repair (IH)	33.2	18.3	.44879518 = 45%	30	15	.5 = 50%

"Mean" is the "average" where you add up all the numbers and then divide by the number of numbers.
"Median" is the "middle" value in the list of numbers.

Comparison of Opioid Prescriptions Pre versus Post Provider Education

COURTESY OF DR. DAVID BARTH

conditions. Unless you can prove that OxyContin is safe and effective for low back pain or headache or fibromyalgia, we can't let you promote for those conditions.' It was very clear that prescribing opioids, especially OxyContin, had taken off at a level much greater than could be clinically needed. There were clearly adverse public health consequences associated with that sharp increase in prescribing. Had the FDA started to enforce the law and started to limit other drug companies from putting their opioids on the market and promoting the same way, I don't think the epidemic would've gotten nearly as bad as it did. Instead, the FDA went in the opposite direction. They allowed the aggressive marketing. They made label changes that actually helped market for chronic pain, and they made it easier for other drug companies to get their opioids on the market," Dr. Kolodny said.

What followed was a steady stream of opioids all trying to compete with OxyContin's billion-dollar success. With the new drugs came a barrage of marketing campaigns, all of which said that their drugs were safe and effective, which was "like pouring fuel on a fire," Dr. Kolodny said. This was allowed to happen because of the close relationship between people in the FDA and the pharmaceutical industry. Dr. Kolodny mentioned Dr. Curtis Wright, the FDA doctor who shortly after overseeing

OxyContin's approval process was working at Purdue. "We've seen many different FDA regulators over the years, who've been involved in regulating analgesics, winding up leaving the FDA and taking jobs either directly for an opioid maker like Purdue or working as consultants in the industry. That's a big part of the problem," he said.

"Another part of the problem was just the individuals who happen to be running the analgesic division [at the FDA]," Dr. Kolodny said. "Bob Rappaport, and now his deputy, [who is] the new director, Sharon Hertz, were both extremely cozy with industry. I think we relied on the experts who were leading the campaign to increase prescribing."

FDA commissioners changed, and in the last years of the Obama administration, opioids were taken more seriously. Still, not enough action was taken. According to Dr. Kolodny, the FDA still hasn't taken effective steps to stem the crisis. During the Obama administration, a report was commissioned from the National Academy of Sciences considering a potential regulatory role for the FDA. The report came out under the new FDA commissioner for the Trump administration, Scott Gottlieb. While Gottlieb endorsed the report and stated the FDA was going to follow its recommendations, nothing has yet happened, according to Dr. Kolodny. "That's well over a year [ago] now, and he really hasn't made any of the changes that the report called for," Dr. Kolodny said.

"It's more of the same," he said. "You'll hear the FDA talk about what it can do that's really outside of its primary regulatory role. The commissioner's talking a lot about coming up with guidance on opioid prescribing for acute pain. That's his big thing. You're still seeing them focus on drug formulations, which don't really do very much. You're not seeing them fix the mistakes that they've made over the years. If they were to follow the recommendations of the National Academy of Sciences, they would stop approving new opioids right now because we can't handle the ones that we currently have.

"[The FDA] just recently approved a new opioid that's 10 times stronger than fentanyl, 500 times stronger than heroin. It's called

Dsuvia. If they'd do what the National Academy of Science recommended, they'd stop putting new opioids on the market, and they'd start going through the current opioids that are on the market and decide which should probably come off. They haven't done that yet, so the new FDA—well, there really is no new FDA," Dr. Kolodny said.

But Dr. Kolodny said doctors are prescribing less opioids. While that's an important first step, he still believes there are far too many opioids out there. Deaths from opioid prescriptions have gone down in some places, but at the same time, deaths from fentanyl have skyrocketed. Yet there has been an expansion of access to treatment, which has shown some positive effects. "I think that one other positive element, which may explain why deaths have stopped going up, is I think more Americans are beginning to access effective treatment," Dr. Kolodny said. "[This] means preventing more Americans from becoming opioid addicted. It means seeing that the millions that are addicted have access to effective treatment. We have a very long way to go on both fronts, but I think we're making progress. More Americans are beginning to access effective treatment. [We are] nowhere near where we need to be, but at least there's a trend that's in the right direction."

"DEALING WITH THIS issue is going to take a combination of measures. We need to limit exposure to the medications. We need better packaging and labeling. We also need consumer products regulations that will result in [pill] bottles that are safer for children. Children as young as four, five, six can get into a pill bottle with a safety cap. We also need to reduce prescribing in this country and tell parents what to do with the medications when they finish. Take them back to the pharmacy. Police stations are taking the medications as well. Treat them as objects of harm and make sure that children don't gain access to them." —**Dr. Julie Gaither, Yale School of Medicine**

CDC GUIDELINE FOR PRESCRIBING OPIOIDS FOR CHRONIC PAIN

Promoting Patient Care and Safety

THE US OPIOID OVERDOSE EPIDEMIC

The United States is in the midst of an epidemic of prescription opioid overdoses. The amount of opioids prescribed and sold in the US quadrupled since 1999, but the overall amount of pain reported by Americans hasn't changed. This epidemic is devastating American lives, families, and communities.

 40

More than 40 people die every day from overdoses involving prescription opioids.[1]

 **165K**

Since 1999, there have been over 165,000 deaths from overdose related to prescription opioids.[1]

 4.3M

4.3 million Americans engaged in non-medical use of prescription opioids in the last month.[2]

PRESCRIPTION OPIOIDS HAVE BENEFITS AND RISKS

Many Americans suffer from chronic pain. These patients deserve safe and effective pain management. Prescription opioids can help manage some types of pain in the short term. However, we don't have enough information about the benefits of opioids long term, and we know that there are serious risks of opioid use disorder and overdose—particularly with high dosages and long-term use.

R_x

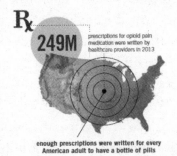 **249M**

prescriptions for opioid pain medication were written by healthcare providers in 2013

enough prescriptions were written for every American adult to have a bottle of pills

[1] Includes overdose deaths related to methadone but does not include overdose deaths related to other synthetic prescription opioids such as fentanyl.
[2] National Survey on Drug Use and Health (NSDUH), 2014

 **CDC**

U.S. Department of Health and Human Services
Centers for Disease Control and Prevention

LEARN MORE I www.cdc.gov/drugoverdose/prescribing/guideline.html

Part of an information packet from the CDC regarding new opioid prescription guidelines, 2016

CDC

THE NEED FOR EFFECTIVE PRESCRIPTION MONITORING PROGRAMS

Access to treatment has expanded over the past few years as communities scramble to cope with large numbers of addicts. Medical insurance companies have added treatment programs to their coverage, and more people are able to obtain the treatment they need. However, the coordination between medical providers is not what it should be. Dr. Sharon Walsh at the University of Kentucky School of Medicine said, "There are many different things that need to be done in order to address this epidemic. Many of these initiatives are already underway, but they're not widespread," she said. "We see the introduction of prescription monitoring programs that are improving across the country. [But] they don't all talk to each other online yet. So, for instance, if you have a prescription monitoring program, you can look and see what your patients are getting from other doctors. But it's not necessarily communicating with the states that are immediately surrounding yours. It's only partially helpful. We need to improve that. There's been some discussion about developing a federal system that would allow really comprehensive data set[s] to be collected and have it be [in] real time. That's another characteristic of the prescription monitoring programs—they're not necessarily always in real time; there's some lag time."

One of the issues that occurs when trying to tamp down the level of prescriptions is "doctor shopping." People who can't get the drugs they want from one doctor simply go to another who will prescribe them. Increased accountability is essential to combating further overprescribing. "One of the other things is education. Education targeted at basically all segments of society," Dr. Walsh said. "Certainly educating physicians. With the new CDC guidelines that have come out about pain prescribing, there is increased emphasis on education. Physicians who are treating opioid addiction already have required elements of education. I think that we need to do a better job of that. We need certainly to increase education of medical students. For a long time, addiction has been missing from the curriculum of medical education.

"I'll talk to doctors and I'll say, 'Do you have any patients who are addicted in your practice?' Sometimes they'll say, 'No, I never see anybody with addiction.' But the fact is, we know based on the epidemiological numbers that addiction is so widespread that every physician is seeing people with addiction. They're just not asking about it," Dr. Walsh said. "We really need to do a better job with regard to that and integrating the crosstalk between pain physicians and addiction physicians that has been lacking in the past. Another area is about education on when to prescribe and how much to prescribe."[233]

BETTER TREATMENTS AVAILABLE

In addition to better education and efforts at limiting prescriptions of opioids, there are also better treatments now available for opioid addiction. Methadone, which for many years was the go-to drug for medication-assisted treatment, is now slowly being replaced by buprenorphine. Buprenorphine has been shown to provide the same withdrawal suppression but without the draining effects of methadone. "We know from many studies that have been done in the United States and across the world that medication-assisted treatment, whether that be with buprenorphine products or with methadone, can be very effective in treating opioid addiction. In suppressing withdrawal, reducing illicit use, reducing injection behaviors, reducing criminal behaviors associated with ongoing drug use, and improving quality of life—that includes improving the ability of people to get their lives back together, to regain employment, to restore their relationships," Dr. Walsh said.

"I think that we're fortunate in the field of addiction because we have a really large science base that's been building for 40 or 50 years. We actually have evidence-based practices, and evidence-based medicine, just like in all other areas of medicine. I think it's very important that we look at the science and we look at the results of the controlled studies to determine what works and what doesn't work," Dr. Walsh said.

Still, for many in recovery, there's a stigma attached to medication-assisted treatment. Many view taking methadone or buprenorphine as exchanging one drug habit for another, even if one is far less damaging. But medication-assisted treatment, even with safer drugs like buprenorphine, should not be viewed as a panacea. There is no one simple cure to addiction, and proper treatment takes years of work on the part of both the addict and medical professionals. It is possible for buprenorphine to be abused, and doctors need to take care when prescribing it. "The other element that is being addressed is that we need to improve training for physicians," Dr. Walsh said. "[Physicians] need to really understand the pharmacology of buprenorphine, and what they can expect with respect to how it works for patients. Just as an example, if a physician adopts a one-size-fits-all type of dosing strategy, where they decide they're going to give the same dose to everybody, that actually sets up an opportunity for buprenorphine to be diverted. Not everyone needs the same dose. If a patient is receiving a dose that is higher than what they need, they can self-treat with that and still have medication left over. They can sell that if they choose to, which of course is illegal, but that may be one way that they're paying for their own treatment as well.

"There is a legitimate concern about the misuse or diversion of buprenorphine to people to whom it's not prescribed," Dr. Walsh said. "We know that because we have data on that. What the data generally shows us is that, when people are given a choice of what type of opioid to abuse, buprenorphine would be at the bottom of the list. It's not that well liked compared to other opioids like oxycodone or heroin, for example. However, we have really inadequate access to treatment. What we frequently see in studies that have looked at buprenorphine diversion is that it's going to somebody that it's not intended for. The reason that people often give for taking buprenorphine or buying buprenorphine off of the street is that they can't get access to treatment and that they're trying to basically self-treat. I think that a lot of the problems with buprenorphine diversion would be reduced if we could increase access for patients to actually receive treatment."

Doctors are currently working on new delivery systems for buprenorphine that will lower the risk for abuse and diversion. "We have a number of new products that are under development right now in the country, and we just recently had one approved by the FDA. [It's] an implant of buprenorphine that works for six months. These types of long-acting formulations, like implants or [birth control] injections, will completely eliminate the problem of buprenorphine diversion. Once the medication is inserted into the patient, that's where it's going to stay, and it's not going to be available for anyone else," Dr. Walsh said.[234]

A buprenorphine patch, Butrans, produced by Purdue Pharma, has been on the market since 2014. In 2017, the FDA approved a once-a-month buprenorphine injection called Sublocade. These medications are helping recovering addicts live normal lives again. Methadone, while effective, has serious side effects and requires people to go to clinics and stand in long lines after filling out paperwork. Delivery systems like the patch or once-a-month injections mean addicts can visit their doctor once a month (or possibly less) and not have to worry about suffering withdrawal.

But many are suspicious of MAT—and not wholly without reason. Harriet Rossetto of Beit T'Shuvah recovery center in Culver City voiced concern that MAT was being pushed by the same pharmaceutical companies that created the crisis in the first place. She pointed to the close relationship between the government and pharmaceutical companies in the past, which allowed the claim to be made that opioids were safe.

The close relationship between government and private industry is a consistent problem in American politics, and it's not unreasonable for people to be wary of solutions promoted by the very same people who caused the crisis to begin with. As noted above, Purdue is currently selling buprenorphine products aimed at combating opioid addiction. While there is significant evidence that MAT reduces drug recidivism and reduces rates of overdose, the medical community claimed that there was significant evidence to show that opioids were safe. It's perfectly understandable then for people who have been on the front lines of combating addiction to want to wash their hands of the whole industry and seek solutions elsewhere.

■ ■ ■

DESPITE THE DEBATE about how to best move forward, there's no doubt that there are solutions. The evidence that the problem of addiction is best solved by treatment, not the criminal justice system, has been prevalent for decades. Now it seems there is the political will to actually make the necessary changes needed to effectively address the crisis. The pharmaceutical industry will try their best to deflect blame and avoid responsibility. It is our responsibility as a society, whether we are personally affected by the crisis or not, to demand justice, to hold these companies and our politicians accountable for the damage done.

CHAPTER 14

Changing the Culture, Ending the Crisis

THROUGHOUT THIS BOOK we've laid out how the public was deceived and exploited for personal gain, even as hundreds of thousands died and countless more ruined their lives or watched loved ones suffer. The breadth of the deception is slowly but methodically being revealed, but its full extent may never be known. (For further information about the Sackler family's false claims, please visit the appendix for an excerpted review of the case against Purdue and the Sacklers by the State of Massachusetts.) The question is: What happens now?

There are hundreds of lawsuits currently pending, countless more in the wings. Communities all over the country have crafted their own solutions and come together to try and contain the damage, expanding the services offered at needle exchanges, having more places for addicts to go when they need help, and in general creating more resources to address the issues caused by the epidemic.

Yet despite these efforts, the data reveals that the problem is only getting worse. More people are becoming addicted, more drugs are flowing into the country, and the number of deaths from drug overdose remains very high. Alongside the record deaths from overdose, suicides in America have reached unprecedented levels.[235] Many of these suicides are a result of the traumas from opioid addiction.

It's clear that the delivery of misinformation about the "safety" of opioids on the part of Big Pharma fueled the rise in opioid addiction and overdose. But there was fertile ground for the epidemic to take hold in the United States. This crisis has penetrated all levels of American society. The areas hardest hit by the opioid epidemic were poor, isolated, vulnerable, and economically devastated. Appalachia, which many believe to have been specifically targeted by pharmaceutical companies, always had poor access to health care. Opioid pills were given as an alternative to broader, more encompassing health treatments, such as physical and talk therapy, to a population pressed for time and money. When those pills in turn fueled a wave of addiction, there were few treatment options available. People who needed help couldn't find it. They could, however, find more opioids. Drugs from both black-market drug dealers selling heroin or from barely legitimate "pain clinics," which provided prescriptions to whoever asked for one. At the time there were few to help them cope with addiction and drug dependency but plenty to make a profit off their suffering.

A LACK OF COMMUNITY AND DRIVE FOR CONSUMPTION

The opioid crisis hit places that had been earlier deprived of economic opportunity. These were places that felt they had been abandoned. Where once there had been factories with well-paying union jobs run by the standard bearers of American industry, there were now rusting hulks of metal. A grim reminder of a once prosperous past and a community forgotten by the outside world.

Many of the doctors we spoke to for the *Do No Harm* documentary and for this book pointed to a lack of community, the lack of a sense of belonging, a lack of hope. "What does it mean to live a meaningful life?"

Dr. Anna Lembke at Stanford University asked. "Because it's certainly not pleasuring yourself at all costs." We live in a society centered around consumption. There is a product for every aspect of human life. We are taught that in order to do something, we need to buy something. We have been conditioned to believe that there is an instant solution to all our problems if only we make the right consumer choice.

Yet, for many in America, those choices are often dangled just out of reach. If our culture is centered around consumption, then what does that say about people who don't have the ability to consume? Furthermore, consumer society is focused on the individual. Consumer products are rarely bought by groups. Individuals spend their money for a product to enhance their lives. Consumer choices are often framed as a means to greater community engagement, but the result is often the opposite: a sort of perverted, long-distance engagement that doesn't facilitate the kind of connection or empathy that face-to-face interactions do.

Combine this with a lack of opportunity and economic mobility, and you have a significant amount of the population feeling alone and isolated. Yet there is another consumer choice to "solve" that problem: substance abuse. At least in the beginning, drug abuse allows the user to feel different, to forget his or her problems, and to create a false sense of belonging. Drug abusers find a sense of community in one another, but the basis of that connection is not actual belonging but a common habit. Addiction's stranglehold on the brain ultimately leads the addict to put his or her own needs above all others, even to the point where he or she steals from, or even commits violence against, family and friends.

SEEING ADDICTION AS A DISEASE

For a long time in America, these behaviors were seen as the result of a poor individual choice and thus the response focused on punishing the individual. The doctors we spoke to stressed the receptivity in our culture to drug abuse; the need to understand addiction as a disease of the brain was the overwhelming message. Addicts lose control of themselves, and unless those issues are treated, the addict will simply repeat the same self-defeating actions again and again. Putting someone in a cell does nothing to address addiction. Prison is simply a very expensive way of getting an addict off the street for a time, only to have them return to the same environment.

Doctors we spoke to were emphatic that it be understood not only that addiction was a disease of the brain, but also that opioid addiction changed the brain in such a way that abstinence-only treatment leaves a person far more prone to relapse. It was stressed that medication-assisted treatment in conjunction with some kind of talk therapy were essential tools to an addict's recovery. Several doctors made the comparison to diabetes, where there is no cure in the normal sense of the word. It's not expected that a diabetic could ever end his or her insulin treatment. Likewise, we should think of MAT as a lifelong endeavor. Fortunately, medical advancements are making it possible that buprenorphine, the preferred drug for MAT, can be administered safely by the patients themselves and given in doses of a month at a time, possibly more. Addiction should be thought of as a condition to be managed rather than "cured."

CHANGING OUR SOCIETY'S CULTURAL NORMS TO EMBRACE COLLECTIVE WELFARE

Yet even with expanded access to treatment, better drugs, and greater awareness of the dangers of opioids, the public health crisis continues seemingly unabated. While rates of prescription opioids have dropped, the number of deaths from black-market drugs has risen. Heroin and fentanyl have created another crisis all their own, and for the first time in modern American history, life expectancy rates have declined. According to CDC director Robert Redfield, the decline is driven by opioid overdoses and suicides.[236]

The opioid crisis was allowed to flourish because of circumstances on the ground in American society. If there is to be a true reversal of the epidemic, then there must be an accompanying reversal in American culture. The sad fact of the matter is that, long before the rise of prescription opioids, social solidarity in America has been eroded, and with it, America's social safety net.

Institutions like public schools and social security were once taken for granted, based on the idea of the collective good. But the idea of collective responsibility for public welfare was challenged by people who asked, "Why should I pay for them?" The rhetoric of making the right consumer choice took over from the idea of collective welfare. People who didn't send their children to public schools and who didn't rely on government support questioned why they should pay for other people's needs. That philosophical approach deepened the fragmentation of community responsibility.

But viewing through the lens of consumer choice is a deeply flawed conception of society. One does pay for someone else, one way or another. It's just a matter of how and where that money is spent. As America's social welfare state was slowly eroded, the prison population exploded. The quality of public education deteriorated and with it the job prospects of many of America's youth. Poor educational opportunities mean diminished possibilities to escape poverty. The correlation between poverty and crime and substance abuse is extremely strong. The response was not the improvement of schools and communities but increased punishment and harsher sentences. Sentences that followed offenders for the rest of their lives, even after they had supposedly paid their debt to society through incarceration.

The irony is that police, prisons, courts, and all the rest of the infrastructure that goes into the criminal justice system is far more expensive than funding schools and providing support services. It has been repeated several times throughout this book that the best way to keep people off opioids is to never enable them to start. Prevention is far more effective, and cheaper, than intervention. Prevention through education at all levels. The same logic applies to society at large. Countries with significant funding for social services and public education have far fewer issues with crime and drug abuse. It's been shown time and again that prisoners who are offered education or technical training while incarcerated are far less likely to end up in prison again.[237]

The issue is that public education and welfare are often framed as a "handout." But prisons are government-funded housing, food, and utilities. Police are government-funded. Courts and parole officers are government-funded, but we don't view those as a "handout." We accept that you can't turn someone away from a hospital emergency room if they can't pay, and yet a public health-care system is seen by many as anathema to the American way of life. The fact is, we have an extremely robust public welfare system in America; it's just widely inefficient in its allocation of resources. America spends more on health care than any other developed country but fails many of those who need help the most.[238]

Thankfully, the pendulum is starting to swing back the other way. The problems caused by the erosion of America's social safety net combined with growing wealth inequality have begun to pile up, and Americans are starting to do something about it. Where once socialized medicine was heresy in American politics, "Medicare for all" has become a standard plank in the platform of many Democratic politicians. Even some Republicans have warmed to the idea because they've acknowledged that the current system is wasteful.[239] The need for treatment rather than punishment, in regard to both prisoners and addicts, has become the accepted wisdom across the political spectrum.

■ ■ ■

YET THE ISSUE remains that there is a lack of hope in American society, alongside feelings of isolation and disconnectedness.[240] We live in a culture that in turn has promoted greater isolation and alienation. Of course, these were not explicit efforts, just the unintended side effects of our modern society.

It's against this backdrop that the fight against the opioid epidemic takes place. It's not simply a matter of better understanding addiction or opioids. The fundamental roots of the crisis lie within our society and how we interact with one another. How we conceive of our society and of our collective future. Former British prime minister Margaret Thatcher once said, "There's no such thing as society. There are individual men and women and there are families."[241] We strongly believe this is fundamentally wrong and that humanity is so much more than individuals and families. Human beings have been social animals since the first human stood upright. The lack of responsibility toward community is precisely the kind of thinking that produced the conditions that allowed the opioid crisis to flourish.

This is not to say we are without choice. We must invest in ourselves and be responsible to our community. A true reversal of the opioid crisis must include a more radical change in America. The individual and society are not mutually exclusive; they are interdependent. We have to understand that if we work toward a common good, we will improve our own lives along the way. The communities that have been devastated by the opioid crisis have come to understand this. Programs that help, not punish, lead to fewer addicts, less crime, and less homelessness. Addiction is best treated through empathy and understanding, not through vilification.

The perception of addiction has taken too long to change. It wasn't until it reached all segments of our society that there was a significant response. It changed because the face of the crisis was suddenly familiar. No segment could look away and say the problem was theirs and not ours. It was only then that people actually began to listen to those who were suffering. To listen to the doctors and the former addicts and their families and friends who had been trying to tell them for so long that this was a disease and that compassion for all was a starting point for a cure.

EPILOGUE

SINCE COMPLETING THE original manuscript of *Do No Harm*, Purdue and the Sackler family have continued to come under increased scrutiny. In March 2019, Purdue reached a settlement with the State of Oklahoma totaling $270 million, money that will go toward funding research and paying for statewide recovery programs.[242] Purdue is facing so many lawsuits and potential payouts that the company is exploring filing for bankruptcy.

In March of 2019, New York attorney general Letitia James alleged in a legal complaint that as investigations against Purdue intensified, the company transferred hundreds of millions of dollars to members of the Sackler family through offshore accounts.[243] This was allegedly done in order to safeguard funds from legal action against the company.

Two months after the Oklahoma settlement was issued, Vermont attorney general TJ Donovan announced that the state was filing a suit against eight members of the Sackler family. "By suing the Sacklers separately, we'll be able to keep pressure on the most culpable family members, even if the filing in bankruptcy court should come as a corporation," Donovan said.[244] Vermont, along with 43 other states, has already filed suits against privately held Purdue.

Many of the institutions that bear the Sackler name—the latest being the Louvre—have ended their relationships with the family, declining any future gifts and distancing themselves from the family. The National Portrait Gallery and the Tate museum in London have both declined any future donations from the family, as have the Guggenheim and Metropolitan Museum of Art in New York City.[245]

In February 2019, protestors led by the performance artist and photographer Nancy Goldin, herself in recovery from opioid addiction sparked by the overprescribing of OxyContin, filled the Guggenheim's main hall with paper leaflets to symbolize Purdue's "blizzard of prescriptions." As a result, the museum announced that it was ending its relationship with the Sackler Trust.

David Sackler, son of Richard Sackler and member of the company's board of directors, has purchased a 10,000-square-foot Bel Air mansion for $22.5 million in cash.[246] David Sackler is the only member of the family's third generation to now sit on the Purdue Pharma board. He runs the investment firm for his family, according to the *New Yorker*.[247]

But while Purdue is contemplating bankruptcy in America, another company that the Sacklers control continues to make money from opioid painkillers overseas. Mundipharma, an association of companies started by Raymond and Mortimer Sackler in 1973[248] and still largely run by the Sackler family, has increased its sale of opioids in Europe and Asia.[249]

Meanwhile, states and local communities have stepped up their efforts to combat the crisis. As a result of a rare nonpartisan effort, new funds have been made available through the Department of Health and Human Services and its internal agency, the Substance Abuse and Mental Health Services Administration (SAMHSA), to states, territories, and Native American tribes.[250] Several states have tried to levy taxes on opioid pills in order to secure funds for combating opioid addiction, but only New York was able to pass such a bill. Intense lobbying efforts by Pharmaceutical Research and Manufacturers of America (PhRMA) led to bills in several states failing after making initial progress through state legislatures. New York's law is currently on hold pending a lawsuit. Because opioids are still prescribed, albeit in far less quantities, PhRMA was able to convince enough lawmakers that it was unfair to tax companies for a legitimate medical need.[251]

As the legal battles continue, new stories emerge almost daily. We, along with millions of others whose lives have been affected by the ongoing opioid and addiction crisis, wait for relief, justice, and closure.

DIRECTORY

American Academy of Pain Medicine (AAPM)

painmed.org

Originally named the American Academy of Algology. Compromised of physicians focused on pain medicine, which was not recognized as a distinct physician specialty until 1983.

American Board of Addiction Medicine (ABAM)

www.abam.net | (301) 656-3378

Offers board certification of addiction medicine physicians across a range of medical specialties. ABAM sets standards for physician education, assesses physicians' knowledge, and requires and tracks lifelong education.

American Medical Association (AMA)

www.ama-assn.org | 1-800-621-8335

Organization founded in 1847 that works to create a healthier future for patients, including advocating against racial and ethnic disparities in health care, scientific advancement, and standards for medical education. The AMA has played an important role in the development of US medicine, including developing a program of medical ethics and numerous initiatives focused on improving public health and public health policy.

American Society of Addiction Medicine (ASAM)

www.asam.org | (301) 656-3920

Representing more than 5,500 physicians, clinicians, and associated professionals in the field of addiction medicine and focused on increasing access and improving the quality of addiction treatment.

Automation of Reports and Consolidated Orders System (ARCOS)

www.deadiversion.usdoj.gov/arcos

An electronic data interchange program. Controlled-substance pharmaceutical manufacturers and distributors are required to report their transactions to the Drug Enforcement Administration (DEA) through an automated reporting system. Drugs are tracked from the point of manufacture through commercial distribution channels to point of sale and distribution at the dispensing/retail level.

Behavioral Health Association of Providers (BHAP)

https://bhap.us | (888) 958-2282

National membership association that provides educational resources, develops standards, and advocates for the advancement of quality and access in addiction treatment and behavioral health.

Beit T'Shuvah (Los Angeles)

beittshuvah.org | (310) 204-5200

Residential addiction treatment center and congregation combining the 12 steps with Judaism. Open to all seeking recovery.

Center for Substance Abuse Treatment (CSAT)

samhsa.gov/about-us/who-we-are/offices-centers/csat | (240) 276-1660

Unit within the Substance Abuse and Mental Health Services Administration (SAMHSA) to increase the availability of treatment and recovery services, including medication-assisted treatment (MAT). CSAT participates in SAMHSA's national outcomes reporting efforts.

Centers for Disease Control and Prevention (CDC)

cdc.gov | (404) 639-3311

Federal agency under the oversight of the US Department of Health and Human Services (HHS) that provides data, resources, and expertise to promote and protect public health from threats and to prevent injury and disease.

Centers for Medicare & Medicaid Services (CMS)

cms.gov | 1-800-633-4227

Federal agency within the US Department of Health and Human Services (HHS) that administers the Medicare program and works in partnership with state governments to administer Medicaid.

The Council on Recovery (Houston, Texas)

councilonrecovery.org | (713) 942-4100

At the forefront of helping individuals and families whose lives have been impacted by alcoholism, drug addiction, and co-occurring mental health disorders.

Drug Enforcement Administration (DEA)

dea.gov | (213) 621-6900

Unit of the US Department of Justice that enforces the Controlled Substances Act of 1970 (CSA), overseeing prescription narcotic distribution and illegal drug interdiction.

Facing Addiction With NCADD

facingaddiction.org | (212) 269-7797

A national nonprofit organization dedicated to finding solutions to the addiction crisis.

Food and Drug Administration (FDA)

fda.gov | (888) 463-6332

Federal agency within the US Department of Health and Human Services (HHS) that oversees the manufacturing and distribution of drugs, medical devices, food, tobacco, and other consumer products.

The Haven at College

thehavenatcollege.com/residence

Sober living home for college students in recovery, currently with branches at seven different universities.

Narcotics Anonymous/Heroin Anonymous (NA/HA)

na.org | heroinanonymous.org

International autonomous organization dedicated to recovery from narcotic/heroin use, abuse, and addiction through the 12 steps. NA/HA is nonprofessional, self-sustaining, and available globally through local meetings.

National Alliance on Mental Illness (NAMI)

nami.org | 1-800-950-6264

Nation's largest grassroots mental health organization dedicated to building better lives for the millions of Americans affected by mental illness.

National Alliance for Recovery Residences (NARR)

narronline.org | (855) 355-6277

Recovery community organization that works on improving access to quality recovery residences through developing standards, support services, placement, education, research, and advocacy.

National Council on Alcoholism and Drug Dependence (NCADD)

ncadd.org

Advocates for the interests of people struggling with or in recovery from alcoholism, drug addiction, and the consequences of alcohol and other drug use.

National Institute on Drug Abuse (NIDA)

drugabuse.gov | (301) 443-1124

Focused on advocating for science in the causes and consequences of drug use and addiction and applying to improve individual and public health through prevention and treatment of substance use disorders (SUDs) and enhancing public awareness of project on addiction.

National Institute of Mental Health (NIMH)

nimh.nih.gov

Supports research on mental disorders.

Prescription Drug Monitoring Program (PDMP)

cdc.gov/drugoverdose/pdmp

Electronic database that tracks controlled substance prescriptions and suspensions in each state for the purpose of identifying potential safety, risk, or abuse issues in access to medication.

Substance Abuse and Mental Health Services Administration (SAMHSA)

samhsa.gov | (877) 726-4727

Under the oversight of the Department of Health and Human Services (HHS) to reduce the impact of substance use disorders (SUDs) and mental illness by making information, services, and research available.

Veterans Health Administration (VHA)

va.gov/health

Largest integrated health-care system in the US, providing care to veterans enrolled in the VA health-care program.

Commonwealth of Massachusetts Hearing *vs.* Purdue Pharma

THE FOLLOWING EXCERPTS are from a lawsuit against Purdue Pharma by the State of Massachusetts. These examples reflect some of the most damning evidence against Purdue and its executives. The claims made here are the result of several years of research on the part of the Massachusetts attorney general's office and are supported by emails and other documents surrendered as part of that investigation. These are claims made by the attorney general and, as of this writing, have not yet been proven in court.

MAURA HEALY, ATTORNEY GENERAL
JANUARY 15, 2019 (RECEIVED)

EXCERPTS

18. Putting patients on opioids puts them at risk. Patients who take opioids at higher doses and for longer periods face higher and higher risk of addiction and death. Compared to our general population, Massachusetts patients who were prescribed opioids for more than a year were 51 times more likely to die of an opioid-related overdose.

19. Purdue took advantage of addiction to make money. For decades, physicians had reserved opioids for treating severe short-term pain, or

for patients near the end of life. But the tradition of limiting opioids to short-term treatment ended after Purdue introduced OxyContin and began marketing it and other opioids with deceptive claims.

20. OxyContin's sole active ingredient is oxycodone, a molecule nearly identical to heroin. Purdue later introduced another dangerous drug, Butrans, which releases opioids into the body from a skin patch. Then Purdue introduced Hysingla, which contains yet another opioid. Almost all of Purdue's business is selling opioids.

21. Since May 2007, Purdue has sold more than 70,000,000 doses of opioids in Massachusetts.

23. The people we lost worked as firefighters, homemakers, carpenters, truck drivers, nurses, hairdressers, fishermen, waitresses, students, mechanics, cooks, electricians, ironworkers, social workers, accountants, artists, lab technicians, and bartenders. They lived and died in every part of our state. The oldest died at age 87. The youngest started taking Purdue's opioids at 16 and died when he was 18 years old.

26. The White House Council of Economic Advisers determined that a middle estimate of the cost of each death from opioid overdose is $9.6 million. By that methodology, the 671 deaths that the Attorney General has already identified in Massachusetts total more than $6 billion.

27. Purdue targeted vulnerable people who could be introduced to its opioids, including elderly patients, veterans, and people who had never taken opioids before. Second, Purdue misled them to take higher and more dangerous doses. Third, Purdue deceived them to stay on its drugs for longer and more harmful periods of time.

33. Each of these in-person sales visits cost Purdue money—on average more than $200 per visit. But Purdue made that money back many

times over, because it convinced doctors to prescribe its addictive drugs. When Purdue identified a doctor as a profitable target, Purdue visited the doctor frequently: often weekly, sometimes almost every day. Purdue salespeople asked doctors to list specific patients they were scheduled to see and pressed the doctors to commit to put the patients on Purdue opioids. By the time a patient walked into a clinic, the doctor, in Purdue's words, had already "guaranteed" that he would prescribe Purdue's drugs. Purdue rewarded high-prescribing doctors with coffee, ice cream, catered lunches, and cash. Purdue has given meals, money, or other gifts to more than 2,000 Massachusetts prescribers.

40. Purdue promoted its opioids to Massachusetts patients with marketing that was designed to obscure the risk of addiction and even the fact that Purdue was behind the campaign. Purdue created a website, In the Face of Pain, that promoted pain treatment by urging patients to "overcome" their "concerns about addiction." Testimonials on the website that were presented as personal stories were in fact by Purdue consultants, whom Purdue had paid tens of thousands of dollars to promote its drugs.

2011-10-24 website capture, In the Face of Pain, PVT0033890–891.

41. Another Purdue publication, the Resource Guide for People with Pain, falsely assured patients and doctors that opioid medications are not addictive:

> "Many people living with pain and even some health-care providers believe that opioid medications are addictive. The truth is that when properly prescribed by a health-care professional and taken as directed, these medications give relief—not a 'high.'"

Resource Guide for People with Pain (2009), pg. 8, PVT0037321.

45. To promote its drugs, Purdue pushed the myth that addiction is a character flaw, and "trustworthy" people don't get addicted to drugs.

49. In Massachusetts, Purdue deceptively promoted opioids for elderly patients, veterans, patients who had never taken opioids, and patients with osteoarthritis—putting thousands more patients at risk.

55. To target veterans, Purdue funded a book, *Exit Wounds*, which was packaged as the story of a wounded veteran but was really part of Purdue's deceptive marketing campaign. The book repeated Purdue's lie that patients would not become addicted to opioids:

> "The pain-relieving properties of opioids are unsurpassed; they are today considered the 'gold standard' of pain medications, and so are often the main medications used in the treatment of chronic pain. Yet, despite their great benefits, opioids are underused. For a number of reasons, health-care providers may be afraid to prescribe them, and patients may be afraid to take them. At the core of this wariness is the fear of addiction, so I want to tackle this issue head-on . . . Long experience with opioids shows that people who are not predisposed to addiction are unlikely to become addicted to opioid pain medications."
>
> *Exit Wounds* (2009), pgs. 106-107, PTN000023114.

56. Purdue held special events to encourage doctors to prescribe opioids to veterans:

Purdue Flyer from 2011

57. Purdue's campaign to target veterans had a terrible cost. Compared to non-Massachusetts veterans, Massachusetts veterans are three times more likely to die from opioid overdose.

68. Purdue earns more money every time a patient moves to a higher dose. For example, Purdue's 2015 prices increased dramatically as patients moved to higher doses:

OxyContin Prices
(10 mg) bottle of 100 tablets $269.17
(15 mg) bottle of 100 tablets $396.28
(20 mg) bottle of 100 tablets $501.99
(30 mg) bottle of 100 tablets $698.15
(40 mg) bottle of 100 tablets $859.72
(60 mg) bottle of 100 tablets $1,217.22
(80 mg) bottle of 100 tablets $1,500.18

A patient taking the lowest dose pill twice a day for a week earns Purdue $38. But if the patient instead takes the highest dose, Purdue collects $210—an increase of 450 percent. Purdue knew its promotion drove patients to higher doses. Purdue's internal analysis "found that there is greater loss in the 60 mg and 80 mg strengths (compared to other strengths) when we don't make primary sales calls." Purdue's business plans emphasized that "OxyContin is promotionally sensitive, specifically with the higher doses, and recent research findings reinforce the value of sales calls." In 2014, when public health experts tried to save patients' lives by warning against high doses of opioids, Purdue pursued a "strategic initiative" to fight back and "maintain 2013 dose mix."
2013-08-19 OxyContin "Initiation, Conversion, and Titration" workshop, PWG000197635; 2013-09-23 OxyContin marketing plan, PWG000062680. 2013-09-23 OxyContin marketing plan, pgs. 35, 57, PWG000062688, -710.

75. Purdue analyzed, down to the last dollar, how much of its profit depended on patients taking higher doses of opioids. In the slide below, Purdue reminded staff that a shift to lower doses, which reduces the danger to patients, would be bad for Purdue's bottom line.

Impact of changes in dose mix
(For illustration purposes)

% shift from 20mg and 15mg down to 10mg

Dose	Forecast (Rx)	Forecast ($)	1% Shift		2% Shift	3% Shift
10 mg	1,226,840	$ 135,005,554	1,242,664	$ 136,746,931	$ 138,488,308	$ 140,229,686
15mg	180,831	$ 33,261,232	179,023	$ 32,928,620	$ 32,596,008	$ 32,263,395
20mg	1,401,616	$ 361,951,330	1,387,599	$ 358,331,817	$ 354,712,303	$ 351,092,790
30mg	519,945	$ 193,796,793	519,945	$ 193,796,793	$ 193,796,793	$ 193,796,793
40mg	1,085,624	$ 577,483,835	1,085,624	$ 577,483,835	$ 577,483,835	$ 577,483,835
60mg	436,272	$ 326,705,155	436,272	$ 326,705,155	$ 326,705,155	$ 326,705,155
80mg	768,198	$ 931,583,802	768,198	$ 931,583,802	$ 931,583,802	$ 931,583,802
Total	5,619,324	$ 2,559,787,701	5,619,324	$ 2,557,576,952	$ 2,555,366,204	$ 2,553,155,456

$2,210,748

$4,421,496

$6,632,244

A small shift of roughly 15K prescriptions from 20mg or 15mg down to 10mg has a $2MM impact

Marketing

PURDUE

2012-08-14 OxyContin ACAM Presentation, slide 28, PWG00062610.

76. When the US Centers for Disease Control issued a national warning against the highest and most dangerous doses of opioids, Purdue studied prescription data to calculate how much profit it would lose if doctors followed the CDC's advice. Purdue determined that the amount at stake in Massachusetts was $23,964,122—that was the extra revenue that Purdue was getting from the most dangerous doses of opioids, every year, in Massachusetts alone.

2016-04-13 April Board meeting Commercial Update, slide 74, PPLPC016000286167.

83. Purdue knew its campaign to push higher doses of opioids was wrong. Doctors on Purdue's payroll admitted in writing that pseudo-addiction was used to describe "behaviors that are clearly characterized as drug abuse" and put Purdue at risk of "ignoring" addiction and "sanctioning abuse." But Purdue nevertheless urged doctors to respond to signs of addiction by prescribing higher doses of Purdue's drugs.

84. Just as Purdue made more money by pushing patients to higher doses, Purdue increased its profits by keeping patients on drugs for longer periods of time. Long-term opioid use causes addiction and death. But for Purdue, keeping patients on drugs longer meant more profits. So Purdue deceived doctors and patients to stay on its drugs longer.

85. According to Purdue's 2015 price list, a patient taking Purdue's 80 mg OxyContin pill twice a day for a week earned Purdue $210. If that same patient could be kept on the drug for a year, Purdue collected far more money: $10,959.

2015-01-12 Price Increase Notification, PWG000045843.

93. One of Purdue's most powerful tactics to keep patients on opioids longer was an opioid savings card that gave patients discounts on their first prescriptions. Discounts could have cut Purdue's revenue if patients took opioids for a short time. But Purdue's internal 10-year plan highlighted its discovery that opioid savings cards kept patients on opioids longer: "more patients remain on OxyContin after 90 days." Purdue determined that opioid savings cards worked like the teaser rate on a long-term and very high-stakes mortgage. According to Purdue's internal analysis, the savings cards had the highest "return on investment" in the entire "OxyContin Marketing Mix." The return on investment for Purdue was 4.28, so that every $1,000,000 Purdue gave away in savings came back to Purdue as $4,280,000 in revenue because patients stayed on dangerous opioids longer.

2012-11-01 Board report, pg. 31, PWG000414917.

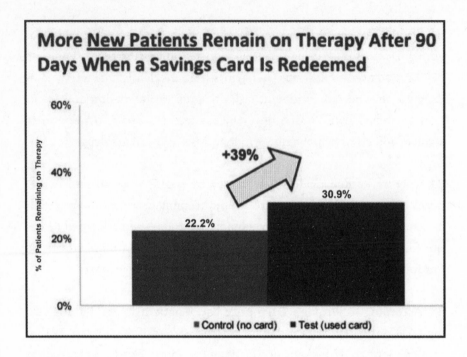

Purdue internal strategy presentation from 2011

2011-12-06 Manager's Meeting Presentation, slide 13, PWG003840379.

94. Keeping more patients on opioids for longer than 90 days was one of Purdue's "2011 Highlights."[38] Purdue's directors and CEO were briefed specifically on "emails targeted towards HCPs [health-care professionals] practicing in Massachusetts" to push opioid savings cards. But it was a public health disaster. The Massachusetts Department of Public Health found that patients who stayed on prescription opioids for more than 90 days were thirty times more likely to die of an overdose.

2012-02-15 10-Year Plan, slide 33, PWG000164240.

2012-11-01 Board report, pg. 17, PWG000413518.

97. Purdue's campaign to "extend average treatment duration" succeeded. A national study of tens of thousands of medical and pharmacy claims records published in the *Journal of General Internal Medicine* found that two-thirds of patients who took opioids for 90 days were still

taking opioids five years later.

Martin et al., Long-term chronic opioid therapy discontinuation rates from the TROUP study. J Gen Intern Med. 2011;26(12):1450-7. Summarized in Purdue's files on pg. 15, PWG000226034.

100. Purdue made deceptive claims about research by its own employees, designed to "highlight" the risks of non-opioid drugs. Purdue deceptively compared the risks of high doses of acetaminophen and NSAIDs (non-steroidal anti-inflammatory drugs, such as aspirin and ibuprofen) with its claim that opioids have "no ceiling dose," to falsely contend that opioids were safer, even though high doses of opioids pose grave risk of addiction and death.

101. Purdue paid for deceptive propaganda by groups designed to appear independent from Purdue, promoting the message that NSAIDs and Tylenol have "life-threatening" side effects, but opioids are "the gold standard of pain medications."

2009 Exit Wounds, pg. 104-106, PTN000023113-114.

106. Purdue also devised and funded third-party publications to say that opioids give patients the "quality of life we deserve."

Treatment Options: A Guide for People Living with Pain, pg. 15, PWG000243995.

109. Purdue further created an unbranded marketing initiative, Opioids with Abuse Deterrent Properties, to encourage prescribers to switch to Purdue opioids. The initiative included a website, ads in medical journals, medical education events touting the benefits of the tamper-resistant drugs, and payments to doctors to promote Purdue opioids.

Introducing Opioids with Abuse-Deterrent Properties (OADP), PVT0024614.

116. Purdue's top targets prescribed Purdue opioids to more of their patients, at higher doses, and for longer periods of time. Compared to Massachusetts doctors and nurses who prescribed Purdue opioids

without seeing reps, Purdue's top targets were at least ten times more likely to prescribe Purdue opioids to patients who overdosed and died.

174. Purdue launched OxyContin in 1996. It became one of the deadliest drugs of all time. The FDA scientist who evaluated OxyContin wrote in his original review: "Care should be taken to limit competitive promotion." The Sacklers did not agree. See, e.g., 2016-03-15 telebriefing by CDC Director Tom Frieden ("We know of no other medication that's routinely used for a nonfatal condition that kills patients so frequently . . . those who got the highest doses of opioids, more than 200 MMEs per day had a 1 in 32 chance of dying in just 2 1/2 years . . . almost all the opioids on the market are just as addictive as heroin."), available at www.cdc.gov/media/releases/2016/t0315-prescribing-opioids-guidelines html.

1995-10 Overall Conclusion to 1995 FDA review, Curtis Wright, #785793.1.

175. At the OxyContin launch party, Richard Sackler spoke as the Senior Vice President responsible for sales. He asked the audience to imagine a series of natural disasters: an earthquake, a volcanic eruption, a hurricane, and a blizzard. He said: "the launch of OxyContin Tablets will be followed by a blizzard of prescriptions that will bury the competition. The prescription blizzard will be so deep, dense, and white . . ." Over the next twenty years, the Sacklers made Richard's boast come true. They created a man-made disaster. Their blizzard of dangerous prescriptions buried children and parents and grandparents across Massachusetts, and the burials continue.

PKY180280951.

176. From the beginning, the Sacklers were behind Purdue's decision to deceive doctors and patients. In 1997, Richard Sackler, Kathe Sackler, and other Purdue executives determined—and recorded in secret internal correspondence—that doctors had the crucial misconception that OxyContin was weaker than morphine, which led them to prescribe

OxyContin much more often, even as a substitute for Tylenol.[65] In fact, OxyContin is more potent than morphine. Richard directed Purdue staff not to tell doctors the truth, because the truth could reduce OxyContin sales. 1997-06-12 email from Richard Sackler, PDD8801141848 (Staff reported: "Since oxycodone is perceived as being a 'weaker' opioid than morphine, it has resulted in OxyContin being used much earlier for non-cancer pain. Physicians are positioning this product where Percocet, hydrocodone, and Tylenol with Codeine have been traditionally used. Since the non-cancer pain market is much greater than the cancer pain market, it is important that we allow this product to be positioned where it currently is in the physician's mind." Richard Sackler replied: "I think you have this issue well in hand. If there are developments, please let me know.");

1997-05-28 email from Richard Sackler PDD1508224773; 1997-04-23 email from Richard Sackler, PDD1701801141.

1997-06-12 email from Richard Sackler, PDD8801141848; 1997-05-28 email from Richard Sackler PDD1508224773; 1997-04-23 email from Richard Sackler, PDD1701801141.

187. As Purdue kept pushing opioids and people kept dying, the company was engulfed in a wave of investigations by state attorneys general, the DEA, and the US Department of Justice. In 2003, Richard Sackler left his position as President of Purdue. After a few more years of investigation, Jonathan, Kathe, and Mortimer Sackler resigned from their positions as Vice Presidents. But those moves were for show. The Sacklers kept control of the company. Their family owned Purdue. They controlled the Board. They paid themselves the profits. And, as alleged in detail below, they continued to direct Purdue's deceptive marketing campaign.

2018-09-05 declaration of Jonathan Sackler; 2018-09-08 declaration of Kathe Sackler; 2018-09-06 declaration of Mortimer Sackler.

190. The Sacklers voted to admit in an Agreed Statement Of Facts that, for more than six years, supervisors and employees intentionally

deceived doctors about OxyContin: "Beginning on or about December 12, 1995, and continuing until on or about June 30, 2000, certain Purdue supervisors and employees, with the intent to defraud or mislead, marketed and promoted OxyContin as less addictive, less subject to abuse and diversion, and less likely to cause tolerance and withdrawal than other pain medications."

2007-05-09 Agreed Statement of Facts, paragraph 20, available at https://www. documentcloud.org/documents/279028-purdue-guilty-plea.

193. Finally, the Sacklers voted to enter into a Consent Judgment in this Court ("2007 Judgment"). The 2007 Judgment ordered that Purdue "shall not make any written or oral claim that is false, misleading, or deceptive" in the promotion or marketing of OxyContin. The judgment further required that Purdue provide fair balance regarding risks and benefits in all promotion of OxyContin. That judgment required fair balance about the risks of taking higher doses for longer periods and the risks of addiction, overdose, and death.

2007-05-15 Consent Judgment, Commonwealth v. Purdue Pharma L.P. et al., No. 07-1967(B), Mass. Super. Ct.

195. The 2007 Judgment and related agreements should have ended the Sacklers misconduct for good. Instead, the Sacklers decided to break the law again and again, expanding their deceptive sales campaign to make more money from more patients on more dangerous doses of opioids.

196. From the 2007 Judgment to 2018, the Sacklers controlled Purdue's deceptive sales campaign. They directed the company to hire hundreds more sales reps to visit doctors thousands more times. They insisted that sales reps repeatedly visit the most prolific prescribers. They directed reps to encourage doctors to prescribe more of the highest doses of opioids. They studied unlawful tactics to keep patients on opioids longer and then ordered staff to use them. They asked for detailed reports about doctors suspected of misconduct, how much money Purdue made from them,

and how few of them Purdue had reported to the authorities. They some-times demanded more detail than anyone else in the entire company, so staff had to create special reports just for them. Richard Sackler even went into the field to promote opioids to doctors and supervise reps face to face.

214. In preparation for an upcoming Board meeting, Richard Sackler instructed staff to give him the spreadsheets underlying their sales analysis, so that he could do his own calculations. The spreadsheets showed that, in 2007, Purdue expected to collect more than half its total revenue from sales of 80 mg OxyContin—its most powerful, most profitable, and most dangerous pill.

2007-10-28 email from Richard Sackler, PPLPC012000159168.

2007-10-28 attachment to email from Edward Mahony, PPLPC012000159170.

217. Staff also told the Sacklers that Purdue received 689 Reports of Concern about abuse and diversion of Purdue's opioids in Q4 2007, and they conducted only 21 field inquiries in response. Staff also reported to the Sacklers that they received 83 tips to Purdue's compliance hotline during the quarter, but Purdue did not report any of them to the authorities.

2008-01-15 Board report, pg. 16, 24, PDD8901733989, -997.

228. The Sacklers learned that another company was planning clinical research to test whether crush-proof opioids are safer for patients.[132] Mor-timer Sackler suggested that Purdue conduct similar studies to find out whether reformulated OxyContin was really safer before selling it to mil-lions of patients. He wrote to Richard Sackler: "Purdue should be leading the charge on this type of research and should be generating the research to support." By 2008, Purdue was working on a crush-proof reformula-tion of OxyContin to our formulation. "Why are we playing catch up . . . ? Shouldn't we have studies like this . . . ?" The Sacklers decided not to do the research because they wanted the profits from a new product,

regardless of whether the deaths continued. Richard didn't want a paper trail, so he instructed Mortimer to call him, and CEO John Stewart met with his staff to plan how to phrase a carefully worded reply.

2008-02-07 email from Robert Kaiko, PPLPC013000244844.

2008-02-12 email from Richard Sackler, PPLPC013000244843.

229. Meanwhile, staff gave Jonathan, Kathe, Mortimer, and Richard Sackler projections indicating that OxyContin sales could plateau. Mortimer demanded answers to a series of questions about why sales would not grow. Richard chimed in at 8:30 p.m. to instruct the staff to find answers "before tomorrow." Staff emailed among themselves about how the Sacklers' demands were unrealistic and harmful and then decided it was safer to discuss the problem by phone.

2008-02-26 email from Edward Mahony, PPLPC012000172585; attachment PPLPC012000172587.

2008-02-26 email from Mortimer Sackler, PPLPC12000172674.

2008-02-26 email from Richard Sackler, PPLPC12000172674.

2008-02-26 email from John Stewart, PPLPC012000172677.

237. On April 18, 2008 Richard Sackler sent Kathe, Ilene, David, Jonathan, and Mortimer Sackler a secret memo about how to keep money flowing to their family. Richard wrote that Purdue's business posed a "dangerous concentration of risk." After the criminal investigations that almost reached the Sacklers, Richard wrote that it was crucial to install a CEO who would be loyal to the family: "People who will shift their loyalties rapidly under stress and temptation can become a liability from the owners' viewpoint." Richard recommended John Stewart for CEO because of his loyalty. Richard also proposed that the family should either sell Purdue in 2008 or, if they could not find a buyer, milk the profits out of the business and "distribute more free cash flow" to themselves.

2008-04-18 email and attached memo from Richard Sackler, PDD9316300629-631.

Op+ions

| 10 mg | 15 mg | 20 mg | 30 mg | 40 mg | 60 mg | 80 mg |

TABLETS NOT ACTUAL SIZE

Through a wide range of tablet strengths, OxyContin® provides options to meet the individual therapeutic needs of your appropriate patient

- Q12h dosing with as few as 2 tablets per day
- When converting from other opioids, the 7 OxyContin, Tablet strengths enable you to closely approximate the calculated conversion dose
- OxyContin• is a single-entity opioid
- You can adjust your patient's dose every 1 to 2 days, if needed, because steady-state plasma concentrations are approximated within 24 to 36 hours

2009 Marketing Campaign

337. In February, 2001 staff reported to the Sacklers that law enforcement was increasingly concerned about lawbreaking by drug companies and the resulting "danger to public safety." Staff also told the Sacklers that Purdue was receiving a rising volume of hotline calls and other compliance matters, reaching an all-time high during Q4 2010. Staff reported to the Sacklers that sales reps had engaged in improper promotion of Purdue opioids, but the company had decided not to report the violations to the government. Staff also reported to the Sacklers about the risks of OxyContin, including that 83 percent of patients in substance abuse treatment centers began abusing opioids by swallowing pills, and that it took, on average, 20 months for a patient to get treatment.

2001-02-03 Board meeting materials, slide 48, PDD8901468062.

340. In April, 2011 the Sacklers met with Sales VP Russell Gasdia to talk about sales. He told them that OxyContin was the best-selling painkiller in America, with more than three billion dollars in annual sales—almost double the second-place drug.

2011-04-14 Board presentation, PPLP004405866, -880.

356. Richard Sackler indeed went into the field to promote opioids to doctors alongside a sales rep. When he returned, Richard argued to the Vice President of Sales that a legally required warning about Purdue's opioids wasn't needed. He asserted that the warning "implies a danger of untoward reactions and hazards that simply aren't there." Richard insisted there should be "less threatening" ways to describe Purdue opioids.

2011-07-20 email from Richard Sackler, PPLPC001000091102.

360. In July 2011, staff assured the Sacklers that Purdue prohibited sales reps from writing their sales pitches to prescribers in email. The Sacklers believed that promoting opioids in oral conversations with doctors and banning employee email, would protect them from investigations of their misconduct.

2011-07-21 Board meeting presentation, PPLP004406488-490.

391. That same month, the Sacklers voted to set Purdue's budget for Sales and Promotion for 2013 at $312,563,000. Staff told the Sacklers that Purdue employed 622 sales reps and, during Q3 2012, they visited prescribers 180,723 times.

Exhibit 1. 2013-01-07 [440] 2013-01-07 Staff told the Sacklers that they continued to reinforce the "Individualize The Dose" program. Staff told the Sacklers that the sales rep visits target for the quarter of 199,466 visits; and that reps visited 7.0 prescribers per day, on average, target of 7.1.

396. In March 2013, staff reported to the Sacklers on the devastation caused by prescription opioids. Staff told the Sacklers that drug overdose

deaths had more than tripled since 1990—the period during which Purdue had made OxyContin the best-selling painkiller. Staff told the Sacklers that tens of thousands of deaths were only the "tip of the iceberg." Staff reported that, for every death, there were more than a hundred people suffering from prescription opioid dependence or abuse.

2013-03-21 Board presentation, PPLP004409513-514.

406. Staff also reported to the Sacklers that they had trained Purdue's sales reps to use new sales materials designed to get patients on higher doses of opioids for longer periods. Staff told the Sacklers that Purdue employed 634 sales reps and, during Q2 2013, they visited prescribers 177,773 times.

2013-07-23 Board report, pgs. 11, 12, 59, PPLPC012000433398.

414. In October 2013, Mortimer Sackler pressed for more information on dosing and "the breakdown of OxyContin market share by strength." Staff told the Sacklers that "the high dose prescriptions are declining," and "there are fewer patients titrating to the higher strengths from the lower ones." In response to the Sacklers' insistent questions, staff explained that sales of the highest doses were not keeping up with the Sacklers' expectations because some pharmacies had implemented "good faith dispensing" policies to double-check prescriptions that looked illegal and some prescribers were under pressure from the DEA.

2013-10-28 email from David Rosen, PPLPC012000448832-833.

2013-10-28 email from David Rosen, PPLPC012000448833.

437. That February 2014 report was the last of its kind. After Q4 2013, Purdue abolished the detailed Quarterly Reports that had created a paper trail of targets for sales visits and been emailed among the Board and staff. In 2013, the City of Chicago served Purdue with a subpoena seeking internal documents about Purdue's marketing of opioids. The Sacklers continued to demand information about sales tactics, and their control of Purdue's deceptive marketing did not change.

2015-11-20 email from Robert Josephson, PPLP004153099; 2013-04-24 email from Burt Rosen, PPLPC012000419813.

442. In 2012, the *Los Angeles Times* had studied coroner's records and revealed that overdoses killed thousands of patients who were taking opioids prescribed by their doctors, refuting the Sacklers' lie that patients who are prescribed opioids don't get addicted and die. The next year, the *Los Angeles Times* revealed that Purdue tracked illegal sales of OxyContin with a secret list of 1,800 doctors code-named Region Zero, but did not report them to the authorities. The "mitigation effort" that the Sacklers ordered was not designed to protect patients from over-doses or from illegal prescribers, but instead to protect the Sacklers from reporters revealing the truth.

2012-11-11 "Legal drugs, deadly outcomes," by Scott Glover and Lisa Girion.

2013-08-11 "OxyContin maker closely guards its list of suspect doctors," by Scott Glover and Lisa Girion.

471. In April 2016, the Sacklers considered exactly how much money was riding on their strategy of pushing higher doses of opioids. The month before, the US Centers for Disease Control announced guide-lines to try to slow the epidemic of opioid overdose and death. The CDC urged prescribers to avoid doses higher than 30 mg of Purdue's OxyCon-tin twice per day. The CDC discouraged twice-a-day prescriptions of all three of Purdue's most profitable strengths—40 mg, 60 mg, and 80 mg. Staff studied how much money Purdue was making from its high-dose strategy and told the Sacklers that $23,964,122 was at risk in Massa-chusetts each year.

2016-04-13 Q1 2016 Commercial Update, slide 74, PPLPC016000286167.

472. In May 2016, Richard Sackler told staff to circulate a *New York Times* story reporting that opioid prescriptions were dropping for the first time since Purdue launched OxyContin twenty years earlier. The *Times* wrote: "Experts say the drop is an important early signal that the

Critical Shifts in The National Discussion about Pain And Opioids

From	To
Undertreatment of Pain	Opioid Epidemic
Abuse	Addiction
Criminal	Victim
FDA	CDC
Benefits Outweigh Risks	Lack of Long-Term Evidence
ADFs as Part of Solution	ADF Value Unproven

2016 Mid-Year Board Update

long-running prescription opioid epidemic may be peaking, that doctors have begun heeding a drumbeat of warnings about the highly addictive nature of the drugs." The only person quoted in favor of more opioid prescribing was a Massachusetts professor whose program at Tufts University was funded by the Sacklers.

2016-05-21 email from Richard Sackler, PPLPC021000841074; 2016-05-20. "Opioid Prescriptions Drop for First Time in Two Decades," by Abby Goodnough and Sabrina Tavernise. The opioid advocate was Dr. Daniel B. Carr, director of Tufts Medical School's program on pain research education and policy.

474. That same month, staff presented the 2016 Mid-Year Update. They warned the Sacklers that shifts in the national discussion of opioids threatened their plans. The deception that Purdue had used to conceal the risks of opioids was being exposed. Staff summarized the problems on a slide:

2016-06-08 Mid-Year Update, slide 18, PPLPC011000099783.

478. Fourth, the Sacklers had long sought to hide behind the approval of Purdue's drugs by the FDA. But FDA approval could not protect the Sacklers when their deceptive marketing led thousands of patients to become addicted and die. The US Centers for Disease Control ("CDC") reported that opioids were, indeed, killing people. The CDC Director said: "We know of no other medication that's routinely used for a non-fatal condition that kills patients so frequently." The 2016 Mid-Year Update warned that the truth was threatening Purdue so frequently."

2016-03-15 briefing by CDC Director Tom Frieden.

488. Staff felt the pressure of the opioid epidemic, even if the billionaire Sacklers did not. In one presentation, staff came close to insubordination and told the Sacklers: "Purdue Needs a New Approach." Their suggestion for a new direction was: "A New Narrative: Appropriate Use."

A New Narrative:
Appropriate Use

The Sacklers led Purdue so far into the darkness that employees proposed "appropriate use" of drugs to reinvent the company. Staff also suggested that the Sacklers create a family foundation to help solve the opioid crisis.

2017-06 Board of Directors: Purdue Mid-Year Pre-Read, slides 36-38, PPLPC011000151189.

489. The Sacklers did not redirect the company toward appropriate use or create the suggested family foundation. Instead, they decided to sell harder. For 2018, the Sacklers approved a target for sales reps to visit prescribers 1,050,000 times—almost double the number of sales visits they had ordered during the heyday of OxyContin in 2010.

2017-06 Board of Directors: Purdue Mid-Year Pre-Read, slides 36-38, PPLPC011000151189.2017-06 Board of Directors: Purdue Mid-Year Pre-Read, slide

147, PPLPC011000151189.

491. On October 17, 2017, Beverly Sackler served her last day on the Board. It was the beginning of the end for the Sackler family. A week later, *The New Yorker* published an article entitled "The Family That Built an Empire of Pain." The story quoted a former FDA Commissioner: "the goal should have been to sell the least dose of the drug to the smallest number of patients." The reporter concluded: "Purdue set out to do exactly the opposite."

2017-10-23 email from Robert Josephson, PPLPC016000318910.2017-10-23 email from Robert Josephson, PPLPC016000318910.

497. On June 12, 2018, the Massachusetts Attorney General filed this suit to hold the Sacklers as well as Purdue accountable. Just as their employees predicted, the Sacklers tried to run. Richard Sackler was the first to go: He resigned from the Board in July. David Sackler quit in August. Theresa Sackler served her last day in September. As of the date of this filing, Ilene, Jonathan, Kathe, and Mortimer remain.

2018-09-05 declaration of David Sackler; 2018-09-07 declaration of Theresa Sackler.

CONCLUSION

831. Holding the defendants accountable is important because of the people they hurt in Massachusetts and because of the defendants' selfish, deliberate choice to break the law. Purdue's leaders knew more than anyone about their addictive drugs. They knew how to get people addicted, how to keep people addicted, and how to collect the most money from the patients who were trapped on their opioids. They used the powers of a billion-dollar corporation to engineer an opioid epidemic.

832. As Purdue's scheme unraveled, in the fall of 2017, Purdue CEO Landau wrote down notes about the opioid crisis. He wrote:

288) DO NO HARM: THE OPIOID EPIDEMIC

"There are:

Too many Rxs being written

Too high a dose

For too long

For conditions that often don't require them

By doctors who lack the requisite training in how to use them appropriately."

833. Craig Landau knew he was building an epidemic the whole time. He joined Purdue in 1999. He helped make OxyContin a billion-dollar drug. His life's work is getting too many people on opioids, at doses that are too high, for far too long.

834. The opioid epidemic is not a mystery to the people who started it. The defendants knew what they were doing.

2017-09-18 email from Craig Landau, PPLPC021000904935.

Maura Healy

Attorney General

State of Massachusetts

PURDUE LETTER TO DR. GARY FRANKLIN

One Stamford Forum
Stamford, CT 06901-3431
www.purduepharma.com

Via Electronic Transmission: mcgs235@lni.wa.gov

May 9, 2007

Gary Franklin, MD, MPH
Chair, Agency Medical Directors Group
Washington State Department of Labor & Industries
PO Box 44321
Olympia, WA 98504-4321

RE: Washington State Interagency Guideline on Opioid Dosing for Chronic Non-Cancer Pain

Dear Dr. Franklin:

This letter is being submitted in response to your recently published *Interagency Guideline on Opioid Dosing for Chronic Non-Cancer Pain*. Purdue Pharma L.P., a privately held pharmaceutical company founded by physicians, is focused on the needs of patients. We are known for our pioneering research on persistent pain, a principal cause of human suffering, and we have extensive experience with clinical issues concerning pain management due to our portfolio of pain medications. We appreciate your efforts to improve patient care and safety when using opioids to treat chronic pain and we share in this goal through extensive educational endeavors and publications. However, we are concerned that some of the restrictions you have placed on opioid prescribing are too stringent and may interfere with access to appropriate and effective pain care for persons suffering from chronic pain.

While deaths involving prescription-opioid analgesics constitute a serious public health problem that needs to be prevented, limiting access to opioids for persons with chronic pain is not the answer. More often accidental deaths involving opioid analgesics are due to abuse or misuse of opioids and not due to the therapeutic use of opioids for chronic pain.[1] Efforts to prevent drug abuse should not prevent patients from getting the treatment they need.

According to your guideline, "high-dose" opioid treatment is a total daily dose of opioid exceeding 120 mg of oral morphine equivalents. For OxyContin® (oxycodone HCl controlled-release) Tablets, this would mean that doses above 40 mg every 12 hours

---

[1] Sabel J. Draft Washington State injury and violence prevention plan. Draft chapter on poisoning. Revised Jan 3, 2007. Department of Health website. Available at: http://www.doh.wa.gov/hsqa/emstrauma/injury/pubs/icpg/default.htm. Accessed March 14, 2007.

Dedicated to Physician and Patient

would be considered "high dose" and should "rarely" be prescribed, and then only after consultation with a pain specialist. The safety and efficacy of OxyContin doses greater than 40 mg every 12 hours in patients with chronic nonmalignant pain has been established in several randomized, controlled clinical trials.[2,3,4] Additionally, a recently published study evaluated the use of OxyContin for up to 36 months in 219 patients with osteoarthritic pain, low back pain, and diabetic neuropathic pain. In this long-term study, the daily dose of OxyContin ranged from 10 mg to 293.5 mg (mean 52.5 mg/day). At entry into this study, 8% and 5% of the patients used daily doses of OxyContin in the range of 80 mg to 99 mg and 100 mg or more, respectively.[5] The clinical rationale for choosing this oral morphine equivalent cutoff dose in the guideline is, therefore, unclear to us. We are concerned that patients requiring more than 40 mg every 12 hours of OxyContin may be undertreated while they are waiting for consultations with pain specialists, as required by the guideline. On your website <http://www.agencymeddirectors.wa.gov/Files/painmanagement.pdf> there is currently a list of 11 pain management specialists in Washington. While we realize this is not an all-inclusive list and that there are probably more pain specialists in Washington, there still may be a limited number of pain specialists available for patients to get the required consultations in a timely manner.

Furthermore, the guideline states that in patients taking more than one opioid, the morphine equivalent dose calculation is based on the dose of all opioids prescribed. Patients on modified-release opioids are often prescribed an immediate-release opioid for breakthrough pain on a p.r.n. basis. Patients may use one rescue dose on one day and maybe two rescue doses on another day and on other days may not require any supplemental analgesia. As such, the daily dose of the opioid for morphine equivalent dose calculation may vary from day to day. The stringent opioid dosing recommendations in the guideline may prevent clinicians from prescribing the recommended supplemental analgesia in order to avoid reaching the dose cutoff and, as a result, patients may suffer from undertreatment of incident or breakthrough pain. Additionally, patients may be considered as using morphine equivalents of greater than 120 mg/day based solely on maximum prescribed amount and not on actual use.

One of the recommendations for assessing the effects of opioid treatment is the use of urine drug testing. The guideline states that a positive result should be interpreted with caution. We agree that urine drug testing may be useful in patients prescribed opioids to help monitor treatment adherence. However, we would like to emphasize that when using urine testing to assess adherence, negative results should also be interpreted with caution. It is well documented in the medical literature that false-negative immunoassay

---

[2] Markenson JA, Croft J, Zhang PG, Richards P. Treatment of persistent pain associated with osteoarthritis with controlled-release oxycodone tablets in a randomized controlled clinical trial. *Clin J Pain*. 2005;21(6): 524-535.
[3] Gimbel JS, Richards P, Portenoy RK. Controlled-release oxycodone for pain in diabetic neuropathy - A randomized controlled trial. *Neurology*. 2003;60(6):927-934.
[4] Zautra AJ, Smith BW. Impact of controlled-release oxycodone on efficacy beliefs and coping efforts among osteoarthritis patients with moderate to severe pain. *Clin J Pain*. 2005;21(6):471-477.
[5] Portenoy RK, Farrar JT, Backonja MM, et al. Long-term use of controlled-release oxycodone for noncancer pain: results of a 3-year registry study. *Clin J Pain*. 2007;23(4):287-299.

Purdue

screening results may occur in patients being treated with synthetic or semi-synthetic opioids such as OxyContin.[6,7,8,9] This may occur due to the standard cutoff values used in many immunoassays, which may be too high to detect levels of oxycodone in urine, due to minimal cross-reactivity of those immunoassays that are calibrated for morphine and codeine detection with synthetic or semi-synthetic opioid analgesics. A negative immunoassay result means that at the time of specimen collection, concentrations for the substance tested were below the threshold limits required for a positive result, or substances in the urine are not being detected by the immunoassay due to specificity of the test. The recommendation in the guideline to discontinue opioids if a patient "fails" a drug test may result in discontinuation of opioids in adherent patients with legitimate medical need for taking opioid analgesics for chronic pain.

The guideline goes further to state that before seeking pain management consultation for morphine equivalent doses above 120 mg/day, one of the conditions that should be met is that the prescriber must ensure that there is no evidence of drug-seeking behaviors. Pseudoaddiction is a term which has been used to describe patient behaviors that may occur when pain is undertreated.[10] It involves the misinterpretation of relief-seeking behaviors due to un- or under-treated pain as drug-seeking behaviors as might be encountered with an abuser. Misunderstanding of these signs may lead the clinician to inappropriately discontinue opioids. In the setting of unrelieved pain, the request for increases in drug dose requires careful assessment, renewed efforts to manage pain, and avoidance of stigmatizing labels. The possibility of pseudoaddiction as the reason for the drug-seeking behaviors is not addressed in the recommendations and instead you imply that these patients should be weaned off of opioids.

Part II of your guidance mentions that opioid treatment may produce significant adverse effects and this is a reason to discontinue opioids. While we agree that an opioid should be discontinued if it causes significant adverse effects that are not otherwise manageable, this does not preclude a trial of another opioid. Some patients appear to tolerate one opioid better than another and it is often useful to try a different opioid if the first is poorly tolerated. Also, some patients respond better to one opioid versus another. Genetic heterogeneity in the nociceptive pathways and in drug metabolism may contribute to the variability in patient responses to opioid analgesics.[11,12,13,14] If a patient

[6] Elias M. Oxycodone in non-malignant pain: Drug diversion or laboratory error. *Pain Clin.* 2001;13(2): 163-164.
[7] Von Seggern RL, Fitzgerald CP, Adelman LC, Adelman JU. Laboratory monitoring of OxyContin (oxycodone): Clinical pitfalls. *Headache.* 2004;44(1):44-47.
[8] Fishman SM, Wilsey B, Yang J, Reisfield GM, Bandman TB, Borsook D. Adherence monitoring and drug surveillance in chronic opioid therapy. *J Pain Symptom Manage.* 2000;20(4):293-307.
[9] Gourlay DL, Heit HA, Caplan YH. Urine drug testing in clinical practice: dispelling the myths and designing strategies. Available at: http://www.familydocs.org/assets/171_UDT%202006.pdf. Accessed April 5, 2007.
[10] American Academy of Pain Medicine, American Pain Society, American Society of Addiction Medicine. Definitions Related to the Use of Opioids for the Treatment of Pain, 2001.
[11] Galer BS, Coyle N, Pasternak GW, Portenoy RK. Individual variability in the response to different opioids: report of five cases. *Pain.* 1992;49:87-91.
[12] Sinatra R. Opioid analgesics in primary care: Challenges and new advances in the management of noncancer pain. *J Am Board Fam Med.* 2006; 19(2):165-77.

3

Purdue

does not appear to obtain reasonable analgesia despite increasing doses of one opioid, many experts recommend that another should be tried.[15]

Highlighted above are some important clinical issues with chronic opioid therapy that we believe need more focus in the guidelines for opioid dosing. We realize that this is an educational pilot program and would appreciate your consideration of these issues as you assess the clinical effectiveness of this guideline. If you need any additional information or would like to discuss any of these concerns, please feel free to contact me.

Sincerely,

Lally Samuel, RPh, MS
Assoc. Director, Medical Services
(203) 588-8165

J. David Haddox, DDS, MD
VP, Risk Management & Health Policy

Enclosure:
OxyContin [package insert]. Stamford, CT: Purdue Pharma LP.

[13] Lotsch J, Starke C, Liefhold J, Geisslinger G. Genetic predictors of the clinical response to opioid analgesics: Clinical utility and future perspectives. *Clin Pharmacokinet.* 2004;43(14):983-1013.
[14] Jackson KC, Lipman AG. Opioid analgesics. In: Lipman AG, ed. *Pain Management for Primary Care Clinicians.* Bethesda, MD: American Society of Health-System Pharmacists; 2004.
[15] American Pain Society. *Guideline for the Management of Pain in Osteoarthritis, Rheumatoid arthritis, and Juvenile Chronic Arthritis.* Glenview, IL: American Pain Society; 2002:83,89.

4

(OXYCODONE HCI CONTROLLED-RELEASED TABLETS)
10 mg 20 mg 40 mg 80 mg 160 mg*
*(80 mg and 160 mg for use in opioid-tolerant patients only)

GT003673-E 00P017

WARNING:

OxyContin is an opioid agonist and a Schedule II controlled substance with an abuse liability similar to morphine.

Oxycodone can be abused in a manner similar to other opioid agonists, legal or illicit. This should be considered when prescribing or dispensing OxyContin in situations where the physician or pharmacist is concerned about an increased risk of misuse, abuse, or diversion.

OxyContin Tablets are a controlled-release oral formulation of oxycodone hydrochloride indicated for the management of moderate to severe pain when a continuous, around-the-clock analgesic is needed for an extended period of time.

OxyContin Tablets are NOT intended for use as a prn analgesic.

OxyContin 80 mg and 160 mg Tablets ARE FOR USE IN OPIOID-TOLERANT PATIENTS ONLY. These tablet strengths may cause fatal respiratory depression when administered to patients not previously exposed to opioids.

OxyContin TABLETS ARE TO BE SWALLOWED WHOLE AND ARE NOT TO BE BROKEN, CHEWED, OR CRUSHED. TAKING BROKEN, CHEWED, OR CRUSHED OxyContin TABLETS LEADS TO RAPID RELEASE AND ABSORPTION OF A POTENTIALLY FATAL DOSE OF OXYCODONE.

DESCRIPTION

OxyContin® (oxycodone hydrochloride controlled-release) Tablets are an opioid analgesic supplied in 10 mg, 20 mg, 40 mg, 80 mg, and 160 mg tablet strengths for oral administration. The tablet strengths describe the amount of oxycodone per tablet as the hydrochloride salt. The structural formula for oxycodone hydrochloride is as follows:

$C_{18}H_{21}NO_4 \cdot HCl$ MW 351.83
The chemical formula is 4, 5α-epoxy-14-hydroxy-3-methoxy-17-methylmorphinan-6-one hydrochloride.

Oxycodone is a white, odorless crystalline powder derived from the opium alkaloid, thebaine. Oxycodone hydrochloride dissolves in water (1 g in 6 to 7 mL). It is slightly soluble in alcohol (octanol water partition coefficient 0.7). The tablets contain the following inactive ingredients: ammonio methacrylate copolymer, hypromellose, lactose, magnesium stearate, polyethylene glycol 400, povidone, sodium hydroxide, sorbic acid, stearyl alcohol, talc, titanium dioxide, and triacetin.

The 10 mg tablets also contain: hydroxypropyl cellulose.

The 20 mg tablets also contain: polysorbate 80 and red iron oxide.

The 40 mg tablets also contain: polysorbate 80 and yellow iron oxide.

The 80 mg tablets also contain: FD&C blue No. 2, hydroxypropyl cellulose, and yellow iron oxide.

The 160 mg tablets also contain: FD&C blue No. 2 and polysorbate 80.

CLINICAL PHARMACOLOGY

Oxycodone is a pure agonist opioid whose principal therapeutic action is analgesia. Other members of the class known as opioid agonists include substances such as morphine, hydromorphone, fentanyl, codeine, and hydrocodone. Pharmacological effects of opioid agonists include anxiolysis, euphoria, feelings of relaxation, respiratory depression, constipation, miosis, and cough suppression, as well as analgesia. Like all pure opioid agonist analgesics, with increasing doses there is increasing analgesia, unlike with mixed agonist/antagonists or non-opioid analgesics, where there is a limit to the analgesic effect with increasing doses. With pure opioid agonist analgesics, there is no defined maximum dose; the ceiling to analgesic effectiveness is imposed only by side effects, the more serious of which may include somnolence and respiratory depression.

Central Nervous System

The precise mechanism of the analgesic action is unknown. However, specific CNS opioid receptors for endogenous compounds with opioid-like activity have been identified throughout the brain and spinal cord and play a role in the analgesic effects of this drug.

Oxycodone produces respiratory depression by direct action on brain stem respiratory centers. The respiratory depression involves both a reduction in the responsiveness of the brain stem respiratory centers to increases in carbon dioxide tension and to electrical stimulation.

Oxycodone depresses the cough reflex by direct effect on the cough center in the medulla. Antitussive effects may occur with doses lower than those usually required for analgesia.

Oxycodone causes miosis, even in total darkness. Pinpoint pupils are a sign of opioid overdose but are not pathognomonic (e.g., pontine lesions of hemorrhagic or ischemic origin may produce similar findings). Marked mydriasis rather than miosis may be seen with hypoxia in the setting of OxyContin® overdose (See **OVERDOSAGE**).

Gastrointestinal Tract And Other Smooth Muscle

Oxycodone causes a reduction in motility associated with an increase in smooth muscle tone in the antrum of the stomach and duodenum. Digestion of food in the small intestine is delayed and propulsive contractions are decreased. Propulsive peristaltic waves in the colon are decreased, while tone may be increased to the point of spasm resulting in constipation. Other opioid-induced effects may include a reduction in gastric, biliary and pancreatic secretions, spasm of sphincter of Oddi, and transient elevations in serum amylase.

Cardiovascular System

Oxycodone may produce release of histamine with or without associated peripheral vasodilation. Manifestations of histamine release and/or peripheral vasodilation may include pruritus, flushing, red eyes, sweating, and/or orthostatic hypotension.

Concentration – Efficacy Relationships

Studies in normal volunteers and patients reveal predictable relationships between oxycodone dosage and plasma oxycodone concentrations, as well as between concentration and certain expected opioid effects, such as pupillary constriction, sedation, overall "drug effect", analgesia and feelings of "relaxation".

As with all opioids, the minimum effective plasma concentration for analgesia will vary widely among patients, especially among patients who have been previously treated with potent agonist opioids. As a result, patients must be treated with individualized titration of dosage to the desired effect. The minimum effective analgesic concentration of oxycodone for any individual patient may increase over time due to an increase in pain, the development of a new pain syndrome and/or the development of analgesic tolerance.

Concentration – Adverse Experience Relationships

OxyContin® Tablets are associated with typical opioid-related adverse experiences. There is a general relationship between increasing oxycodone plasma concentration and increasing frequency of dose-related opioid adverse experiences such as nausea, vomiting, CNS effects, and respiratory depression. In opioid-tolerant patients, the situation is altered by the development of tolerance to opioid-related side effects, and the relationship is not clinically relevant.

As with all opioids, the dose must be individualized (see **DOSAGE AND ADMINISTRATION**), because the effective analgesic dose for some patients will be too high to be tolerated by other patients.

PHARMACOKINETICS AND METABOLISM

The activity of OxyContin Tablets is primarily due to the parent drug oxycodone. OxyContin Tablets are designed to provide controlled delivery of oxycodone over 12 hours.

Breaking, chewing or crushing OxyContin Tablets eliminates the controlled delivery mechanism and results in the rapid release and absorption of a potentially fatal dose of oxycodone.

Oxycodone release from OxyContin Tablets is pH independent. Oxycodone is well absorbed from OxyContin Tablets with an oral bioavailability of 60% to 87%. The relative oral bioavailability of OxyContin to immediate-release oral dosage forms is 100%. Upon repeated dosing in normal volunteers in pharmacokinetic studies, steady-state levels were achieved within 24-36 hours. Dose proportionality and/or bioavailability has been established for the 10 mg, 20 mg, 40 mg, 80 mg, and 160 mg tablet strengths for both peak plasma levels (Cmax) and extent of absorption (AUC). Oxycodone is extensively metabolized and eliminated primarily in the urine as both conjugated and unconjugated metabolites.

The apparent elimination half-life of oxycodone following the administration of OxyContin® was 4.5 hours compared to 3.2 hours for immediate-release oxycodone.

Absorption

About 60% to 87% of an oral dose of oxycodone reaches the central compartment in comparison to a parenteral dose. This high oral bioavailability is due to low pre-systemic and/or first-pass metabolism. In normal volunteers, the $t^{1/2}$ of absorption is 0.4 hours for immediate-release oral oxycodone. In contrast, OxyContin Tablets exhibit a biphasic absorption pattern with two apparent absorption half-lives of 0.6 and 6.9 hours, which describes the initial release of oxycodone from the tablet followed by a prolonged release.

Plasma Oxycodone by Time

Dose proportionality has been established for the 10 mg, 20 mg, 40 mg, and 80 mg tablet strengths for both peak plasma concentrations (Cmax) and extent of absorption (AUC) (see Table 1 below). Another study established that the 160 mg tablet is bioequivalent to 2 x 80 mg tablets as well as to 4 x 40 mg for both peak plasma concentrations (Cmax) and extent of absorption (AUC) (see Table 2 below). Given the short half-life of elimination of oxycodone from OxyContin®, steady-state plasma concentrations of oxycodone are achieved within 24-36 hours of initiation of dosing with OxyContin Tablets. In a study comparing 10 mg of OxyContin every 12 hours to 5 mg of immediate-release oxycodone every 6 hours, the two treatments were found to be equivalent for AUC and Cmax, and similar for Cmin (trough) concentrations. There was less fluctuation in plasma concentrations for the OxyContin Tablets than for the immediate-release formulation.

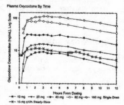

TABLE 1
Mean [% coefficient variation]

Regimen/ Dosage Form	AUC (ng·hr/mL)†	Cmax (ng/mL)	Tmax (hrs)	Trough Conc. (ng/mL)
Single Dose				
10 mg OxyContin	100.7 [26.0]	10.6 [20.1]	2.7 [44.1]	n.a.
20 mg OxyContin	207.5 [35.9]	21.4 [36.6]	3.2 [57.9]	n.a.
40 mg OxyContin	423.1 [33.3]	39.3 [34.0]	3.1 [77.4]	n.a.
80 mg OxyContin*	1085.5 [32.5]	98.5 [32.1]	2.1 [52.3]	n.a.
Multiple Dose				
10 mg OxyContin Tablets q12h	103.6 [38.6]	15.1 [31.0]	3.2 [69.5]	7.2 [48.1]
5 mg immediate-release q6h	99.0 [35.2]	15.5 [28.6]	1.6 [49.7]	7.4 [50.9]

TABLE 2
Mean [% coefficient variation]

Regimen/ Dosage Form	AUC— (ng·hr/mL)†	Cmax (ng/mL)	Tmax (hrs)	Trough Conc. (ng/mL)
Single Dose				
4x40 mg OxyContin*	1935.3 [34.7]	152.0 [28.6]	2.56 [42.5]	n.a.
2x80 mg OxyContin*	1959.3 [30.1]	153.4 [25.1]	2.78 [59.3]	n.a.
1x160 mg OxyContin*	1856.4 [30.5]	156.4 [24.8]	2.54 [36.4]	n.a.

†for single-dose AUC=AUC₀-inf; for multiple-dose AUC=AUC₀-τ

*data obtained while volunteers received naltrexone which can enhance absorption.

OxyContin® is NOT INDICATED FOR RECTAL ADMINISTRATION. Data from a study involving 21 normal volunteers show that OxyContin Tablets administered per rectum resulted in an AUC 39% greater and a Cmax 9% higher than tablets administered by mouth. Therefore, there is an increased risk of adverse events with rectal administration.

Food Effects

Food has no significant effect on the extent of absorption of oxycodone from OxyContin. However, the peak plasma concentration of oxycodone increased by 25% when a OxyContin 160 mg Tablet was administered with a high-fat meal.

Distribution

Following intravenous administration, the volume of distribution (Vss) for oxycodone was 2.6 L/kg. Oxycodone binding to plasma protein at 37°C and a pH of 7.4 was about 45%. Once absorbed, oxycodone is distributed to skeletal muscle, liver, intestinal tract, lungs, spleen, and brain. Oxycodone has been found in breast milk (see **PRECAUTIONS**).

Metabolism

Oxycodone hydrochloride is extensively metabolized to noroxycodone, oxymorphone, and their glucuronides. The major circulating metabolite is noroxycodone with an AUC ratio of 0.6 relative to that of oxycodone. Noroxycodone is reported to be a considerably weaker analgesic than oxycodone. Oxymorphone, although possessing analgesic activity, is present in the plasma only in low concentrations. The correlation between oxymorphone concentrations and opioid effects was much less than that seen with oxycodone plasma concentrations. The analgesic activity profile of other metabolites is not known.

The formation of oxymorphone, but not noroxycodone, is mediated by cytochrome P450 2D6 and, as such, its formation can, in theory, be affected by other drugs (see **Drug-Drug Interactions**).

Excretion

Oxycodone and its metabolites are excreted primarily via the kidney. The amounts measured in the urine have been reported as follows: free oxycodone up to 19%; conjugated oxycodone up to 50%; free oxymorphone 0%; conjugated oxymorphone ≤ 14%; both free and conjugated noroxycodone have been found in the urine but not quantified. The total plasma clearance was 0.8 L/min for adults.

Special Populations

Elderly

The plasma concentrations of oxycodone are only nominally affected by age, being 15% greater in elderly as compared to young subjects.

Gender

Female subjects have, on average, plasma oxycodone concentrations up to 25% higher than males on a body weight adjusted basis. The reason for this difference is unknown.

Renal Impairment

Data from a pharmacokinetic study involving 13 patients with mild to severe renal dysfunction (creatinine clearance <60 mL/min) show peak plasma oxycodone and noroxycodone concentrations 50% and 20% higher, respectively, and AUC values for oxycodone, noroxycodone, and oxymorphone 60%, 50%, and 40% higher than normal subjects, respectively. This is accompanied by an increase in sedation but not by differences in respiratory rate, pupillary constriction, or several other measures of drug effect. There was an increase in $t^{1}/_{2}$ of elim-

ination for oxycodone of only 1 hour (see **PRECAUTIONS**).

Hepatic Impairment

Data from a study involving 24 patients with mild to moderate hepatic dysfunction show peak plasma oxycodone and noroxycodone concentrations 50% and 20% higher, respectively, than normal subjects. AUC values are 95% and 65% higher, respectively. Oxymorphone peak plasma concentrations and AUC values are lower by 30% and 40%. These differences are accompanied by increases in some, but not other, drug effects. The $t^{1}/_{2}$ elimination for oxycodone increased by 2.3 hours (see **PRECAUTIONS**).

Drug-Drug Interactions (see PRECAUTIONS)

Oxycodone is metabolized in part by cytochrome P450 2D6 to oxymorphone which represents less than 15% of the total administered dose. This route of elimination may be blocked by a variety of drugs (e.g., certain cardiovascular drugs including amiodarone and quinidine as well as polycyclic anti-depressants). However, in a study involving 10 subjects using quinidine, a known inhibitor of cytochrome P450 2D6, the pharmacodynamic effects of oxycodone were unchanged.

Pharmacodynamics

A single-dose, double-blind, placebo- and dose-controlled study was conducted using OxyContin® (10, 20, and 30 mg) in an analgesic pain model involving 182 patients with moderate to severe pain. Twenty and 30 mg of OxyContin were superior in reducing pain compared with placebo, and this difference was statistically significant. The onset of analgesic action with OxyContin occurred within 1 hour in most patients following oral administration.

CLINICAL TRIALS

A double-blind placebo-controlled, fixed-dose, parallel group, two-week study was conducted in 133 patients with chronic, moderate to severe pain, who were judged as having inadequate pain control with their current therapy. In this study, 20 mg OxyContin q12h but not 10 mg OxyContin q12h decreased pain compared with placebo, and this difference was statistically significant.

INDICATIONS AND USAGE

OxyContin Tablets are a controlled-release

oral formulation of oxycodone hydrochloride indicated for the management of moderate to severe pain when a continuous, around-the-clock analgesic is needed for an extended period of time.

OxyContin is **NOT** intended for use as a prn analgesic.

Physicians should individualize treatment in every case, initiating therapy at the appropriate point along a progression from non-opioid analgesics, such as non-steroidal anti-inflammatory drugs and acetaminophen to opioids in a plan of pain management such as outlined by the World Health Organization, the Agency for Healthcare Research and Quality (formerly known as the Agency for Health Care Policy and Research), the Federation of State Medical Boards Model Guidelines, or the American Pain Society.

OxyContin is not indicated for pain in the immediate postoperative period (the first 12-24 hours following surgery), or if the pain is mild, or not expected to persist for an extended period of time. OxyContin is only indicated for postoperative use if the patient is already receiving the drug prior to surgery or if the postoperative pain is expected to be moderate to severe and persist for an extended period of time. Physicians should individualize treatment, moving from parenteral to oral analgesics as appropriate. (See American Pain Society guidelines.)

CONTRAINDICATIONS

OxyContin® is contraindicated in patients with known hypersensitivity to oxycodone, or in any situation where opioids are contraindicated. This includes patients with significant respiratory depression (in unmonitored settings or the absence of resuscitative equipment), and patients with acute or severe bronchial asthma or hypercarbia. OxyContin is contraindicated in any patient who has or is suspected of having paralytic ileus.

WARNINGS

OXYCONTIN TABLETS ARE TO BE SWALLOWED WHOLE, AND ARE NOT TO BE BROKEN, CHEWED OR CRUSHED. TAKING BROKEN, CHEWED OR CRUSHED OXYCONTIN TABLETS LEADS TO RAPID RELEASE AND ABSORPTION OF A POTENTIALLY FATAL DOSE OF OXYCODONE.

OxyContin 80 mg and 160 mg Tablets ARE FOR USE IN OPIOID-TOLERANT PATIENTS

ONLY. These tablet strengths may cause fatal respiratory depression when administered to patients not previously exposed to opioids.

OxyContin 80 mg and 160 mg Tablets are for use only in opioid-tolerant patients requiring daily oxycodone equivalent dosages of 160 mg or more for the 80 mg tablet and 320 mg or more for the 160 mg tablet. Care should be taken in the prescribing of these tablet strengths. Patients should be instructed against use by individuals other than the patient for whom it was prescribed, as such inappropriate use may have severe medical consequences, including death.

Misuse, Abuse and Diversion of Opioids

Oxycodone is an opioid agonist of the morphine-type. Such drugs are sought by drug abusers and people with addiction disorders and are subject to criminal diversion. Oxycodone can be abused in a manner similar to other opioid agonists, legal or illicit. This should be considered when prescribing or dispensing OxyContin in situations where the physician or pharmacist is concerned about an increased risk of misuse, abuse, or diversion.

OxyContin has been reported as being abused by crushing, chewing, snorting, or injecting the dissolved product. These practices will result in the uncontrolled delivery of the opioid and pose a significant risk to the abuser that could result in overdose and death (see **WARNINGS** and **DRUG ABUSE AND ADDICTION**).

Concerns about abuse, addiction, and diversion should not prevent the proper management of pain.

Healthcare professionals should contact their State Professional Licensing Board, or State Controlled Substances Authority for information on how to prevent and detect abuse or diversion of this product.

Interactions with Alcohol and Drugs of Abuse

Oxycodone may be expected to have additive effects when used in conjunction with alcohol, other opioids, or illicit drugs that cause central nervous system depression.

DRUG ABUSE AND ADDICTION

OxyContin® is a mu-agonist opioid with an abuse liability similar to morphine and is a Schedule II controlled substance.

Oxycodone, like morphine and other opioids used in analgesia, can be abused and is subject to criminal diversion.

Drug addiction is characterized by compulsive use, use for non-medical purposes, and continued use despite harm or risk of harm. Drug addiction is a treatable disease, utilizing a multi-disciplinary approach, but relapse is common.

"Drug-seeking" behavior is very common in addicts and drug abusers. Drug-seeking tactics include emergency calls or visits near the end of office hours, refusal to undergo appropriate examination, testing or referral, repeated "loss" of prescriptions, tampering with prescriptions and reluctance to provide prior medical records or contact information for other treating physician(s). "Doctor shopping" to obtain additional prescriptions is common among drug abusers and people suffering from untreated addiction.

Abuse and addiction are separate and distinct from physical dependence and tolerance. Physicians should be aware that addiction may not be accompanied by concurrent tolerance and symptoms of physical dependence in all addicts. In addition, abuse of opioids can occur in the absence of true addiction and is characterized by misuse for non-medical purposes, often in combination with other psychoactive substances. OxyContin, like other opioids, has been diverted for non-medical use. Careful record-keeping of prescribing information, including quantity, frequency, and renewal requests is strongly advised.

Proper assessment of the patient, proper prescribing practices, periodic re-evaluation of therapy, and proper dispensing and storage are appropriate measures that help to limit abuse of opioid drugs.

OxyContin consists of a dual-polymer matrix, intended for oral use only. Abuse of the crushed tablet poses a hazard of overdose and death. This risk is increased with concurrent abuse of alcohol and other substances. With parenteral abuse, the tablet excipients, especially talc, can be expected to result in local tissue necrosis, infection, pulmonary granulomas, and increased risk of endocarditis and valvular heart injury. Parenteral drug abuse is commonly associated with transmission of infectious diseases such as hepatitis and HIV.

Respiratory Depression

Respiratory depression is the chief hazard from oxycodone, the active ingredient in OxyContin®, as with all opioid agonists. Respiratory depression is a particular problem in elderly or debilitated patients, usually following large initial doses in non-tolerant patients, or when opioids are given in conjunction with other agents that depress respiration.

Oxycodone should be used with extreme caution in patients with significant chronic obstructive pulmonary disease or cor pulmonale, and in patients having a substantially decreased respiratory reserve, hypoxia, hypercapnia, or pre-existing respiratory depression. In such patients, even usual therapeutic doses of oxycodone may decrease respiratory drive to the point of apnea. In these patients alternative non-opioid analgesics should be considered, and opioids should be employed only under careful medical supervision at the lowest effective dose.

Head Injury

The respiratory depressant effects of opioids include carbon dioxide retention and secondary elevation of cerebrospinal fluid pressure, and may be markedly exaggerated in the presence of head injury, intracranial lesions, or other sources of pre-existing increased intracranial pressure. Oxycodone produces effects on pupillary response and consciousness which may obscure neurologic signs of further increases in intracranial pressure in patients with head injuries.

Hypotensive Effect

OxyContin may cause severe hypotension. There is an added risk to individuals whose ability to maintain blood pressure has been compromised by a depleted blood volume, or after concurrent administration with drugs such as phenothiazines or other agents which compromise vasomotor tone. Oxycodone may produce orthostatic hypotension in ambulatory patients. Oxycodone, like all opioid analgesics of the morphine-type, should be administered with caution to patients in circulatory shock, since vasodilation produced by the drug may further reduce cardiac output and blood pressure.

PRECAUTIONS

General

Opioid analgesics have a narrow therapeutic index in certain patient populations, especially when combined with CNS depressant drugs, and should be reserved for cases where the benefits of opioid analgesia outweigh the known risks of respiratory depression, altered mental state, and postural hypotension.

Use of OxyContin® is associated with increased potential risks and should be used only with caution in the following conditions: acute alcoholism; adrenocortical insufficiency (e.g., Addison's disease); CNS depression or coma; delirium tremens; debilitated patients; kyphoscoliosis associated with respiratory depression; myxedema or hypothyroidism; prostatic hypertrophy or urethral stricture; severe impairment of hepatic, pulmonary or renal function; and toxic psychosis.

The administration of oxycodone may obscure the diagnosis or clinical course in patients with acute abdominal conditions. Oxycodone may aggravate convulsions in patients with convulsive disorders, and all opioids may induce or aggravate seizures in some clinical settings.

Interactions with other CNS Depressants

OxyContin should be used with caution and started in a reduced dosage ($^1\!/_3$ to $^1\!/_2$ of the usual dosage) in patients who are concurrently receiving other central nervous system depressants including sedatives or hypnotics, general anesthetics, phenothiazines, other tranquilizers, and alcohol. Interactive effects resulting in respiratory depression, hypotension, profound sedation, or coma may result if these drugs are taken in combination with the usual doses of OxyContin.

Interactions with Mixed Agonist/Antagonist Opioid Analgesics

Agonist/antagonist analgesics (i.e., pentazocine, nalbuphine, and butorphanol) should be administered with caution to a patient who has received or is receiving a course of therapy with a pure opioid agonist analgesic such as oxycodone. In this situation, mixed agonist/antagonist analgesics may reduce the analgesic effect of oxycodone and/or may precipitate withdrawal symptoms in these patients.

Ambulatory Surgery and Postoperative Use

OxyContin is not indicated for pre-emptive analgesia (administration pre-operatively for the management of postoperative pain).

OxyContin is not indicated for pain in the immediate postoperative period (the first 12 to 24 hours following surgery) for patients not previously taking the drug, because its safety in this setting has not been established.

OxyContin is not indicated for pain in the postoperative period if the pain is mild or not expected to persist for an extended period of time.

OxyContin is only indicated for postoperative use if the patient is already receiving the drug prior to surgery or if the postoperative pain is expected to be moderate to severe and persist for an extended period of time. Physicians should individualize treatment, moving from parenteral to oral analgesics as appropriate (See American Pain Society guidelines).

Patients who are already receiving OxyContin® Tablets as part of ongoing analgesic therapy may be safely continued on the drug if appropriate dosage adjustments are made considering the procedure, other drugs given, and the temporary changes in physiology caused by the surgical intervention (see DOSAGE AND ADMINISTRATION).

OxyContin and other morphine-like opioids have been shown to decrease bowel motility. Ileus is a common postoperative complication, especially after intra-abdominal surgery with opioid analgesia. Caution should be taken to monitor for decreased bowel motility in postoperative patients receiving opioids. Standard supportive therapy should be implemented.

Use in Pancreatic/Biliary Tract Disease

Oxycodone may cause spasm of the sphincter of Oddi and should be used with caution in patients with biliary tract disease, including acute pancreatitis. Opioids like oxycodone may cause increases in the serum amylase level.

Tolerance and Physical Dependence

Tolerance is the need for increasing doses of opioids to maintain a defined effect such as analgesia (in the absence of disease progression or other external factors). Physical dependence is manifested by withdrawal symptoms after abrupt discontinuation of a drug or upon administration of an antagonist. Physical dependence and tolerance are not unusual during chronic opioid therapy.

The opioid abstinence or withdrawal syndrome is characterized by some or all of the following: restlessness, lacrimation, rhinorrhea, yawning, perspiration, chills, myalgia, and mydriasis. Other symptoms also may develop, including: irritability, anxiety, backache, joint pain, weakness, abdominal cramps, insomnia, nausea, anorexia, vomiting, diarrhea, or increased blood pressure, respiratory rate, or heart rate.

In general, opioids should not be abruptly discontinued (see DOSAGE AND ADMINISTRATION: Cessation of Therapy).

Information for Patients/Caregivers

If clinically advisable, patients receiving OxyContin Tablets or their caregivers should be given the following information by the physician, nurse, pharmacist, or caregiver:

1. Patients should be aware that OxyContin Tablets contain oxycodone, which is a morphine-like substance.

2. Patients should be advised that OxyContin Tablets were designed to work properly only if swallowed whole. OxyContin Tablets will release all their contents at once if broken, chewed, or crushed, resulting in a risk of fatal overdose.

3. Patients should be advised to report episodes of breakthrough pain and adverse experiences occurring during therapy. Individualization of dosage is essential to make optimal use of this medication.

4. Patients should be advised not to adjust the dose of OxyContin® without consulting the prescribing professional.

5. Patients should be advised that OxyContin may impair mental and/or physical ability required for the performance of potentially hazardous tasks (e.g., driving, operating heavy machinery).

6. Patients should not combine OxyContin with alcohol or other central nervous system depressants (sleep aids, tranquilizers) except by the orders of the prescribing physician, because dangerous additive effects may occur, resulting in serious injury or death.

7. Women of childbearing potential who become, or are planning to become, pregnant should be advised to consult their physician regarding the effects of analgesics and other drug use during pregnancy on themselves and their unborn child.

298) DO NO HARM: THE OPIOID EPIDEMIC

8. Patients should be advised that OxyContin is a potential drug of abuse. They should protect it from theft, and it should never be given to anyone other than the individual for whom it was prescribed.

9. Patients should be advised that they may pass empty matrix "ghosts" (tablets) via colostomy or in the stool, and that this is of no concern since the active medication has already been absorbed.

10. Patients should be advised that if they have been receiving treatment with OxyContin for more than a few weeks and cessation of therapy is indicated, it may be appropriate to taper the OxyContin dose, rather than abruptly discontinue it, due to the risk of precipitating withdrawal symptoms. Their physician can provide a dose schedule to accomplish a gradual discontinuation of the medication.

11. Patients should be instructed to keep OxyContin in a secure place out of the reach of children. When OxyContin is no longer needed, the unused tablets should be destroyed by flushing down the toilet.

Use in Drug and Alcohol Addiction

OxyContin is an opioid with no approved use in the management of addictive disorders. Its proper usage in individuals with drug or alcohol dependence, either active or in remission, is for the management of pain requiring opioid analgesia.

Drug-Drug Interactions

Opioid analgesics, including OxyContin®, may enhance the neuromuscular blocking action of skeletal muscle relaxants and produce an increased degree of respiratory depression.

Oxycodone is metabolized in part to oxymorphone via cytochrome P450 2D6. While this pathway may be blocked by a variety of drugs (e.g., certain cardiovascular drugs including amiodarone and quinidine as well as polycyclic antidepressants), such blockade has not yet been shown to be of clinical significance with this agent. Clinicians should be aware of this possible interaction, however.

Use with CNS Depressants

OxyContin, like all opioid analgesics, should be started at $1/3$ to $1/2$ of the usual dosage in patients who are concurrently receiving other central nervous system depressants including sedatives or hypnotics, general anesthetics, phenothiazines, centrally acting antiemetics, tranquilizers, and alcohol because respiratory depression, hypotension, and profound sedation or coma may result. No specific interaction between oxycodone and monoamine oxidase inhibitors has been observed, but caution in the use of any opioid in patients taking this class of drugs is appropriate.

Carcinogenesis, Mutagenesis, Impairment of Fertility

Studies of oxycodone to evaluate its carcinogenic potential have not been conducted.

Oxycodone was not mutagenic in the following assays: Ames Salmonella and E. coli test with and without metabolic activation at doses of up to 5000 μg, chromosomal aberration test in human lymphocytes in the absence of metabolic activation at doses of up to 1500 μg/mL and with activation 48 hours after exposure at doses of up to 5000 μg/mL, and in the in vivo bone marrow micronucleus test in mice (at plasma levels of up to 48 μg/mL). Oxycodone was clastogenic in the human lymphocyte chromosomal assay in the presence of metabolic activation in the human chromosomal aberration test (at greater than or equal to 1250 μg/mL) at 24 but not 48 hours of exposure and in the mouse lymphoma assay at doses of 50 μg/mL or greater with metabolic activation and at 400 μg/mL or greater without metabolic activation.

Pregnancy

Teratogenic Effects — Category B: Reproduction studies have been performed in rats and rabbits by oral administration at doses up to 8 mg/kg and 125 mg/kg, respectively. These doses are 3 and 46 times a human dose of 160 mg/day, based on mg/kg basis. The results did not reveal evidence of harm to the fetus due to oxycodone. There are, however, no adequate and well-controlled studies in pregnant women. Because animal reproduction studies are not always predictive of human response, this drug should be used during pregnancy only if clearly needed.

Labor and Delivery

OxyContin® is not recommended for use in women during and immediately prior to labor and delivery because oral opioids may cause respiratory depression in the newborn. Neonates whose mothers have been taking oxycodone chronically may exhibit respiratory depression and/or withdrawal symptoms, either at birth and/or in the nursery.

Nursing Mothers

Low concentrations of oxycodone have been detected in breast milk. Withdrawal symptoms can occur in breast-feeding infants when maternal administration of an opioid analgesic is stopped. Ordinarily, nursing should not be undertaken while a patient is receiving OxyContin because of the possibility of sedation and/or respiratory depression in the infant.

Pediatric Use

Safety and effectiveness of OxyContin have not been established in pediatric patients below the age of 18. **It must be remembered that OxyContin Tablets cannot be crushed or divided for administration.**

Geriatric Use

In controlled pharmacokinetic studies in elderly subjects (greater than 65 years) the clearance of oxycodone appeared to be slightly reduced. Compared to young adults, the plasma concentrations of oxycodone were increased approximately 15% (see **PHARMACOKINETICS AND METABOLISM**). Of the total number of subjects (445) in clinical studies of OxyContin, 148 (33.3%) were age 65 and older (including those age 75 and older) while 40 (9.0%) were age 75 and older. In clinical trials with appropriate initiation of therapy and dose titration, no untoward or unexpected side effects were seen in the elderly patients who received OxyContin. Thus, the usual doses and dosing intervals are appropriate for these patients. As with all opioids, the starting dose should be reduced to $1/3$ to $1/2$ of the usual dosage in debilitated, non-tolerant patients. Respiratory depression is the chief hazard in elderly or debilitated patients, usually following large initial doses in non-tolerant patients, or when opioids are given in conjunction with other agents that depress respiration.

Laboratory Monitoring

Due to the broad range of plasma concentrations seen in clinical populations, the varying degrees of pain, and the development of tolerance, plasma oxycodone measurements are usually not helpful in clinical management. Plasma concentrations of the active drug substance may be of value in selected, unusual or complex cases.

DO NO HARM DOCUMENTARY SERIES FOR TELEVISION

EPISODE #1. AN ODYSSEY OF IGNORANCE & GREED

The Opioid Epidemic is the worst man-made epidemic in the history of our nation. More people die each year from an opioid overdose than in automobile accidents. The statistics are staggering. This episode traces how an aggressive pharmaceutical mass marketing campaign for the new drug OxyContin misled doctors and the public into our current crisis of death and addiction. The FDA and health-care organizations became coconspirators in endorsing long-term use of opioids despite no scientific proof they were nonaddictive. This episode shows the direct link between prescription opioids and heroin addiction. It spotlights experts, journalists, and public health crusaders combating the special interests and informing the world. Meanwhile, scientists search to find better, safer drugs to combat pain. As the US becomes more aware of prescription opioid dangers, Big Pharma now takes their dangerous marketing campaign to third-world countries. And the battle continues.

EPISODE #2. GROUND ZERO

Rural America was among the earliest and hardest hit by prescription opioid addiction and overdose deaths. The stories in this episode center primarily in Kentucky, ground zero of the epidemic. Whole communities have been devastated. Some schools don't hold parent-teacher meetings because many of the parents are either dead, in rehab, or in jail. Regional health experts, local government, law enforcement, journalists, and the DEA all weigh in on the crisis.

In Vermont and New Hampshire hospitals, local law enforcement and even the fire department are implementing new programs to deal with the crisis and save lives. Founded by grieving parents who lost children to heroin, two grassroots movements in Kentucky are changing laws and battling for reform so that other parents will not lose their children. And yet despite heroic efforts, people continue to die.

EPISODE #3.
ROCKY ROAD TO RECOVERY

This episode shines a light on the plight of the millions of Americans who suffer from opioid addiction. Nearly everyone knows someone or has a family member who is addicted or died from an opioid overdose. On this episode we meet people, young, old, and in between, on the rocky road to recovery. They tell their harrowing stories and current victories and struggles with the disease. Experts discuss the difficulty of finding treatment and maintaining sobriety in a system that is in overload. Various methods of treatment are candidly discussed. Among the stories is that of the young woman scientist fresh out of college who in 1963 discovered methadone could be an effective treatment for addiction. We meet a heroic Vermont pediatrician who changed his practice to include addiction treatment for young patients. Some of the stories of those in recovery have positive outcomes others do not. But the overall message of this episode is a life-affirming hope for a better future.

LOCATION INTERVIEWS

Seattle

- Interviews included Dr. Michael Von Korff, an epidemiologist and researcher who focuses on pain management and how patients adapt to chronic pain; Dr. Gary Franklin, pain-management expert and research professor in the Department of Environmental and Occupational Health Sciences and in the Department of Medicine (Neurology) at the University of Washington and Dr. David Tauben, chief of Pain Medicine at the University of Washington.
- Dr. Richard Ries, professor of Psychiatry, director of the Addictions Division at UW Medicine and Harborview Medical was interviewed with several recovering addicts.
- Psychiatrist Dr. Andrew Saxon, director of Center of Excellence in Substance Abuse Treatment and Education at the VA Puget Sound Health Care System and director of Addiction, Psychiatry Residency Program at the University of Washington.

New York

- Katherine Eban, journalist for *Fortune Magazine*.
- Dr. Lewis Nelson, professor and chair, Department of Emergency Medicine, director.
- Dr. Sam Ball, president and chief executive officer of The National Center on Addiction and Substance Abuse.
- Dr. George Woody, professor in the Department of Psychiatry at the University of Pennsylvania, who has written and researched extensively on opioid addiction.
- Dr. Andrew Kolodny, chief medical officer, Phoenix House, and executive director of PROP, a leader in exposing the opioid crisis and facilitating change in the medical community.
- David Crow, senior US business correspondent at *Financial Times*, covering telecoms, technology and pharmaceuticals.

Crow says there's an irony that drug companies will profit a second time around from the sales of abuse deterrent opioids. He believes, "Big Pharma isn't trying to stop the party. There's a dark underworld."

■ Dr. Mary Jeanne Kreek is senior attending physician and professor of Laboratory of the Biology of Addictive Diseases at Rockefeller University. Dr. Kreek is a pioneer in investigating the biological basis of opioid addiction developed the use of methadone therapy for heroin addiction.

Kentucky

■ Interviews included staff and physicians who run the Center on Drug and Alcohol Research (CDAR) at the University of Kentucky: director Dr. Sharon Walsh; clinical support, Nikki Milward; Epidemiologist Dr. Jennifer Havens, whose primary research is in opioid and substance abuse; and psychiatrist Dr. Michelle Lofwall, who treats opioid addicts and conducts clinical research on improving the treatment of addiction.

■ DEA agent Thomas Gorman talks about the efforts to stop drug trafficking in heroin.

■ Psychiatrist Dr. Kelly Clark, president-elect of the American Society of Addiction Medicine, practices addiction medicine in Appalachian Kentucky. She discusses the breakdown of the family and death of parents of overdose.

■ Reporter Laura Ungar with the Louisville *Courier-Journal* shares her groundbreaking investigation into the heroin epidemic in Kentucky and rides along as we travel to Appalachia, including areas hardest hit by the opioid crisis.

■ Van Ingram, executive director, Kentucky Office of Drug Control Policy, is at the forefront of dealing with crisis on the state government level.

■ Attorney General Andy Beshear receives a check for $450,000— part of funding won by the state in one of the precedent setting lawsuits against Purdue Pharmaceuticals to go toward recovery centers.

- Holly Specht (founder of Northern Kentucky Hates Heroin) and a group of 80 parents gather for a candlelight march in Ft. Thomas, Kentucky, where they pray and share their personal stories of loss.

- Hazard, Kentucky, police chief Minor Allen speaks about what law enforcement in Appalachia is doing to fight the war against increasing opioid and heroin use.

- Chad's Hope was the first recovery center founded in Manchester, Kentucky, where director Wendell McCormack deals daily with residents whose lives have been destroyed by opioid and heroin addiction. Several addicts, all working blue-collar jobs, including in the mines, talk about their struggles with heroin.

- Karyn Hascal, president of The Healing Place, a free recovery center in Louisville, can't keep up with the demand for beds.

- Charlotte Wethington of Morning View, Kentucky, created Casey's Law after her 23-year-old son died of an opioid overdose. The law enables parents, relatives, or friends to seek involuntary, court-ordered treatment for a loved one struggling with addiction.

Boulder, Colorado

- Assistant research professor Dr. Peter Grace of the University of Colorado, Boulder, explains his important new findings: the use of opioids may have a long-term negative effect on chronic pain by actually increasing it.

Boston

- Dr. Jane Ballantyne, an anesthesiologist who practices and teaches in both Seattle and Boston, is widely recognized as a researcher and educator in acute and chronic pain management. She is the current president of PROP.

Philadelphia

■ Dr. Jeanmarie Perrone, professor of Emergency Medicine, Hospital of the University of Pennsylvania, witnesses drug overdoses when victims are rushed to the ER.

Los Angeles

■ Addicts attempt to turn their lives around at nationally recognized residential not-for-profit treatment center, Beit T'Shuvah.

■ Dr. Joel Hay is a professor of Pharmaceutical Economics and Policy & Professor of Health Policy and Economics at USC. Dr. Hay discloses the economic impact of opioid sales on the pharmaceutical industry and how pharmaceutical companies are able to market drugs to the medical community by creating alternative avenues. He discusses the FDA's reliance on Big Pharma as a dangerous conflict of interest and why it fails to follow up once a drug has been approved.

Costa Mesa, California

■ Joseph DeSanto, MD, a physician practicing Addiction Medicine, was treating addicts at a recovery center and then became addicted to painkillers himself. He has been in recovery for the past year. His license to practice medicine has been suspended.

Stanford, California

■ Dr. Aashish Manglik, instructor of Molecular & Cellular Physiology, Stanford University, investigates the potential for a nonaddictive pain killer based on a newly identified compound, PZM21.

■ Dr. Anna Lembke is an assistant professor of psychiatry and behavioral sciences at Stanford University School of Medicine. She is a diplomate of the American Board of Psychiatry and

Neurology, and a diplomate of the American Board of Addiction Medicine. She is the program director for the Stanford University Addiction Medicine Fellowship, and chief of the Stanford Addiction Medicine Dual Diagnosis Clinic.

- Dr. Lembke is author of the book on the opioid epidemic, *Drug Dealer, MD: How Doctors Were Duped, Patients Got Hooked, and Why It's So Hard to Stop*. She points to Big Pharma for misleading doctors about the science and safety of opioids.

Vermont

- Dr. Fred Holmes was a practicing small-town pediatrician when he encountered an increasingly big problem among his adolescent patients: their easy access and subsequent addiction to opioid painkillers and heroin.
- Burlington police chief Brandon del Pozo inherited an opioid/heroin crisis when he took office but immediately took action: providing every parole car with the overdose antidote Narcan.
- The Howard Center provides help for those dealing with substance abuse. CEO Bob Bick talks about the impact of opioid and heroin addiction on the community and the challenge their patients face in weaning off these overprescribed drugs.

New Hampshire

- Interview with state attorney general Foster about the legal implications of the opioid epidemic and what New Hampshire is doing to bring suit against Big Pharma.
- A profile of the Dartmouth-Hitchcock Hospital treatment program for opioid addicted expectant mothers and their newborn infants. RN, PhD, pediatric nurse Daisy Goodman leads the Expectant Mom program.
- Interview with 71-year-old woman in recovery from substance abuse disorder by her psychotherapist, Dr. Jennifer Kinsey

New Haven, Connecticut

- Dr. Julie Gaither, PhD, MPH, RN, and postdoctoral fellow in Biostatistics at Yale University is lead author of a team at Yale that analyzed the data on children admitted to US hospitals. The researchers discovered that in a 16-year period from 1997 to 2012, the number of children, ages 1 to 19, who were hospitalized for opioid poisoning nearly doubled. In toddlers and preschoolers, the rates more than doubled.

San Francisco

- Opioid addiction among adolescents and college-aged young adults is increasing. The Haven at College, founded in 2012, is a unique college residential living facility and outpatient center for students in recovery that now exists on five campuses across the country, including the University of San Francisco, which started in 2017 two years ago. Program director Jon Anderson talks about the need for such a facility on campuses as does USF director of Counseling and Psychological Services Barbara Thomas. Student Haley Kaplan shares her personal story of addiction and recovery. Her father, Scott Kaplan, provides a cautionary tale for other parents.

Andrew Kolodny, MD
PROP Founder

Michelle Lofwall, MD
University of KY

Frederick Holmes, MD
Vermont Pediatrician

Brandon del Pozo
Chief, Burlinghton VT

Mike Moore
Attorney

Georges Benjamin, MD
Executive Director, APHA

Lewis Nelson, MD
Rutgers NJ, School Medicine

Jeanmarie Perrone, MD
UPenn - Medicine

Aashish Manglik, MD
UCSF

Anna Lembke, MD
Stanford University

Minor Allen
Chief, Hazard KY

Andrew J Saxon, MD
University of WA

Jane C. Ballantyne, MD
UW Medicine

Harry Wiland, Gary M. Franklin, MD (UWA)
and Dale Bell

Barbara J Thomas, PhD
USF

Harriet Rossetto and Rabbi Mark Borovitz
Beit T'Shuvah

Harriet Ryan
LA Times

Michael Von Korff, MD
KPWA Res. Ins.

David Crow
Financial Times

ACKNOWLEDGMENTS

I WANT TO acknowledge the incredible work and dedication that my business and film partners Dale Bell and Beverly Baroff have steadfastly offered over the past 20 years. Thanks to Margie Friedman, Waleska Santiago, Martin Thiel, Jonathan Bell, and Troy Mathews. Without their unflagging participation, *Do No Harm* never would have happened. This book was written with the extraordinary contribution of Peter Segall. Thank you, Peter. Finally, I want to especially thank Andrew Kolodny, MD, and his dedicated band of physicians and health-care professionals who joined together to fight back against the forces of greed and evil. Without their persistent effort, the progress now being made in mitigating—and eventually defeating—the opioid epidemic would not be possible.

I want to acknowledge with full appreciation Turner Publishing Company's Managing Editor, Heather Howell, and editors Lara Asher and Lauren Langston Stewart for the extraordinary work they have done in bringing the book to life. I especially want to thank Executive Editor, Stephanie Beard for the confidence she has shown in greenlighting *Do No Harm*. Finally, I want to say that this book would not have happened without the effort on the part of my agent, Gerrie Sturman.

I hope the book lives up to their expectations.

ENDNOTES

1. https://www.nytimes.com/2014/02/11/us/heroins-small-town-toll-and-a-mothers-pain.html

2. https://www.hhs.gov/opioids/about-the-epidemic/index.html

3. https://www.cdc.gov/mmwr/volumes/67/wr/mm675152e1.htm?s_cid=mm675152e1_w

4. OxyContin: Purdue Pharma's painful medicine, Fortune magazine, November 9, 2011, Katherine Eban,

5. NIDA, Opioid Overdose Crisis, Revised March 2018.

6. https://www.wsj.com/articles/SB10001424127887324478304578173342657044604

7. NIDA, Opioid Overdose Crisis, Revised March 2018.

8. http://www.documentcloud.org/documents/2815968-Seriousgenericcompetition.html#document/p2, Original July 16, 1990 document taken from Maloy Moore, the Los Angeles Times

9. https://www.nytimes.com/2007/05/10/business/11drug-web.html, Barry Meier

10. N Engl J Med. 1980;302:123, Porter J, Jick H. Addiction rare in patients treated with narcotics. N Engl J Med. 1980;302:123

11. HHS Public Access, 2013 Nov; 35(11): 1728-1732.

12. NIDA Newsletter, March 2018.

13. New York Times, Barry Mier, May 29, 2018

14. Phillips DM. JCAHO pain management standards are unveiled. Joint Commission. JAMA. 2000; 284(4):428-9./

15. https://www.cincinnati.com/story/news/2013/10/09/who-fueled-the-opioid-explosion-/4073201/

16. https://www.jointcommission.org/assets/1/6/Pain_Std_History_Web_Version_05122017.pdf, *The Joint Commission Pain Standards: Origins and Evolution, May 5, 2017*

17. http://www.donoharmseries.org. *Do No Harm* documentary interview with Andrew Kolodny, MD. 2016.

18. http://www.donoharmseries.org. *Do No Harm* documentary interview with Dr. Richard Ries. 2018.

19. https://www.painmanagementnursing.org/article/S1524-9042(00)04110-2/pdf

20. Puntillo K, Neighbor M, O'Neil N, Nixon R. Accuracy of emergency nurses in assessment of patients' pain. Pain Manag Nurs. 2003;4(4):171-5.

21. (McCaffery, 1968, cited in Rosdahl & Kowalski, 2007, p. 704).

22. Rosdahl & Kowalski, 2007, p. 704

23. https://www.statnews.com/wp-content/uploads/2017/11/2017-11-02-FINAL-Kenova-v-JCA-HO-class-action-complaint.pdf

24. Cincinnati Enquirer, Dec. 17, 2013).

25. https://www.cdc.gov/mmwr/volumes/65/rr/rr6501e1.htm?CDC_AA_refVal=https%3A%2F%2Fwww.cdc.gov%2Fmmwr%2Fvolumes%2F65%2Frr%2Frr6501e1er.htm

26. Bloomberg News, May 2017

27. NPR reporting on Altarum, a not for profit reporting on health economics, February 2018.

28. https://www.cdc.gov/drugoverdose/epidemic/index.html

29. https://www.cdc.gov/mmwr/volumes/67/wr/mm6734a2.htm, August 31, 2018

30. https://www.cdc.gov/media/releases/2018/p0329-drug-overdose-deaths.html

31. How OxyContin Became America's Most Widely Abused Prescription Drug, May 16, 2016

32. C.D.C. Painkiller Guidelines Aim to Reduce Addiction Risk, Sabrina Tavernise. NYT, March 16, 2016.

33. Pain News Network, June 16, 2016

34. MedPage Today, June 16, 2016.

35. Bloomberg News, May 10, 2017

36. https://www.deamuseum.org/ccp/opium/history.html

37. https://www.theatlantic.com/china/archive/2013/10/how-humiliation-drove-modern-chinese-history/280878/

38. https://museumofhealthcare.wordpress.com/2015/07/20/laudanum-freedom-from-pain-for-the-price-of-addiction/

39. https://www.smithsonianmag.com/history/inside-story-americas-19th-century-opiate-addiction-180967673/

40. ibid.

41. ibid.

42. https://www.npr.org/sections/parallels/2018/01/14/571184153/on-the-hunt-for-poppies-in-mexico-americas-biggest-heroin-supplier

43. www.worldofmolecules.com/drugs/oxycodone.htm, World of Molecules. September 28, 2018

44. https://pubchem.ncbi.nlm.nih.gov/compound/Oxycodone

45. http://www.donoharmseries.org. *Do No Harm* documentary interview with Andrew Kolodny., June 2018

46. http://www.nber.org/papers/w24475

47. https://www.nejm.org/doi/10.1056/NEJMra1508490?url_ver=Z39.88-2003&rfr_id=ori%3Arid%3Acrossref.org&rfr_dat=cr_pub%3Dwww.ncbi.nlm.nih.gov

48. https://www.federalregister.gov/documents/2018/04/19/2018-08111/controlled-substances-quotas

49. http://www.nber.org/papers/w24475

50. https://www.ncbi.nlm.nih.gov/pmc/articles/PMC5105018/

51. https://harpers.org/archive/2016/04/legalize-it-all/

52. https://www.independent.co.uk/arts-entertainment/obituary-john-ehrlichman-1071331.html

53. https://www.aclu.org/other/drug-war-new-jim-crow

54. https://www.cnn.com/2018/06/28/us/mass-incarceration-five-key-facts/index.html

55. https://www.washingtonpost.com/news/fact-checker/wp/2015/07/07/yes-u-s-locks-people-up-at-a-higher-rate-than-any-other-country/?noredirect=on&utm_term=.452d6753c17c

56. http://www.drugpolicy.org/issues/race-and-drug-war

57. https://www.npr.org/2017/11/04/562137082/why-is-the-opioid-epidemic-overwhelming-ly-white

58. https://www.washingtonpost.com/graphics/2017/national/fentanyl-overdoses/?noredi-rect=on&utm_term=.a5609850f19b

59. https://calgaryherald.com/news/local-news/training-sniffer-dogs-is-a-tricky-job-when-just-a-trace-of-fentanyl-is-enough-to-kill

60. Vertosick, Frank T. Why We Hurt: The Natural History of Pain. New York: Harcourt, 2001.

61. Foreman, Judy. A Nation in Pain: Healing Our Nation's Biggest Health Problem. Oxford: Oxford University Press, 2014.

62. https://www.iasp-pain.org/AboutIASP/Content.aspx?ItemNumber=1129

63. https://www.cdc.gov/nchs/data/hus/2016/080.pdf

64. https://www.brookings.edu/bpea-articles/mortality-and-morbidity-in-the-21st-century/

65. http://www.portlandeyeopener.com/AA-12-Steps-12-Traditions.pdf

66. ttps://www.washingtonpost.com/news/morning-mix/wp/2017/06/02/how-the-opioid-crisis-traces-back-to-a-five-sentence-scholarly-letter-from-1980/?utm_term=.3f35fc414a90

67. https://www.wsj.com/articles/SB10001424127887324478304578173342657044604

68. https://www.newyorker.com/magazine/2017/10/30/the-family-that-built-an-empire-of-pain

69. https://www.drugabuse.gov/drugs-abuse/opioids/opioid-overdose-crisis. 2019

70. https://www.mahf.com/mahf-inductees/

71. https://www.nytimes.com/2007/05/10/business/11drug-web.html

72. *https://www.mahf.com/mahf-inductees/*, Arthur Sackler obituary

73. https://www.ncbi.nlm.nih.gov/pmc/articles/PMC3278148/, Direct-to-Consumer Pharmaceutical Advertising

74. http://articles.latimes.com/1987-05-31/news/mn-9302_1_medical-advertising

75. https://www.newyorker.com/magazine/2017/10/30/the-family-that-built-an-empire-of-pain, Patrick Radden Keefe

76. Quinones, Sam. Dreamland: The True Tale of America's Opiate Epidemic. New York, NY: Bloomsbury Press, 2015.

77. https://www.newyorker.com/magazine/2017/10/30/the-family-that-built-an-empire-of-pain, Patrick Radden Keefe

78. ibid.

79. ibid.

80. ibid.

81. Quinones, Sam. Dreamland: The True Tale of America's Opiate Epidemic. New York, NY: Bloomsbury Press, 2015.

82. https://www.mahf.com/mahf-inductees/

83. *https://www.newyorker.com/magazine/2017/10/30/the-family-that-built-an-empire-of-pain*, Patrick Radden Keefe

84. *http://sandbox.asm.org/microbe/images/stories/images/sept2010/origins.pdf*, Henry Welch, FDA, and the Origins of the ICAAC

85. http://www.documentcloud.org/documents/2815969-Launchteamminutes.html#document/p2, Internal Purdue memo.

86. *http://www.documentcloud.org/documents/2815968-Seriousgenericcompetition.html#document/p1*, Internal Purdue memo.

87. http://www.documentcloud.org/documents/2815968-Seriousgenericcompetition.html#document/p1

88. http://www.documentcloud.org/documents/2815968-Seriousgenericcompetition.html#document/p1, Internal Purdue memo.

89. *http://www.documentcloud.org/documents/2815975-Pressreleaseversionone.html#document/p1*, Purdue Press Release

90. https://www.ncbi.nlm.nih.gov/pmc/articles/PMC2622774/#bib12, The Promotion of OxyContin, Commercial Triumph Public Health Tragedy. American Public Health Association. Art Van Zee, MD

91. ibid.

92. ibid

93. *https://www.ncbi.nlm.nih.gov/pubmed/1623766*. The effects of pharmaceutical firm enticements on physician prescribing patterns. There's no such thing as a free lunch

94. *https://www.ncbi.nlm.nih.gov/pubmed/1623766*

95. *http://www.documentcloud.org/documents/2815965-Bonustime.html#document/p1*, Internal Purdue memo.

96. http://www.sackler.org/about/, Sackler's philanthropy.

97. ibid.

98. https://www.washingtonpost.com/news/business/wp/2018/09/08/the-man-who-made-billions-of-dollars-from-oxycontin-is-pushing-a-drug-to-wean-addicts-off-opioids/?utm_term=.de96720dee6b

99. https://www.purduepharma.com/about/#&panel1-5

100. ibid.

101. https://www.courant.com/news/connecticut/hc-xpm-2001-09-02-0109020319-story.html

102. https://www.ncbi.nlm.nih.gov/pmc/articles/PMC4142099/, *Controlled Drug Delivery Systems, Kinam Park.*

103. *https://patents.google.com/patent/US4330338A/en, Pharmaceutical Coating Compositions.*

104. *https://www.bmj.com/content/suppl/2005/07/18/331.7509.DC1, Dame Cicely Saunders Dies.*

105. *http://www.stchristophers.org.uk/about/history/pioneeringdays, Pioneering Days of Pallative Care*

106. https://www.nytimes.com/1994/08/20/obituaries/john-j-bonica-pioneer-in-anesthe-sia-dies-at-77.html

107. http://www.documentcloud.org/documents/2821671-1992-OxyContin-patent.html#document/p1

108. http://www.latimes.com/projects/oxycontin-part1/, OxyContin's 12-Hour Problem. Harriet Ryan.

109. http://www.documentcloud.org/documents/2822902-Sales-Manager-on12-hour-Dosing.html#document/p2

110. http://www.documentcloud.org/documents/2815975-Pressreleaseversionone.html#document/p10, Purdue Pushes 'Pseudo-Addiction.'

111. http://www.documentcloud.org/documents/2815975-Pressreleaseversionone.html#document/p10, Purdue Pushes 'Pseudo-Addiction.'

112. https://www.hsgac.senate.gov/imo/media/doc/REPORT-Fueling%20an%20Epidemic-Exposing%20the%20Financial%20Ties%20Between%20Opioid%20Manufacturers%20and%20Third%20Party%20Advocacy%20Groups.pdfs

113. https://www.hsgac.senate.gov/imo/media/doc/REPORT-Fueling%20an%20Epidemic-Exposing%20the%20Financial%20Ties%20Between%20Opioid%20Manufacturers%20and%20Third%20Party%20Advocacy%20Groups.pdf

114. https://www.researchgate.net/profile/J_Haddox

115. https://www.jointcommission.org/assets/1/6/Pain_Std_History_Web_Version_05122017.pdf

116. https://www.wsj.com/articles/SB10001424127887324478304578173342657044604, Catan and Perez.

117. https://www.jointcommission.org/assets/1/6/Pain_Std_History_Web_Version_05122017.pdf

118. https://www.nytimes.com/2019/02/21/health/oxycontin-sackler-purdue-pharma.html, Sackler Testimony Conflicts with Federal Investigation, Barry Meier.

119. https://www.francopsychological.com › fpa-resources › when-is-it-addiction

120. https://www.statnews.com/2018/06/06/oxycontin-purdue-sackler-barry-meier-book/

121. https://www.nytimes.com/2018/05/29/health/purdue-opioids-oxycontin.html

122. https://www.nytimes.com/2018/05/29/health/purdue-opioids-oxycontin.html

123. *https://www.ncbi.nlm.nih.gov/pmc/articles/PMC2622774/, Promotion and Marketing of Opioids, Art Van Zee, MD.*

124. https://www.newyorker.com/magazine/2017/10/30/the-family-that-built-an-empire-of-pain

125. http://i.bnet.com/blogs/purdue-agreed-facts.pdf

126. https://www.nytimes.com/2007/05/10/business/11drug-web.html?module=inline,OxyContin Make to Pay $600 million, Barry Meier.

127. ibid.

128. ibid.

129. https://www.nytimes.com/2004/02/22/nyregion/rudy-politician-s-empire-giuliani-selling-his-public-image-branches-for-private.html, Rudy Brances Out for Private Profit, Eric Lipton.

130. https://www.nytimes.com/2018/07/05/podcasts/the-daily/opioid-crisis-purdue-oxycontin.html, How the Opioid Crisis Started, Michael Barbaro.

131. https://www.nytimes.com/2007/12/28/us/politics/28oxycontin.html?module=inline,Drug Maker Turned to Guiliani for Help, Barry Meier and Eric Lipton.

132. https://www.nytimes.com/2018/07/05/podcasts/the-daily/opioid-crisis-purdue-oxycontin.html, How the Opioid Crisis Started, Michael Barbaro.

133. https://archive.org/details/DrugAddictsAreHumanBeingsTheStoryOfOurBillion-dollarDrugRacketHow_485

134. http://news.bbc.co.uk/2/shared/spl/hi/uk/06/prisons/html/nn2page1.stm

135. https://www.ncbi.nlm.nih.gov/pmc/articles/PMC2715956/

136. https://dash.harvard.edu/bitstream/handle/1/8846740/Pacheco.pdf?sequence=1&isAllowed=y

137. Quinones, Dreamland

138. https://ajph.aphapublications.org/doi/full/10.2105/AJPH.2005.071647

139. https://www.washingtonpost.com/news/retropolis/wp/2017/09/29/the-greatest-drug-fiends-in-the-world-an-american-opioid-crisis-in-1908/?utm_term=.0e9569da6f79

140. https://ajph.aphapublications.org/doi/pdf/10.2105/AJPH.62.7.995

141. https://www.washingtonpost.com/news/retropolis/wp/2017/09/29/the-greatest-drug-fiends-in-the-world-an-american-opioid-crisis-in-1908/?utm_term=.d17272548e01

142. https://www.npr.org/sections/health-shots/2016/10/01/495031077/how-we-got-here-treating-addiction-in-28-days

143. https://heller.brandeis.edu/facguide/person.html?emplid=fed1af017db070b94ce59c-13714f1e7970a787ad

144. https://www.hsgac.senate.gov/hearings/unintended-consequences-medicaid-and-the-opioid-epidemic, January 17, 2018

145. https://www.judiciary.senate.gov/imo/media/doc/paulozzi_testimony_03_12_08.pdf

146. https://www.pharmaceutical-journal.com/news-and-analysis/reformulated-oxycontin-reduces-abuse-but-many-addicts-have-switched-to-heroin/20068119.article?firstPass=false

147. https://www.acsh.org/news/2017/10/12/opioid-epidemic-6-charts-designed-deceive-you-11935

148. https://deohs.washington.edu/faculty/franklin_gary

149. http://www.donoharmseries.org. *Do No Harm* documentary interview with Gary Franklin, *MD*, 2016.

150. https://www.aspph.org/washingtons-franklin-authors-position-statement-on-opioids/

151. https://www.painresearchforum.org/forums/interview/108641-shifting-landscape-opioids-pain-conversation-jane-ballantyne

152. https://en.wikipedia.org/wiki/Michael_Von_Korff

153. http://www.donoharmseries.org. *Do No Harm* documentary interview with Gary Franklin. 2016.

154. https://addiction.surgeongeneral.gov/sites/default/files/fact-sheet-general.pdf

155. http://www.bri.ucla.edu/people/christopher-j-evans-phd

156. http://www.donoharmseries.org. *Do No Harm* documentary interview with Dr. Chris Evans. 2017.

157. https://odcp.ky.gov/Pages/default.aspx

158. https://www.drugabuse.gov/drugs-abuse/opioids/opioid-overdose-crisis#seven

159. https://www.opiant.com/team/dr-sharon-walsh/

160. https://www.thehealingplace.org

161. https://www.asam.org/about-us/leadership/alternates/biography-michelle-lofwall

162. http://donoharmseries.org. *Do No Harm* interview with Dr. Fred Holmes. 2017.

163. http://donoharmseries.org. *Do No Harm* documentary interview with Haley, 2017.

164. http://www.ctnnortheastnode.org/event/science-series-perinatal-substance-use-disorders-rationale-integrated-care-daisy-goodman-cnm-dnp-mph/, Daisy Goodman RN PhD. bio. 2018.

165. https://www.vnews.com/Report-Drug-crisis-taking-toll-on-New-Hampshire-newborns-14438941

166. http://donoharmseries.org. *Do No Harm* documentary interview with Diana Salzinger. 2018.

167. http://donoharmseries.org. *Do No Harm* documentary interview with Dr. Daisy Goodman. 2018

168. https://www.webmd.com/children/news/20161031/opioid-overdoses-up-nearly-200-percent-among-kids-teens#2

169. http://donoharmseries.org. *Do No Harm* documentary interview Dr. Julie Gaither. 2018.

170. http://donoharmseries.org. *Do No Harm* documentary interview with Shayna Akin. 2018.

171. *https://beittshuvah.org/*

172. http://donoharmseries.org. *Do No Harm* documentary interview with Dr. Joseph DeSanto. 2017

173. ibid.

174. https://www.uwmedicine.org/bios/richard-ries

175. http://www.donoharmseries.org. *Do No Harm* documentary interview with Dr. Fred Holmes.

176. https://www.theatlantic.com/health/archive/2018/04/how-france-reduced-heroin-overdoses-by-79-in-four-years/558023/

177. https://www.rockefeller.edu/our-scientists/heads-of-laboratories/1198-mary-jeanne-kreek/

178. https://www.ncbi.nlm.nih.gov/pmc/articles/PMC1511970/

179. http://donoharmseries.org. *Do No Harm* documentary interview with Dr. Kreek 2018.

180. https://indro-online.de/en/the-history-of-methadone/

181. https://en.wikipedia.org/wiki/Methadone

182. http://anesthesiology.pubs.asahq.org/article.aspx?articleid=1946793

183. http://donoharmseries.org. *Do No Harm* documentary interview Shayna Akin, 2018.

184. https://www.nbcnews.com/nightly-news/video/this-opioid-addiction-treatment-helped-france-combat-its-own-epidemic-1268114499857

185. http://www.donoharmseries.org. *Do No Harm* documentary interview with Dr. Ries. 2017.

186. ibid.

187. http://donoharmseries.org. *Do No Harm* documentary interview with Dr. Ries. 2017

188. https://beittshuvah.org/about-us/our-team/harriet-rossetto/

189. http://depts.washington.edu/psychadd/faculty.shtml, Andrew Saxon,MD bio. 2019

190. http://donoharmseries.org. *Do No Harm* documentary interview with Dr. Andrew Saxon. 2017.

191. http://donoharmseries.org. *Do No Harm* documentary on location in San Diego speaking before Californina AGs. 2014.

192. https://www.prainc.com/qa-police-chief-brandon-del-pozo/

193. http://www.donoharmseries.org. *Do No Harm* documentary interview with Chief del Pozo. 2018

194. https://www.narcan.com/

195. http://www.donoharmseries.org. *Do No Harm* documentary interview with Chief del Pozo. 2018

196. ibid.

197. https://www.cincinnati.com/story/life/2016/04/10/standing-against-heroin-for-her-son/81492158/. Woman of the Year

198. http://www.donoharmseries.org. *Do No Harm* documentary interview with Charlotte Wethington. 2018

199. ibid.

200. https://www.courier-journal.com/story/news/crime/2018/03/01/caseys-law-forces-drug-treatment-addicts-kentucky/1042235001/

201. https://www.nhpr.org/post/future-safe-stations-one-many-questions-under-nhs-new-addiction-plan#stream/0

202. https://www.nhpr.org/post/future-safe-stations-one-many-questions-under-nhs-new-addiction-plan#stream/0

203. https://www.bloomberg.com/news/features/2017-10-05/the-lawyer-who-beat-big-tobacco-takes-on-the-opioid-industry

204. http://www.donoharmseries.org. *Do No Harm* documentary interview with Mike Moore. 2019.

205. https://www.statnews.com/2019/02/22/a-secretive-billionaires-role-in-promoting-oxycontin-emerges-in-new-documents/

206. https://mms.mckesson.com/product/1040645/Egalet-US-Inc-69344011311

207. http://www.donoharmseries.org. *Do No Harm* documentary interview with Mike Moore. 2019.

208. purduepharma.com

209. http://www.donoharmseries.org. *Do No Harm* documentary interview with Mike Moore. 2019.

210. ibid.

211. https://www.nytimes.com/interactive/2019/07/17/upshot/drug-overdose-deaths-fall.html?action=click&module=Top%20Stories&pgtype=Homepage

212. http://www.donoharmseries.org. *Do No Harm* documentary interview with Mike Moore. 2019.

213. https://www.wsj.com/articles/purdue-pharma-preparing-for-possible-bankruptcy-filing-11551721519

214. ibid.

215. https://www.cdc.gov/drugoverdose/epidemic/index.html

216. http://www.donoharmseries.org. *Do No Harm* documentary interview with Karyn Hascal. 2019.

217. https://www.nytimes.com/2019/01/31/health/opioids-purdue-pharma-sackler.html?rref=collection%2Fbyline%2Fbarry-meier&action=click&contentCollection=undefined&region=stream&module=stream_unit&version=latest&contentPlacement=1&pgtype=collection

218. https://www.ncbi.nlm.nih.gov/pmc/articles/PMC2622774/

219. https://www.verywellmind.com/basic-facts-about-oxycontin-67709

220. https://medicine.wustl.edu/news/podcast/switching-from-oxycontin-to-heroin/

221. https://www.documentcloud.org/documents/5715954-Massachusetts-AGO-Amended-Complaint-2019-01-31.html

222. https://www.workingpartners.com/over-600-lawsuits-against-opioid-companies-become-one-federal-court-case/

223. http://www.donoharmseries.org. *Do No Harm* documentary interview with Lewis Nelson, MD. 2018.

224. ibid.

225. June 20, 2017 by Lizette Alvarez, https://www.nytimes.com/2017/06/20/us/delray-beach-addiction.html

226. https://www.nytimes.com/2017/06/20/us/delray-beach-addiction.html

227. http://www.donoharmseries.org.DoNoHarmdocumentaryinterviewwithLewisNelson,MD. 2018.

228. ibid.

229. ibid.

230. http://www.donoharmseries.org.DoNoHarmdocumentaryinterviewwithDavidTauben,MD. 2018

231. ibid.

232. http://www.donoharmseries.org.DoNoHarmdocumentaryinterviewwithRichardBarth,MD. 2018

233. http://www.donoharmseries.org.DoNoHarmdocumentaryinterviewwithDr.SharonWalsh. 2018

234. ibid.

235. https://www.nytimes.com/2019/03/07/us/deaths-drugs-suicide-record.html?action=click&module=Well&pgtype=Homepage&section=US

236. https://www.cdc.gov/media/releases/2018/s1129-US-life-expectancy.html

237. https://www.thenation.com/article/prison-education-reduces-recidivism-by-over-40-percent-why-arent-we-funding-more-of-it/

238. https://www.reuters.com/article/us-health-spending/u-s-health-spending-twice-other-countries-with-worse-results-idUSKCN1GP2YN

239. https://thehill.com/hilltv/what-americas-thinking/412552-majority-of-republicans-say-the-support-medicare-for-all-poll

240. https://www.washingtonpost.com/education/2018/11/02/major-depression-american-youth-rising-new-report-says/?utm_term=.6dc1ace64818

241. https://www.theguardian.com/politics/2013/apr/08/margaret-thatcher-quotes

242. https://www.washingtonpost.com/national/health-science/purdue-pharma-state-of-oklahoma-reach-settlement-in-landmark-opioid-lawsuit/2019/03/26/69aa5cda-4f11-11e9-a3f7-78b7525a8d5f_story.html?utm_term=.55ddffa909ee

243. https://www.nytimes.com/2019/03/28/health/new-york-lawsuit-opioids-sacklers-distributors.html?rref=collection%2Fbyline%2Froni-caryn-rabin&action=click&contentCollection=undefined&region=stream&module=stream_unit&version=latest&contentPlacement=9&pgtype=collection

244. https://vtdigger.org/2019/05/21/vermont-sues-sackler-family-members-oxycontin-marketing/

245. https://www.vox.com/future-perfect/2019/3/26/18282383/sackler-opioids-purdue-museums-donation

246. https://www.tmz.com/2018/03/08/oxycontin-heir-buys-bel-air-mansion/

247. https://www.newyorker.com/magazine/2017/10/30/the-family-that-built-an-empire-of-pain

248. http://www.mundipharma.ie/history

249. https://www.bloomberg.com/news/articles/2019-03-30/oxycontin-billionaires-chase-global-profits-to-offset-u-s-woes

250. https://www.hhs.gov/about/news/2019/03/20/hhs-releases-additional-487-million-to-states-territories-to-expand-access-to-effective-opioid-treatment.html

251. https://www.mprnews.org/story/2018/03/30/penny-a-pill-funding-fades-under-pressure-from-pharmaceutical-industry

INDEX

Page numbers in *italics* indicate images.

ABOUT THE AUTHOR

HARRY WILAND is one of the founders of the Media Policy Center (MPC). He is currently the Co-President and Co-CEO of MPC (www.mediapolicycenter.org) in Santa Monica, CA. Wiland graduated Brooklyn College with a major in Chemistry and from Columbia University with a MFA in Film & Television. He has written, produced and directed public television and multimedia for over 35 years. With business partner, Dale Bell, they founded the 501c3 Media Policy Center and developed its multimedia model. Wiland has been a Director Member of the Directors Guild of America since 1985, and a member of the Academy of Television Arts & Sciences since 2003. In 2006, he and Dale Bell were elected Ashoka Lifetime Fellows (www.ashoka.org); they are the only media professionals to be so honored. Current public television projects include the documentary series Do No Harm: The Opioid Epidemic and Our Kids: Narrowing the Opportunity Gap hosted by Harvard Professor Robert D Putnam.